Social Network Analytics

This book presents the cutting-edge techniques of social network analytics, focusing on both the positive and negative aspects of social media. While platforms like X, Facebook, and LinkedIn serve as powerful tools for product promotion and crisis management, they also present challenges such as the spread of misinformation, cyberbullying, and hateful content. This book explores these dimensions while highlighting the advancements in social media analytics, specifically through the lens of emerging technologies like artificial intelligence, machine learning, and deep learning. This book is intended for data engineers, researchers, practitioners, and students in the fields of data science, social computing, and artificial intelligence.

This book

- Explores state-of-the-art deep learning methodologies tailored for social network analysis, including Convolutional Neural Networks (CNNs), Recurrent Neural Networks (RNNs), and Graph Neural Networks (GNNs), to uncover hidden patterns and trends within social media data.
- Examines the application of large language models, such as GPT (Generative Pre-trained Transformer), in analysing and generating text-based content. Readers will gain practical insights into using these models for content generation, summarisation, and classification tasks.
- Provides detailed coverage of sentiment analysis techniques, enabling readers to extract valuable insights from user-generated content and helping organisations better understand public opinion.
- Explores methodologies for detecting communities within social networks, uncovering hidden structures, relationships, and influential nodes or communities.
- Offers insights into predicting user behaviour on social media platforms, including engagement, preferences, and click-through rates, equipping readers with tools to drive informed decision-making.

Social Network Analytics

Empowering Data Engineering with Deep Learning and Large Language Models

Edited By

Pradeep Kumar Roy, Asis Kumar Tripathy, Abhinav Kumar, and Yulei Wu

CRC Press
Taylor & Francis Group
Boca Raton London New York

CRC Press is an imprint of the
Taylor & Francis Group, an informa business
A CHAPMAN & HALL BOOK

First edition published 2027
by CRC Press
2385 NW Executive Center Drive, Suite 320, Boca Raton FL 33431

and by CRC Press
4 Park Square, Milton Park, Abingdon, Oxon, OX14 4RN

CRC Press is an imprint of Taylor & Francis Group, LLC

Library of Congress Cataloging-in-Publication Data
Names: Roy, Pradeep Kumar editor | Tripathy, Asis Kumar editor | Kumar,
Abhinav, 1993- editor | Wu, Yulei editor
Title: Social network analytics : empowering data engineering with deep
learning and large language models / edited by Pradeep Kumar Roy, Asis
Kumar Tripathy, Abhinav Kumar, and Yulei Wu.
Description: First edition. | Boca Raton: CRC Press, 2026. | Includes
bibliographical references. | Identifiers: LCCN 2026013323 (print) |
LCCN 2026013324 (ebook) | ISBN 9781041006909 hardback | ISBN 9781003611110 ebook
Subjects: LCSH: Social sciences—Network analysis | Social
networks—Research—Methodology | Deep learning (Machine learning) |
Natural language processing (Computer science)
Classification: LCC HM741 .S6324 2026 (print) | LCC HM741 (ebook)
LC record available at https://lccn.loc.gov/2026013323
LC ebook record available https://lccn.loc.gov/2026013324

ISBN: 9781041006909 (hbk)
ISBN: 9781041006923 (pbk)
ISBN: 9781003611110 (ebk)

DOI: 10.1201/9781003611110

Typeset in Times
by codeMantra

Contents

Preface

Over the past decade, social networks have evolved from channels of communication and entertainment into complex ecosystems that influence public discourse, shape business strategy, and mirror human behaviour at a global scale. They capture an ever-expanding spectrum of emotions, opinions, and events, reflecting both the potential and the fragility of our digital society. The unprecedented scale, velocity, and diversity of social media data offer vast opportunities for insight generation, yet they also pose pressing challenges of authenticity, fairness, interpretability, and societal trust.

This edited volume explores the dynamic intersection of Artificial Intelligence (AI), Deep Learning, Large Language Models (LLMs), and Social Network Analytics in understanding and managing these complexities. These chapters collectively present advances in computational modelling, ethical design, and application-driven frameworks that enable deeper insight into human communication and its digital expressions. Together, they illustrate how modern AI can uncover behavioural patterns, forecast emerging trends, and strengthen social resilience while emphasising responsible and interpretable deployment.

This book begins with foundational perspectives on the role of AI in social network analysis and the global impact of digital ecosystems. It then transitions into specialized studies that examine the psychological and social implications of online behaviour, including depression detection, mental health monitoring, and the analysis of offensive or discriminatory content. These discussions are particularly contextualized within Indian linguistic and cultural landscapes, reflecting the growing need for inclusivity and sensitivity in low-resource environments.

Subsequent chapters focus on applied and domain-specific advances, including personalised advertising, brand value prediction, fake news detection, and explainable models for disaster damage assessment. The inclusion of digital agriculture and perception analysis underscores the expanding role of social network data in developmental and sustainability-driven contexts. By integrating ethical AI principles, interpretability mechanisms, and region-aware modelling, the volume bridges technical innovation with human and societal values.

This book aims to serve as a comprehensive reference for researchers, practitioners, and policymakers seeking to harness advanced AI for meaningful and responsible social network analytics. It brings together diverse perspectives, empirical studies, and practical insights to illuminate the path towards building intelligent, ethical, and inclusive digital ecosystems that can positively shape the connected world.

We express our sincere gratitude to all contributing authors, reviewers, and collaborators for their scholarly commitment. We hope this volume encourages continued innovation and critical reflection on how AI can empower societies to communicate more responsibly, inclusively, and intelligently in the years ahead.

Pradeep Kumar Roy
Asis Kumar Tripathy
Abhinav Kumar
Yulei Wu

About the Editors

Pradeep Kumar Roy earned a BTech degree in Computer Science and Engineering from BPUT Odisha. He earned his MTech and PhD degrees in Computer Science and Engineering from the National Institute of Technology Patna in 2015 and 2018, respectively. He received a Certificate of Excellence for securing a top rank in the MTech course. He is currently an assistant professor in the Decision Science and Information Systems area, IIM Nagpur Maharashtra, India.

Asis Kumar Tripathy is a professor at the School of Computer Science Engineering and Information Systems, Vellore Institute of Technology, Vellore, India. He has more than ten years of teaching experience. He completed his PhD from the National Institute of Technology, Rourkela. His areas of research interest include wireless sensor networks, cloud computing, the Internet of Things, and advanced network technologies. He has several publications in refereed journals, reputed conferences, and book chapters to his credit.

Abhinav Kumar is currently an assistant professor in the Department of Computer Science and Engineering, Motilal Nehru National Institute of Technology Allahabad (MNNIT Allahabad), Prayagraj, India. Prior to joining MNNIT Allahabad, he worked as an assistant professor in the Department of CSE at IIIT Surat and Siksha "O" Anusandhan (Deemed to be University), Bhubaneswar, Odisha. He earned a PhD in Computer Science and Engineering from the Department of CSE at the National Institute of Technology Patna, India.

Dr. Yulei Wu is an associate professor working across the Faculty of Engineering and the Bristol Digital Futures Institute, University of Bristol, UK. He is also affiliated with the Smart Internet Lab and is a member of the High-Performance Networks Research Group. He earned his PhD in Computing and Mathematics and BSc (1st Class Hons.) degree in Computer Science from the University of Bradford, UK, in 2010 and 2006, respectively. Before joining the University of Bristol, Dr. Wu worked at the University of Exeter and the Chinese Academy of Sciences (CAS).

Contributors

Dibya Ranjan Das Adhikary
Department of Computer Science and Engineering
Siksha "O" Anusandhan, Deemed to be University
Bhubaneswar, Odisha, India

Shankar Biradar
Manipal Institute of Technology
Manipal Academy of Higher Education
Manipal, Karnataka, India

Prabhat Dansena
Department of Computer Science and Engineering
C. V. Raman Global University
Bhubaneswar, Odisha, India

Rahul Dixit
Department of Artificial Intelligence, Sardar Vallabhbhai National Institute of Technology
Surat, Gujarat, India

Ashish Kumar Dwivedi
Department of Computer Science and Engineering
LNM Institute of Information Technology
Jaipur, Rajasthan, India

Shivnath Ghosh
Department of Computer Science & Engineering
Brainware University
Kolkata, West Bengal, India

Ankit Jha
Department of Computer Science and Engineering
LNM Institute of Information Technology
Jaipur, Rajasthan, India

Shikha Jha
Department of Environmental Science and Engineering
IIT ISM Dhanbad
Dhanbad, Jharkhand, India

Sanjana Kavatagi
Manipal Institute of Technology
Manipal Academy of Higher Education
Manipal, Karnataka, India

Upkar Kedia
Department of Computer Science and Engineering
Indian Institute of Information Technology
Ranchi, Jharkhand, India

Abhinav Kumar
Department of Computer Science and Engineering
Motilal Nehru National Institute of Technology
Allahabad, Uttar Pradesh, India

Vijay Kumar
Department of Computer Science and Engineering
Motilal Nehru National Institute of Technology
Allahabad, Uttar Pradesh, India

Kirti Kumari
Department of Computer Science and Engineering
Indian Institute of Information Technology
Ranchi, Jharkhand, India

Ruchi Kumari
Department of Computer Science and Engineering
Indian Institute of Information Technology
Ranchi, Jharkhand, India

Dev Sourav Panda
Bosch Global Software Technologies Private Limited
Bangalore, Karnataka, India

Rajnish Pandey
Department of Information Technology
Dr. Ram-Manohar Lohia Avadh University
Ayodhya, Uttar Pradesh, India

Rajat Pandit
Department of Computer Science
West Bengal State University
Berunanpukuria, West Bengal, India

Rajendra Shivaji Patil
Department of Computer Science and Engineering
LNM Institute of Information Technology
Jaipur, Rajasthan, India

Amitava Podder
Department of Computer Science & Engineering
Brainware University
Kolkata, West Bengal, India

Rashmi Rachh
Department of Computer Science and Engineering
Visvesvaraya Technological University
Belagavi, Karnataka, India

Rimjhim
Department of Computer Science and Engineering
National Institute of Technology
Warangal, Telangana, India

Piyal Roy
Department of Computer Science & Engineering
Brainware University
Kolkata, West Bengal, India

Kumar Saurav
Department of Marketing
IQ City United World School of Business
Kolkata, West Bengal, India

Jyoti Prakash Singh
Department of Computer Science and Engineering
National Institute of Technology
Patna, Bihar, India

Laxminath Tripathy
Department of Computer Science and Engineering
Siksha "O" Anusandhan, Deemed to be University
Bhubaneswar, Odisha, India

Dharamveer Yadav
Department of Computer Science and Engineering
Katihar Engineering College
Katihar, Bihar, India

1 The Role of Artificial Intelligence in Social Network Analysis

Dev Sourav Panda and Rahul Dixit

1.1 INTRODUCTION

Every exchange in the realm of digital interactions paints a distinct picture waiting to be explored. Social Network Analysis (SNA) [1–5] offers insights into the sophisticated system of interpersonal connections prevalent in today's society, as it has today become prevalent principles and practices of relationships between human beings. When people, groups, and organizations are represented by nodes that interact through relationships, SNA raw data can be transformed into stunning visuals, accentuating key participants, emerging communities, and significant shifts. Online settings have exploded with a wealth of data that traditional methods cannot cope with due to their volume and intricacy; hence, this approach focuses on enhancing methods of traditional techniques. SNA not only illuminates the underlying social processes of the information society, but it also opens the eyes to new analytical frontiers that must be developed at full speed in response to rapidly evolving technology. The development of our cyber networks triggered the uncontrollable demand for sophisticated technologies and uncovered the transformative promise of Artificial Intelligence (AI).

Now, AI accelerates the powerful tools offered by advanced methods. Drawing on deep learning, graph neural networks (GNNs), and language models, AI enhances insights about our data by performing real-time analyses on extensive datasets using sophisticated computational techniques. These methods reveal previously hidden behaviors and improve the accuracy of traditional SNA techniques. In so doing, AI not only accelerates the pace of the discovery, but it also removes barriers such as data noise, model complexity, and sheer volume. When Social Network Intelligence is integrated with complex algorithms, static data transforms into dynamic, actionable insights through AI. Such potent synergy between SNA and AI does not simply transform data interpretation; rather, it forms a pivotal reason why this research is timely and essential.

Motivated by the need to understand modern society in the context of technology, the exploration of AI-powered SNA requires immediate attention. Outdated strategies have been strained due to the vastness of datasets, thus enabling the opportunity to overcome these challenges – improving access, scalability, and interpretability. This focus is directed toward the rapid advancement of emerging digital networks and the capability to perform synchronized analyses, ensuring that theoretical developments

DOI: 10.1201/9781003611110-1

seamlessly integrate with real-world practices. This focus logically leads us to investigate the corresponding academic literature that tackles these questions.

Shifting toward an academic perspective highlights numerous works that offer both motivation and guidance toward solving the pressing issues of SNA augmented with AI. As an example, Mahsa Nooribakhsh et al. [6] used machine learning algorithms to ascertain digital community structures and mentioned problems associated with real-time analyses scalability, while Jain et al. [7] looked into information diffusion with graph algorithms and had issues with interpretability and speed. Also, Kazemi [8] concentrated on natural language processing (NLP) for Microsoft Zoom sentiment analysis and dealt with the rapid spread of misinformation, while Krenn et al. [9] applied deep learning to predict network evolution and focused on ethically transparent forecasting. All of these studies highlight emerging gaps and persistent matters uniquely framing the scope of this chapter.

This chapter aims to provide a cohesive plan for the development of SNA powered by AI and agentic AI with the inspiration from the previous findings. It aims to describe contemporary strategies that improve precision, scalability, and ethical sharpness in network analysis. Sections 1.2 and 1.3 outline the theoretical and practical approaches we take toward data quality, real-time processing, model explainability, and rapidly evolving applications along with their challenges and ethical considerations. Sections 1.4 and 1.5 demonstrate how profound the capabilities of AI are in transforming the appreciation of complex social networks and hypothesizing what is yet to come, providing some future extensions of this chapter.

1.2 KEY AI TECHNIQUES IN SOCIAL NETWORK ANALYSIS

The advancement of the social network's intricate patterns and behaviors is AI's powerful, and multifaceted, responsibility. This section elaborates and examines the scope of SNA to appreciate its technologies in both isolation and collaboration. It aims to build a story from underlying deep learning models [10–12] to the refinement of LLMs (Large Language Models) and AI agents along the lines of technological evolution and performance optimization. The focus is on constructing a cognitive framework that moves readers from basic neural models to autonomous agents capable of reasoning and interfacing with networks. This section is arranged such that the readers are first introduced to systemically more straightforward AI techniques, subsequently revealing stronger, contextually aware ones, all while ensuring the architecture is rational and applicable in everyday life. This bypasses the "black-box" common misconception in traditional AI techniques. Each step improves upon computation speed, scalability, and interpretability alongside ease of use, proving that streamlined techniques yield enhanced decision networks that outline SNA's framework.

Figure 1.1 represents an AI-powered SNA framework with adaptive model selection. The framework begins with the acquisition of social data, followed by data extraction, preprocessing of raw social inputs, and feature extraction. These steps collectively prepare the data for intelligent model selection and analysis. The processed data is then passed to an Adaptive SNA Model Selector, which intelligently chooses from a set of advanced models such as deep learning models, GNNs, LLMs, and

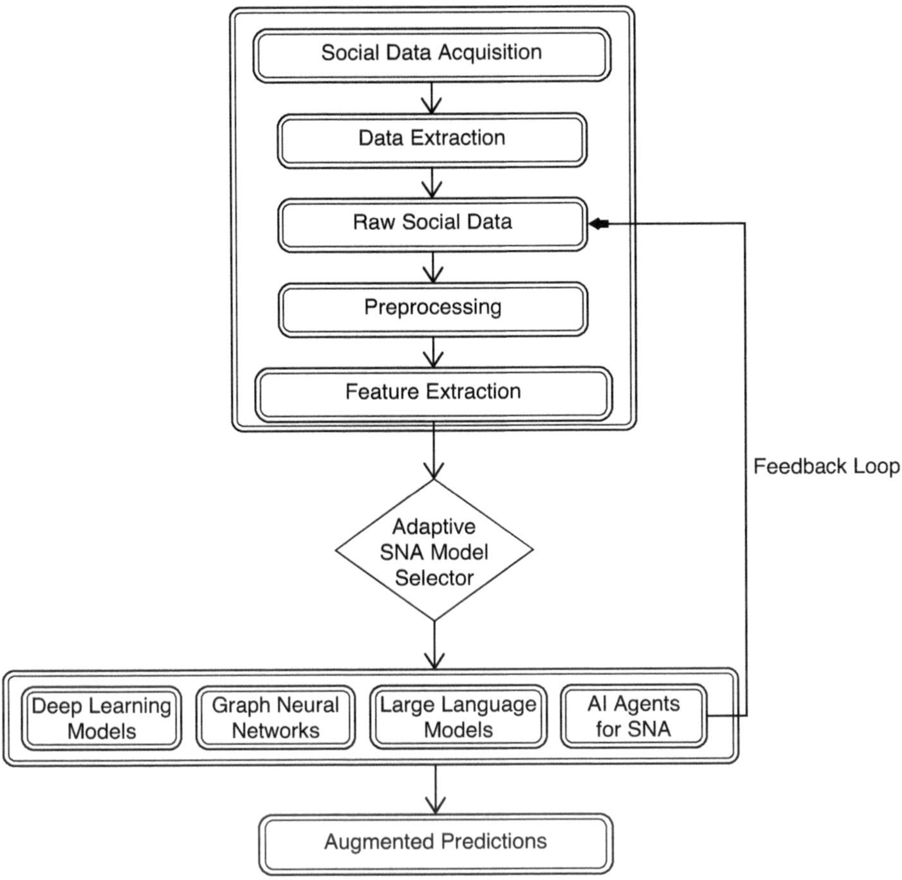

FIGURE 1.1 AI-powered social network analysis framework with adaptive model selection.

AI Agents (which feed into a Feedback Loop to refine data processing and improve future analyses) for SNA. The selected model generates Augmented Predictions. Each block in this figure reflects an additional layer of intelligence embedded within the system. As we move downward through the framework, the system progressively enhances its ability to understand context, anticipate complex relationships, and generate intelligent, autonomous outputs. This layered and adaptive architecture enables scalable, context-aware, and high-accuracy SNA, making it well suited for dynamic cyber and social environments.

In recent years, the landscape of SNA has been significantly transformed by the integration of cutting-edge AI techniques. As social platforms generate vast and complex datasets, traditional analytical methods fall short in capturing the depth of relationships, influence dynamics, and contextual nuances present within networks. To address these challenges, AI has introduced a new era of intelligent analysis. Among the most impactful advancements are deep learning techniques, which uncover hidden patterns in large-scale social data; GNNs, which enable structure-aware learning directly over networked data; LLMs, which provide powerful capabilities for understanding and generating human-like social content; and AI Agents, which autonomously analyze, adapt, and interact within dynamic social ecosystems. The following subsections delve into these key techniques, highlighting their individual contributions and collective impact on modern SNA.

1.2.1 Deep Learning's Impact on Social Networks

The development of deep learning has automated the process of learning hierarchical representations from massive volumes of data, transforming the scale of advancement in AI. In SNA, deep learning frameworks have become extremely useful in understanding user behavior, content propagation within communities, and the intricate structure of communities themselves. These frameworks excel at capturing and understanding unstructured data including user-generated data (text and images), behavioral data (click-streams and timelines), and interactions, all of which are difficult to represent using conventional machine learning approaches [13,14].

Initially, deep learning frameworks were developed for image and speech recognition, but they have been successfully extended to tasks in SNA through the addition of embedding techniques, content–context blending, and sequence modeling. Their utility in SNA stems from the fact that they can work on huge datasets to extract hidden social insights from chaotic, high-dimensional datasets. This subsection looks at the model's architecture in relation to SNA, its real applications, and models that have surpassed traditional methods.

Algorithm 1.1: Deep Learning Framework for Core SNA Tasks

Input: Graph $G=(V,E)$, Feature matrix X, Labels Y (for node classification), Seed nodes (for influence estimation)

Output: Task-specific results: $\hat{Y}$ (labels), S (link scores), $\mathcal{C}$ (communities), I (influence scores)

1: **Start**
2: **if** task is NodeClassification **then**
3: Initialize neural network f_θ
4: Generate node embeddings: $Z \leftarrow f_\theta(X)$
5: Apply Softmax: $\hat{Y} \leftarrow \text{Softmax}(Z)$
6: Compute loss: $L \leftarrow \text{CrossEntropy}\left(\hat{Y},Y\right)$
7: Update θ via backpropagation
8: **return** $\hat{Y}$
9: **else if** task is LinkPrediction **then**
10: Initialize encoder network f_θ
11: Generate embeddings: $Z \leftarrow f_\theta(X)$
12: **for** each node pair (u, v) in candidate pairs **do**
13: Compute similarity: $s_{uv} \leftarrow \sigma\left(Z_u^\top Z_v\right)$

end for
Compute loss: $L \leftarrow \text{Binary Cross Entropy}(s_{uv}, \text{label}_{uv})$
Update θ via backpropagation
return Link scores $S = \{s_{uv}\}$
else if task is CommunityDetection **then**
Initialize autoencoder AE_θ
Encode features: $Z \leftarrow AE_\theta.\text{encode}(X)$
Cluster nodes: $\mathcal{C} \leftarrow \text{KMeans}(Z)$
return Community clusters $\mathcal{C}$
else if task is InfluenceEstimation **then**
Initialize influence model f_θ
Generate embeddings: $Z \leftarrow f_\theta(X)$
for each node $v \in V$ **do**
Aggregate influence: $I_v \leftarrow \sum_{u \in \mathcal{N}(v)} \alpha_{uv} \cdot Z_u$
end for
Rank nodes based on I_v
return Influence scores I
else
return Unsupported Task
end if
End

The application of deep learning in SNA usually adheres to a feature-centric pipeline where social entities, such as users, posts, and links, are converted into numerical vectors either through feature engineering or embedding layers. These vectors undergo a series of processes in which they are passed through multiple hidden layers that recognize abstract, task-oriented representations, which culminate into making predictions or being assigned into clusters. The structure might change depending on the particular application, such as classification, link prediction, or influence estimation, but the overarching trend is the same. These architectures have a general purpose and are currently utilized across various SNA activities. For example, the simpler Feedforward Neural Networks (FNN) are usually applied to community detection. Temporal modeling, which includes forecasting the interaction posts or the states of users over time, is well accomplished by Recurrent Neural Networks (RNNs) especially with Long Short-Term Memory (LSTM) and Gated Recurrent Unit (GRU) architectures. Convolutional Neural Networks (CNNs) are primarily utilized in computer vision, but have also been adapted to help with local structural patterns on ego networks or content-driven influence graphs. In social networks, deep learning frameworks can be trained to automatically execute the below tasks.

- **User profiling and segmentation**, by examining post history combined with interaction frequency.
- **Fake account and bot detection**, based on the sequential nature of user activity intertwined with content specifics.
- **Interest clustering and personalized recommendations**, where user behavior with the system is encoded in dense vectors to discover similar users.

To resolve these problems, deep learning models can be augmented with specific task heads and corresponding training techniques. Algorithm 1.1 represents a deep learning framework tailored for solving core SNA tasks, including node classification, link prediction, community detection, and influence estimation. The algorithm takes as input a graph $G = (V, E)$, a feature matrix X, and task-specific data, such as labels Y for node classification or seed nodes for influence estimation. The framework operates as follows:

- **Node Classification**: A neural network f_θ is initialized, and node embeddings Z are generated by passing the feature matrix X through the network. The embeddings are then processed through a softmax function to predict node labels $\hat{Y}$. The cross-entropy loss between predicted labels $\hat{Y}$ and true labels Y is computed, and the model parameters θ are updated via backpropagation.
- **Link Prediction**: An encoder network f_θ is used to learn node embeddings Z. For each candidate node pair (u, v), the similarity s_{uv} is computed as $s_{uv} = \sigma\left(Z_u^\top Z_v\right)$, where σ represents an activation function (e.g., sigmoid). The binary cross-entropy loss between predicted similarity scores s_{uv} and ground truth labels is minimized, and model parameters θ are updated via backpropagation.
- **Community Detection**: An autoencoder AE_θ is initialized, and node features X are encoded into embeddings Z by the encoder. These embeddings are then clustered using the K-means algorithm to identify communities within the graph. The community clusters C are returned.
- **Influence Estimation**: An influence model f_θ is initialized to generate node embeddings Z. For each node v, the influence score I_v is aggregated by summing over the neighboring nodes $u \in N(v)$, weighted by the influence coefficient α_{uv}, as $I_v = \sum_{u \in N(v)} \alpha_{uv} \cdot Z_u$. The nodes are ranked based on their influence scores I_v, and the influence scores I are returned.

If the task is not recognized, the algorithm returns an "Unsupported Task" message. Throughout the process, model parameters θ are updated using backpropagation where applicable, and the algorithm outputs task-specific results such as predicted labels, link scores, community clusters, or influence scores, depending on the task at hand.

Table 1.1 presents a detailed comparison of three major SNA tasks using deep learning techniques. The table highlights their distinct objectives, applicable deep learning models, and typical use cases, offering a functional understanding of how deep learning adapts to diverse analytical needs in social networks.

The modular design of Algorithm 1.1 allows for greater flexibility in tackling different types of SNA problems with deep learning. By decoupling each functionality into individual node heads – like node labeling, relationship forecasting, structural discovery, and influence measurement – we are able to manage reduced model complexity and enhanced tuning and scaling. Also, these task-specific heads can gain additional peripheral value from elements like precomputed embeddings, transfer

TABLE 1.1
Comparison of Key SNA Tasks Using Deep Learning Techniques

SNA Task	Objective and DL Techniques	Common Applications
Link prediction	Predict missing or future links between nodes using autoencoders, graph embeddings like DeepWalk and Node2Vec, and GCN-based link scoring methods	Friend recommendation, knowledge graph completion, discovering hidden relationships
Influence analysis	Model how influence spreads across a network using RNNs, Graph Attention Networks (GAT), or temporal GNNs for dynamic influence tracking	Viral marketing, content virality prediction, and misinformation spread modeling
Community detection	Detect densely connected groups using spectral autoencoders, variational graph autoencoders (VGAE), or deep clustering techniques	User segmentation, behavior profiling, and targeted content delivery

learning from other social graphs, and even multi-task learning where several related tasks are trained in conjunction. Although effective, most of these deep models neglect to fully utilize the explicit graph topology and multi-hop dependencies. Each unit of work – a node, edge, or a cluster – will be treated as an instance, which is feature-based without network context and entirely structural. This limitation has created a need for, and was the impetus behind, the rise of GNNs, which blend deep learning with graph theory by informing neighboring nodes and propagating features within their neighborhoods. GNNs provide for the integration of attribute and structure representation that is fundamentally holistic, thus driving superior performance on graph-based social network tasks.

1.2.2 The Rise of Graph Neural Networks in Social Insights

The evolution of social networks goes hand in hand with the more expressive methods that go beyond conventional deep learning approaches. The nature of social networks is inherently graphic as users are represented as nodes, while the interactions they engage in such as friendships, follows, likes, and comments form the edges of the graph. The effectiveness of deep learning models is limited when dealing with topological information despite their proficiency in extracting local or sequential patterns. This is why GNNs are introduced to utilize the intrinsic structure of the information and offer solving power. GNNs are designed to process graph-structured inputs and therefore extend the applications of social neural networks to interactions, behaviors, and relationships within the social graph [15–19].

Message passing is what binds GNNs together. Unlike classical networks where each input is processed discreetly, GNNs iterate on a node's representation by including information from its neighbors. Every layer of a GNN is implemented as a two-phase operation: first, it gathers (or "collects") messages from the adjacent nodes, and second, it modifies the state of the current node using the aggregated messages along with the node's previous state. The iterative processes guarantee that embeddings of each node incorporate, in addition to the features of the node, a blended, contextualized view of its local neighborhood. The architecture generally includes several graph convolution layers (GCN), then applies non-linearities such as ReLU, and optionally, a readout layer that aggregates the node's embeddings into a summary at the graph level.

GNNs have introduced structure-aware learning to the forefront far beyond the capabilities of classic deep learning approaches. Whereas CNNs and RNNs operate on flat and sequentially ordered data, respectively, GNNs accept graphs for what they are irregular. This feature makes it possible for GNNs to model social dynamics, where a node's value depends on both its attributes and the influences of its neighbors. Therefore, node classification, link prediction, community detection, and influence estimation tasks become easier and more accurate, particularly in sparse or incomplete social datasets.

Performing strongly in SNA tasks, several GNN architectures have stood out. The Graph Convolutional Network (GCN) performs well on semi-supervised tasks with only some nodes labeled, while the rest are devoid of labels. Inductive learning is made possible with GraphSAGE, which generates embeddings for unseen nodes, making it ideal for social networks that evolve over time. Graph Attention Networks (GAT) enrich neighbor aggregation by introducing attention weights to the aggregation, letting the model focus on the most influential connections. For more intricate networks with diverse types of nodes and edges, HetGNN and HAN (Heterogeneous Attention Networks) specialize in those areas.

Algorithm 1.2: GNN-Based Modular Framework for Social Network Tasks

Input: Graph $G = (V, E)$, Node features X, Task type

Output: Task-specific predictions

1: Construct adjacency matrix A and feature matrix X
2: Initialize GNN model parameters θ
3: **for** each layer $l = 1$ to L **do**
4: $H^{(l)} \leftarrow \sigma\left(\hat{A}H^{(l-1)}W^{(l)}\right)$ {Graph convolution}
5: **end for**
6: $Z \leftarrow H^{(L)}$ {Final node embeddings}
7: **if** Task type = Node Classification **then**
8: $\hat{Y} \leftarrow \text{Softmax}(Z)$
9: **else if** Task type = Link Prediction **then**
10: **for** each node pair (u, v) **do**
11: $s_{uv} \leftarrow \sigma\left(Z_u^\top Z_v\right)$

```
end for
else if Task type = Community Detection then
C ← KMeans(Z)
else if Task type = Influence Estimation then
for each node v ∈ V do
I_v ← Σ_{u∈N(v)} α_uv · Z_u
end for
end if
```

Algorithm 1.2 presents a modular GNN framework designed to address various SNA tasks. The process begins by taking a graph $G=(V, E)$, where V represents nodes and E represents edges, along with node feature matrix X and the specific type of task to be performed. First, the adjacency matrix A and the feature matrix X are constructed to represent the graph structure and node attributes, respectively. The GNN model parameters are then initialized. For each layer in the GNN, graph convolution operations are applied to iteratively update node representations by aggregating information from neighboring nodes. After passing through all layers, the final node embeddings Z are obtained. Depending on the specified task, different modules are activated. For node classification, a softmax function is applied to the embeddings to generate class probabilities. For link prediction, the similarity between node pairs is computed using their embedding vectors. In the case of community detection, the embeddings are clustered using the K-means algorithm to identify node communities. Lastly, for influence estimation, each node's influence is calculated by aggregating weighted contributions from its neighbors. This flexible and task-specific design makes the framework highly adaptable to diverse analytical needs within social networks.

Even with their impressive capabilities for structural reasoning, GNNs have many open issues. They are fundamentally dependent on the completeness and quality of the graph data available. Edges that are not present or extra noisy connections can give rise to faulty embeddings. In addition, most GNN models are expensive from a computational cost perspective, especially on large-scale graphs, which is often the case in practical social network systems. Scalability, over-smoothing of node features, and the limited ability to deal with the temporal evolution of graphs pose ongoing research problems.

To overcome these gaps and reason with more nuanced unstructured data such as text and user interactions, we focus on LLMs now. These models augment the GNNs structural reasoning processes with more profound semantic comprehension, which allows a more thorough examination of social networks. The following section examines the role of LLMs in SNA as a unique intersection of language and structure where profound change is possible.

1.2.3 Large Language Models Transforming Social Analysis

As social networks continue to evolve, the combination of written text, the user's goal, and contextual subtleties becomes crucial for deriving relevant meanings. Although GNNs have effective applications in structural dependence modeling, they are still struggling with rich unstructured user-generated data including posts, comments, hashtags, and descriptions of multimedia. This is exactly what makes LLMs so valuable [20–23]. With large datasets, social networks can be analyzed more easily. Thanks to machines' capability of interpreting, summarizing, classifying, and reasoning with massive volumes of text as offered by LLMs like OpenAI's GPT-series, Google's PaLM, and Meta's LLaMA.

LLMs use self-attention to analyze text with long-range dependencies such as those found in social network interactions due to their transformer-based architectures. In addition, these models undergo a pre-training and fine-tuning process, which further increases their adaptability to domain-specific SNA tasks because they are trained on vast disciplinary corpora. LLMs also build on critical elements of the architecture such as multi-head attention, layer normalization, and residual connections. Following the outlined design, LLMs achieve unprecedented levels of coherence in responses alongside sentiment detection, intention interpretation, and nuanced comprehension.

The distinguishing characteristic of LLMs in comparison to traditional NLP models and even GNNs is the ability to work under zero-shot or few-shot learning settings, which allows for effortless generalization without extensive retraining. In SNA, this enables powerful capabilities such as fake news detection, bot detection, opinion mining, trend analysis, semantic user profiling, and misinformation cascade detection. They can also be used with graph-based models where the linguistic context is incorporated into the network structure, thus giving rise to hybrid architectures that integrate semantic and structural representations.

Algorithm 1.3: LLM-Driven Semantic Processing in Social Network Analysis

Input: Social text corpus $T = \{t_1, t_2, \ldots, t_n\}$, Task type

Output: Task-specific predictions

Start
for each document $t_i \in T$ **do**
Tokenize *ti* into input sequence X_i
Pass X_i through pre-trained LLM: $H_i \leftarrow \text{LLM}(X_i)$
Extract contextual embedding z_i from H_i
end for
if task is TopicModeling **then**
Cluster embeddings $\{z_i\}$ into latent topics
else if task is SentimentAnalysis **then**
Classify z_i into sentiment polarity
else if task is BotDetection **then**
Compare z_i to known bot behavior profiles
else if task is FakeNewsDetection **then**
Use classifier on z_i to verify content authenticity
end if
End

Algorithm 1.3 outlines an LLM-driven semantic processing framework tailored for various SNA tasks. The algorithm begins by taking a corpus of social text data $T = \{t_1, t_2, \ldots, t_n\}$, along with the specific task to be performed. Each document t_i in the corpus is first tokenized into an input sequence X_i, which is then processed through a pre-trained LLM (such as Bidirectional Encoder Representations from Transformers (BERT) or Generative Pre trained Transformer (GPT)-based models) to generate high-dimensional contextual embeddings H_i. From these, the relevant semantic representation z_i is extracted for each document. Depending on the task, the next step varies. For topic modeling, the embeddings $\{z_i\}$ are clustered into meaningful latent topic groups. For sentiment analysis, each embedding is classified to determine sentiment polarity. In the case of bot detection, the model compares each embedding against known behavioral patterns typical of bots. For fake news detection, a classifier is applied to determine the authenticity of the content. This LLM-based pipeline enables refined analysis of social texts, making it well suited for tasks that require deep contextual and semantic analysis.

Along with that potential, LLMs also come with their own set of challenges. They are expensive in terms of computation, memory, and processing power. In addition, interpretability is another challenge as it is unclear how the model's decisions are reached. Alarms also arise with biased data used to train the models, influencing the outcomes to present unfair or unbalanced SNA insights. To solve the stated problems and fully exploit the opportunities, LLMs are now being integrated with dynamic reasoning abilities, memory, and goal-oriented planning into agentic systems. These AI agents, comprising fully integrated LLMs, are the next branch of evolutionary development of intelligence in SNA – not only understanding language, but also capable of autonomous decision-making in intricate social frameworks. In the following section, we analyze the impact of AI agents on the evolution of SNA where the integration of LLMs with autonomy and interactivity in multi-agent systems is redefining the discipline.

1.2.4 AI Agents Shaping the Future of Social Networks

The launch of agentic AI marks a new era in the field of SNA, with the development of new AI capabilities like distributed reasoning and the completion of tasks without any human intervention. Unlike traditional static models, AI agents have autonomy, interactivity, goal orientation, and the capability to collaborate with other agents. These systems can now adapt to the environment because of ever-changing social structures and trends, and now Assistant AI systems can continuously interpret dynamically evolving environments, acting according to the change [24–26].

Agentic AI systems that include numerous intelligent agents connected with each other are not only analyzers but also advanced proactive bots capable of exploration, profiling users, grading influence, tracking misinformation, and modeling engagements. The generated model becomes much more powerful, explainable, and scalable for SNA. These agents are capable of dynamic strategy adaption through inter-agent communication in a multi-agent setting. In this architecture, a total of four primary agent types that interact with each other:

- **Ingestion Agent**: The Ingestion Agent is responsible for collecting raw social data from diverse platforms and sources. It performs initial data cleansing, formatting, and filtering to ensure the quality and consistency of the information. This preprocessed data is then structured and made ready for semantic interpretation and downstream processing.
- **Semantic Agent**: The Semantic Agent utilizes LLMs to transform textual data into meaningful vector representations. By capturing contextual relationships and semantic nuances, it enables a deeper understanding of unstructured content. These embeddings are essential for tasks like similarity search and feeding information into graph-based models.
- **Graph Agent**: The Graph Agent builds structured knowledge graphs using the outputs from the semantic layer. It enables efficient retrieval of relationships, reasoning over node connections, and the execution of core SNA tasks such as link prediction and community detection. The agent serves as the analytical backbone for knowledge-driven insights.
- **Orchestration Agent**: The Orchestration Agent oversees the entire system, coordinating the tasks of all other agents. It manages memory, maintains context over time, and facilitates user interaction. By directing the flow of information between agents, it ensures coherent, efficient, and goal-oriented processing throughout the system.

Algorithm 1.4: Agentic AI-Based Social Network Analysis

Input: Social Graph $G(V, E)$, User Profiles U, Historical Interaction Data H

Output: Agent Decisions $\mathcal{D}$ for Node Classification, Link Prediction, Community Detection, and Influence Estimation

Initialize multi-agent system with roles: *Observer, Analyzer, Predictor*, and *Coordinator*
Load LLM-powered semantic context processor for each agent
Construct Knowledge Graph $\mathcal{K}$ from G, U, and H
for each node $vi \in V$ **do**
Observer Agent gathers context from neighboring nodes
Analyzer Agent computes semantic node embeddings using LLM
Predictor Agent performs:
– Node Classification
– Link Prediction
– Community Detection
– Influence Estimation
Coordinator Agent consolidates predictions to form decision $\mathcal{D}_{v_i}$
end for
Aggregate all $\mathcal{D}_{v_i}$ into final decision set $\mathcal{D}$
return $\mathcal{D}$

Each agent is optimized for specific sub-tasks and utilizes memory modules and vector databases for persistence and context. Together, they form a highly responsive and goal-oriented analytical system. Algorithm 1.4 shows an agentic AI-based framework for SNA, designed to perform a range of predictive tasks using a collaborative multi-agent system. The input includes a social graph $G(V,E)$, user profile data U, and historical interaction records H. The framework initializes multiple intelligent agents, each assigned a specific role, i.e., Observer, Analyzer, Predictor, and Coordinator, to process and analyze the network. Each agent is equipped with an LLM-powered semantic context processor to enhance understanding and decision-making. A Knowledge Graph K is first constructed by integrating the social graph, user data, and past interactions. For each node v_i in the graph, the **Observer Agent** collects contextual information from its neighbors, while the Analyzer Agent computes semantic embeddings using the LLM. The Predictor Agent leverages these embeddings to carry out key tasks such as node classification, link prediction, community detection, and influence estimation. The Coordinator Agent then synthesizes all predictions into a final decision D_{v_i} for each node. These decisions are aggregated to produce a comprehensive decision set D, enabling accurate, context-aware analysis of social networks through distributed AI.

The agentic system structure is modular and composable, which offers unparalleled flexibility and unparalleled performance. When compared to deep learning models, GNNs, and even LLMs, AI agents outperform with their contextual acuity, load adaptability, task specialization, and long-term cognitive planning. A comparative overview of AI techniques used in SNA is presented in Table 1.2. The table highlights how different approaches, including deep learning, GNNs, LLMs, and AI Agents, align with specific SNA tasks such as node classification, sentiment analysis,

TABLE 1.2
Functional Comparison of Various AI Techniques for Social Network Analysis

AI Technique	SNA Tasks	Example Models	Key Capabilities
Deep learning	Node classification, link prediction, community detection	CNN, RNN, LSTM	Captures complex non-linear patterns; effective for temporal dynamics
Graph neural networks	Node and edge classification, influence modeling, fraud detection	GCN, GAT, GraphSAGE	Utilizes graph structure; models both local and global dependencies
Large language models	Text-based social insights, sentiment analysis, topic modeling	GPT, BERT, RoBERTa	Contextual understanding of text; zero/few-shot learning capabilities
AI Agents	Automated reasoning, real-time simulations, decision-making support	ReAct, AutoGPT, LangGraph	Adaptive learning; multi-source integration; human-like interaction

TABLE 1.3
Technical Comparison of AI Paradigms for Social Network Analysis

AI Technique	Scalability	Context Awareness	Autonomy	Adaptability
DL models	Medium	Low	No	Low
GNNs	High	Medium	No	Medium
LLMs	High	High	No	High
AI agents	Very high	Very high	Yes	Very high

and decision-making simulations. Each technique is illustrated with representative models and is evaluated based on key capabilities. This structured comparison aids in understanding the suitability of each technique depending on the analytical objectives, data type, and complexity of the social network being analyzed. Table 1.3 shows a technical comparison of AI paradigms for SNA based on scalability, context awareness, autonomy, and adaptability. According to the table, DL models have medium scalability and low context awareness, autonomy, and adaptability. GNNs feature high scalability and medium context awareness but lack autonomy and adaptability. LLMs exhibit high scalability and context awareness but no autonomy and low adaptability. AI agents outperform all other models, demonstrating very high scalability, context awareness, autonomy, and adaptability.

1.3 APPLICATIONS OF AI IN SOCIAL NETWORK ANALYSIS

The advancement of AI technologies has helped in transforming SNA to work more efficiently, which in turn has made it easier to understand the intertwining of human relationships in this age. SNA not only enhances sociological understanding at a deeper level, but also improves user experience, reduces disinformation and risks, and simultaneously takes care of community welfare. There are three forms of integration between AI and SNA which we will review that have been remarkably transformative. The following subsections highlight some of the key application areas of AI in SNA.

1.3.1 Augmented Personalization and Consumer Understanding

Within the context of trying to achieve maximum engagement from users, user personalization has proven to take the greatest share of attention, absolutely fueled by AI. Businesses like Netflix and Amazon are heavily leveraging SNA to offer clients tailored services, which has skyrocketed engagement. AI receives social graphs of friends, followers, and shared content to automatically assist users via recommendation systems. Beyond personalized data, AI examines networks in aggregate; suppose your friends are suddenly purchasing retro sneakers, then chances are you'll be bombarded with advertisements for those shoes on your social platforms. Such AI systems are used by businesses to enhance understanding of the consumer journey.

AI-powered algorithms enable marketers to define customer segments better, identify possible influencers within small groups, and even predict future spending behavior.

Consider the example of a fashion retailer who, through SNA, discovers that a niche Instagram community is patronizing an emerging street-wear trend. If they act in time, they can capitalize on the trend before it goes mainstream. Put simply, AI transforms fragmented user behaviors into actionable business intelligence, allowing organizations to outmaneuver competition in meeting and anticipating customer service expectations.

1.3.2 AI in Detecting Cybersecurity Threats and Fake News

The internet provides more than just information; it offers a virtual battleground. Unscrupulous agents try to sabotage organizations and influence the public using social networks, phishing, or some other form of disinformation. AI-powered SNA brings some semblance of order into the chaos by monitoring and reconstructing suspicious traffic patterns on networks in record time. For instance, GNN-based anomaly detection can spot a new set of fake accounts that are repetitively performing automated propaganda tasks. Imagine AI detecting a cluster of newly created social media profiles all sharing the same highly contentious narrative while the public was being urged to "get together." AI perceives such a situation as deception at scale and recognizes it as a coordinated attack.

Aside from the structural gaps, LLMs also help investigate the fundamental nature of the content. NLP technologies have the capability to detect patterns within language that are indicative of disinformation, hate speech, or well-organized fraudulent activities. For instance, an AI model could identify a sophisticated phishing attack comprised of several messages spread across different platforms, all employing the same deceptive phrases to trick users into revealing personal information. These models are now being used widely by technology firms and regulators intent on automating threat detection; fraud, cyber bullying, and propaganda content are detected and evaluated at a graph level to ascertain user protection vs. exploitation. With everything malefic in constant flux, defenders are guaranteed speed due to AI.

1.3.3 AI for Understanding Online Communities and Social Trends

The social fabric of the internet has communities springing up unexpectedly due to a shared interest, belief, or objective. The ability to see followers and their participation with the content only scratches the surface. AI-enabled analysis of social networks makes it possible to determine how a community is built, spot and analyze focal points and key actors, and track the movement of ideas within and between the groups. One example might be an environmental campaign on Reddit that sparks a movement that shapes policy discourse on X (formerly Twitter) and later, on X, or mainstream media.

AI also has a unique talent for spotting potential trends that are about to gain popularity. AIs can analyze user-generated content, sentiment, and engagement metrics to detect when niche discussions are starting to rise. Picture it as watching for a ripple before a wave hits. A classic example is how businesses harness AI to scout communities on Discord or TikTok, where they anticipate an outburst of interest, be it for an exciting new fashion trend or a social cause that is just starting to gain traction.

From entertainment firms eager to cash in on the latest fads to NGOs assessing public sentiment around important issues, AI-driven SNA is becoming essential in helping steer hot digital environments for today's fast-moving world.

While the prospects of AI in SNA are thrilling, they come with major challenges. The same technologies that tailor experiences, identify potential dangers, and construct social maps fundamentally transform environments, raising a new set of intricate problems. In what ways can we protect user privacy when social graphs are analyzed through the lenses of AI? Can such large-scale models remain untainted by bias as they cross the boundaries of billions of users? While AI offers unprecedented capabilities in SNA, we need to reflect on what responsibility looks like in this context. The following section discusses the most important constructive challenges – the technological and moral challenges – AI needs to face so that sociological imagination SNA continues to enrich human society.

1.4 CHALLENGES AND ETHICAL CONSIDERATIONS

There is no denying the excitement associated with AI's ever-increasing potential. Yet, with advancements in technology, there also lies a set of accompanying challenges. This is no different with the integration of AI in SNA. The accuracy of the AI models and the insights they provide are just the tip of the iceberg. Beneath the surface concerns that need to be addressed for a safe and responsible AI deployment lies the resolution of real-world problems. This section aims to overview the multifaceted issues ranging from the technical challenges of scaling AI to questions of fairness, ethics, privacy, and everything in between.

1.4.1 Data Quality and Scalability Challenges

The most prominent characteristic of AI systems is data. However, when it comes to data, not all data is created equal. Social networks have a great potential to generate data on a large scale. But the information systems collected will most definitely contain errors, not be complete, and, in the worst-case scenario, not even follow a logical structure. Trying to construct social connections for millions of users will without a doubt contain a lot of missing information. Not to mention bots, which skew engagement metrics. AI models, more so the graph-based ones like GNNs, determine the overall outcomes based on the input provided; hence, the possibility of providing poor quality data will lead to models building incorrect trust and usability.

Another sample of a technical challenge is that of scalability. Although AI technology may flourish in a controlled research setting, scaling that success to encompass platforms like Facebook or LinkedIn is a different challenge altogether. The computational demands of processing massive social graphs that contain millions, if not billions, of nodes and edges are astounding. To deal with this magnitude, techniques in distributed learning, graph sampling, and model optimization became necessities. Even with these techniques, however, there remains a balancing act between the performance achieved and the costs incurred. The efficient analysis of growing networks presents a cost and complexity conundrum.

1.4.2 Ethical Issues: Transparency, Bias, and Fairness in AI Models

The technical issues of scalability sink deeper into ethical considerations. The "black-box" problem of many AI models, including those based on deep learning or GNNs, makes it virtually impossible to provide reasoned explanations for particular predictions or recommendations. For instance, in an SNA system driven by AI, an account recommending system may suggest the removal of certain accounts due to the detection of "suspicious behavior." In such scenarios, users without access to the reasoning behind the decision will oftentimes struggle to validate it, making it impossible to corroborate any such choices without the understanding of rationale in the case explanation. The absence of transparency in a model makes trust impossible, and the lack of it can be dangerous in sensitive areas such as content moderation or fraud detection.

Equally important is bias. AI models will only be as fair as the data they are trained on. Social networks, by their very nature, tend to encode socially constructed historical biases. If the data develops bias to a specific demographic or area, the model's outputs will reflect those inequalities. Take, for instance, an AI system that has been trained on the data coming from metropolitan users. It is very likely that the system overlooks some trends or relevant behaviors from the rural population. Biases are resolved with intentional actions such as bias audits, fairness-aware learning, and evaluating the model's outcomes for biases relative to treatment among different user groups in longitudinal studies.

1.4.3 Mitigating AI Influence on Privacy and Security

Privacy and security concerns are essential parts of ethics. AI users do rely a lot on social networks, texts, and other sensitive types of information. In this aspect, the data itself breaks down and no longer serves its intended purpose. The data can also be used for detection services. Moreover, could the model unintentionally expose user-controlled relationships or sensitive behavioral patterns embedded within? This is not just an unrealistic threat, telling people overly personal details without intending to was proven by some recommender systems that suggested friends based on contacts through hit-the-big-button interactions because they used private settings.

Preserving these methods makes security easier with techniques that don't give out other sorts of self-preservation discriminately. These include methods like differential privacy, federated learning, and data anonymization. While these techniques increase security, disabling measures tends to toggle model performance instead. So, organizations invariably find themselves pleasured in the fine middle between gainful performance and privacy.

With regard to cybersecurity, AI models have their own weaknesses in the form of adversarial attacks. Threat actors can modify the input data to deceive an AI system to make erroneous predictions, such as getting past spam detection systems or evading fake news classifiers. Therefore, designing strong, secure, and privacy preserving compliant AI for SNA is not merely best practice – it's imperative.

Today, social networks would be impossible to navigate without AI, but it is evident that the path is fraught with many technological and ethical intersections.

From supporting problems and data quality to social issues like fairness, transparency, and even privacy, AI-driven SNA functions in a multifaceted, high-pressure context. Nevertheless, these are not insurmountable challenges; on the contrary, they are ripe for innovation and improvement. Beyond today's obstacles lies a new frontier where advancements in AI, combined with much stronger moral reasoning, will transform how we interact with and manage an externally dominated society. The next section looks at these emerging frontiers not just in terms of the developing goals of AI-enabled SNA, but also in terms of the broader digital society and how SNA will shape its evolution.

1.5 FUTURE DIRECTIONS AND TRENDS

The future outlook suggests that the combination of new AI techniques with SNA will transform human behavior in the world as we know it. Something like deep reinforcement learning is becoming progressively more important for modeling and predicting relationships within networks because they evolve and are likely to be useful in personalized marketing as well as community detection. At the same time, federated learning is going to solve privacy issues with decentralized model training where networks would gain from user data without receiving sensitive data. This is immensely relevant in healthcare and finance, as they prioritize data privacy. Also, the merger of some machine learning techniques based on graphs with NLP has now made it easier to extract more useful information from texts within social networks. Not only are sentiment analysis and trend detection enhanced by AI, but these tasks are done with increasingly predictive precision, making the SNA far more intelligent and efficient. With such capabilities, AI-driven SNA can be acted upon in real time.

That being said, there is some work to be done in the AI-powered SNA ecosystem. As social networks expand on a global scale, businesses need to supply durable Automation Solutions' ever-changing organizational and computational infrastructure. Interpretable AI models pose another concern – though insights from deep learning algorithms are useful, the reasoning behind predictions often remains opaque. Such opacity poses severe problems in decision-making dependent domains like cybersecurity. Trust and transparency hacks pose different yet critical problems where trust within AI frameworks is a separate fundamental focus. Models built on discriminatory datasets reinforce existing social biases and perpetuate inequality. These challenges will be critical as AI takes center stage in SNA, which requires building algorithms that are not only efficient but also accountable, transparent, and equitable. Ethical concerns around surveillance, data collection, monitoring, and AI ethics support jurisdiction laws on privacy will shape the responsible use of AI in SNA.

The development of AI will, in turn, facilitate the evolution of social platforms, making them more intelligent and more responsive to user needs. Utilizing advanced algorithms such as LLMs and GNNs, platforms can provide tailored experiences that proactively address user expectations, thus improving personalization from self-service portals to e-commerce and even customer relations. Self-care and remote virtual care are parts of advanced digital health ecosystems that extend AI-powered SNA effects beyond virtual spaces and into real-world implications for public health and politics. In public health, for example, AI can facilitate tracking of diseases, allowing more accurate responses to emerging public health threats. Political applications are equally important, as AI technologies can monitor and report public sentiment in real time, enabling responsive governance. AI's ability to process copious amounts of data is what will ultimately aid in developing a more integrated, informed, and resilient society. With such benefits achieved, however, one must still tread carefully and ethically so that the technology does not widen the inequality gap by making decisions without transparency.

1.6 CONCLUSION

The impact of AI technologies on SNA presents several unresolved opportunities and obstacles to overcome. The problems posed by modern social networks require analysis beyond the capabilities of contemporary data processing AI systems. Inversely, the performance AI models provide must not interfere with their scalability once the model achieves sufficient power; that remains a challenge. In addition, AI offers profound value in the insights it provides. Unfortunately, the lack of interpretability, commonly branded "black-box" models, makes them unsuitable for sensitive fields like cybersecurity, among others, where understanding the logic behind predictions is critical. No less challenging is bias. AI learns from historical data, and thus biased systems, if not properly handled, risk amplifying societal inequalities – heightening the need to build more transparent and fair models. This work has traced the evolution of AI in SNA, highlighting key techniques such as deep learning, GNNs, LLMs, and AI Agents, and their role in improving prediction accuracy, behavior modeling, and system-level automation across various domains. However, this study is limited to a conceptual exploration and lacks empirical validation across real-world datasets.

The future of SNA will aid in enabling AI to enhance natural and human-like interactions with machines. In furtherance of that goal, machine learning and NLP alongside graph analysis will ensure the user interface is personalized, improving workplace AI adoption. With each passing day, with the introduction of AI agents, AI gets to become more integrated into our lives, and that will elevate the ethical challenges posed by its use. Maintaining trust in AI technologies requires fairness, accountability, and transparency in the models used. Future research should focus on benchmarking AI-driven SNA models on heterogeneous datasets, integrating explainable AI techniques to address the "black-box" issue, and developing governance frameworks to ensure responsible AI use – particularly in sensitive domains. Improvements in bias mitigation, model interpretability, and ethical auditing are essential to ensure that the benefits of AI-powered SNA are equitably distributed and trustworthy.

REFERENCES

1. Nirmal Varghese Babu and E Grace Mary Kanaga. Sentiment analysis in social media data for depression detection using artificial intelligence: a review. *SN Computer Science*, 3(1):74, 2022.
2. Man Hung, Evelyn Lauren, Eric S Hon, Wendy C Birmingham, Julie Xu, Sharon Su, Shirley D Hon, Jungweon Park, Peter Dang, and Martin S Lipsky. Social network analysis of covid-19 sentiments: Application of artificial intelligence. *Journal of Medical Internet Research*, 22(8):e22590, 2020.

3. Juhwan Kim, Sunghae Jun, Dongsik Jang, and Sangsung Park. Sustainable technology analysis of artificial intelligence using bayesian and social network models. *Sustainability*, 10(1):115, 2018.
4. Shazia Tabassum, Fabiola SF Pereira, Sofia Fernandes, and Joao Gama. Social network analysis: an overview. *Wiley Interdisciplinary Reviews: Data Mining and Knowledge Discovery*, 8(5):e1256, 2018.
5. Serkan Ucer, Tansel Ozyer, and Reda Alhajj. Explainable artificial intelligence through graph theory by generalized social network analysis-based classifier. *Scientific Reports*, 12(1):15210, 2022.
6. Mahsa Nooribakhsh, Marta Fern´andez-Diego, Fernando Gonz´alez-Ladr´on-De-Guevara, and Mahdi Mollamotalebi. Community detection in social networks using machine learning: a systematic mapping study. *Knowledge and Information Systems*, 66(12):7205–7259, 2024.
7. Lokesh Jain, Rahul Katarya, and Shelly Sachdeva. Opinion leaders for information diffusion using graph neural network in online social networks. *ACM Transactions on the Web*, 17(2):1–37, 2023.
8. Ashkan Kazemi. Human-Centered Natural Language Processing for Countering Misinformation. PhD thesis, 2024.
9. Mario Krenn, Lorenzo Buffoni, Bruno Coutinho, Sagi Eppel, Jacob Gates Foster, Andrew Gritsevskiy, Harlin Lee, Yichao Lu, Jo˜ao P Moutinho, Nima Sanjabi, et al. Forecasting the future of artificial intelligence with machine learning-based link prediction in an exponentially growing knowledge network. *Nature Machine Intelligence*, 5(11):1326–1335, 2023.
10. Ash Mohammad Abbas. Social network analysis using deep learning: applications and schemes. *Social Network Analysis and Mining*, 11(1):106, 2021.
11. Andrei Romascanu, Hannah Ker, Renee Sieber, Sarah Greenidge, Sam Lumley, Drew Bush, Stefan Morgan, Rosie Zhao, and Mikael Brunila. Using deep learning and social network analysis to understand and manage extreme flooding. *Journal of Contingencies and Crisis Management*, 28(3):251–261, 2020.
12. Qiaoyu Tan, Ninghao Liu, and Xia Hu. Deep representation learning for social network analysis. *Frontiers in Big Data*, 2:2, 2019.
13. Malik Khizar Hayat, Ali Daud, Abdulrahman A Alshdadi, Ameen Banjar, Rabeeh Ayaz Abbasi, Yukun Bao, and Hussain Dawood. Towards deep learning prospects: insights for social media analytics. *IEEE Access*, 7:36958–36979, 2019.
14. Donghyuk Shin, Shu He, Gene Moo Lee, Andrew B Whinston, Suleyman Cetintas, and Kuang-Chih Lee. Enhancing social media analysis with visual data analytics: a deep learning approach. *MIS Quarterly*, 44(4):1459–1492, 2020.
15. Wenqi Fan, Yao Ma, Qing Li, Yuan He, Eric Zhao, Jiliang Tang, and Dawei Yin. Graph neural networks for social recommendation. In *The World Wide Web Conference*, pp. 417–426, Singapore, 2019.
16. Wenqi Fan, Yao Ma, Qing Li, JianpingWang, Guoyong Cai, Jiliang Tang, and Dawei Yin. A graph neural network framework for social recommendations. *IEEE Transactions on Knowledge and Data Engineering*, 34(5):2033–2047, 2020.
17. Xiao Li, Li Sun, Mengjie Ling, and Yan Peng. A survey of graph neural network based recommendation in social networks. *Neurocomputing*, 549:126441, 2023.
18. Shengjie Min, Zhan Gao, Jing Peng, Liang Wang, Ke Qin, and Bo Fang. Stgsn—a spatial–temporal graph neural network framework for timeevolving social networks. *Knowledge-Based Systems*, 214:106746, 2021.
19. Kartik Sharma, Yeon-Chang Lee, Sivagami Nambi, Aditya Salian, Shlok Shah, Sang-Wook Kim, and Srijan Kumar. A survey of graph neural networks for social recommender systems. *ACM Computing Surveys*, 56(10):1–34, 2024.

20. Julie Jiang and Emilio Ferrara. Social-llm: Modeling user behavior at scale using language models and social network data. arXiv preprint arXiv:2401.00893, 2023.
21. Ritesh Tandon. Social media texts classification and analysis based on large language models (llms). *Journal of Emerging Technologies and Innovative Research*, 11(9):a751–a757, 2024.
22. Kailai Yang, Tianlin Zhang, Ziyan Kuang, Qianqian Xie, Jimin Huang, and Sophia Ananiadou. Mentallama: interpretable mental health analysis on social media with large language models. In *Proceedings of the ACM Web Conference 2024*, pp. 4489–4500, Singapore, 2024.
23. Jingying Zeng, Richard Huang, Waleed Malik, Langxuan Yin, Bojan Babic, Danny Shacham, Xiao Yan, Jaewon Yang, and Qi He. Large language models for social networks: applications, challenges, and solutions. arXiv preprint arXiv:2401.02575, 2024.
24. Antonino Ferraro, Antonio Galli, Valerio La Gatta, Marco Postiglione, Gian Marco Orlando, Diego Russo, Giuseppe Riccio, Antonio Romano, and Vincenzo Moscato. Agent-based modelling meets generative ai in social network simulations. In *International Conference on Advances in Social Networks Analysis and Mining*, pp. 155–170. Rende, Italy, Springer, 2024.
25. Chen Gao, Xiaochong Lan, Zhihong Lu, Jinzhu Mao, Jinghua Piao, Huandong Wang, Depeng Jin, and Yong Li. S3: Social-network simulation system with large language model-empowered agents. arXiv preprint arXiv:2307.14984, 2023.
26. Nikolaos Mavridis. Artificial agents entering social networks. In *A Networked Self*, pp. 299–311. Zizi Papacharissi, Routledge, 2010.

2 Unraveling the Impact of Social Networks

A Comprehensive Overview

Ruchi Kumari, Shikha Jha, and Kumar Saurav

2.1 INTRODUCTION

Social networks are known as platforms where people can share their thoughts, expressions, and experiences with different people and organizations. This establishes the connections between people, businesses, and organizations, and the boundary is spread to all people using social networks directly or indirectly. They share emotions, gather information, and aspire to achieve a dream that, with hard work and passion, may be fulfilled. This becomes possible because social media networks have the ability to connect people and their ideas across boundaries. It has broadened as the integration of artificial intelligence (AI) models has enabled communication through social networks, from simple communication platforms to complex systems. These models have strengthened the network through the formation of social media groups. In this, the group members are empowered to influence strategically and ultimately enhance different skills.

Different social networking platforms like LinkedIn, Facebook, and Instagram are growing day by day with the increase in the number of users every day. The purpose of joining these platforms is different for different people; some join them for entertainment only, some for gathering information, some for seeking help or a job, etc. Because it facilitates users to share information across geographical boundaries within a fraction of a second. Nowadays, Instagram has become a hub for visual description, connecting people via shared moments, interests, and innovative expressions while serving as a marketing hub for businesses and individuals. Thus, the social network is a depiction of social structures constituted of members, individuals, or organizations, and the bond that connects them. These bonds develop trust and understanding from an informal bond to a formal bond and familiar connections. The elaborate structure of the social network is developed by its members and the dynamic connections between them.

In view of the above changes, the study focuses on applying advanced sentiment analysis models, particularly Long Short-Term Memory (LSTM)–based architectures, networks like Graphical Network Neurons (GNNs), and transformer-based models like BRET, LLM, etc., for executing users' work and public opinion from social media data. While earlier studies primarily relied on basic statistical methods or traditional machine learning models (e.g., SVMs, Naive Bayes), the proposed study compiles deep learning to achieve a more refined, context-aware interpretation

DOI: 10.1201/9781003611110-2

of sentiment (Krishna et al., 2023; Olaniyan et al., 2023). This shift from traditional techniques to deep models significantly increases the accuracy and precision of predictions, especially to handle slang, emojis, sarcasm, and informal language often found in social networks.

Although it is undeniable that, when there are benefits of social media, there are also harms of it, it totally depends on its usage. It is useful, productive, and resourceful, but it can be harmful as well when not used properly. Different benefits include being a medium/platform for sharing ideas and knowledge, forming a common platform to spread the ideas, and helping in businesses to get innovative ideas. It can act as a social campaign, focusing on the issues of society or the common person. However, its challenges are unavoidable like cyber fraud, online harassment, and privacy loss. These challenges have been affecting common people, and it is very important that these issues are addressed. Excess or ill use of social media is resulting in emotional, cognitive, and mental harm to the user. The harm is even physical, in terms of eye-sight loss, sleep loss, and others. Fake news or manipulated information, spread through these platforms, has been a serious issue for users and society. It forms a negative opinion about the users, and the spread of false content makes the user depressed in a way. Data privacy and ethical information are other critical concerns that should be linked with the usage of social media networks.

Despite the benefits, there is a research gap in terms of the use of social media that focuses on sentiment analysis, which can evolve to various languages and trends in real time, especially across different regions and diverse cultural backgrounds. A deep learning framework that helps in the integration of different languages by attention mechanisms and pictorial insights has been addressed in the paper. Recent studies have focused on the need for a sentiment analysis system that can understand the user context, emotion intelligence, and multimodal content, which helps in the usage of social networks to a wide variety of people including regional and local people (e.g., Singh & Singh, 2024; Yue et al., 2023). Additionally, the future scope includes real-time prediction systems associated with social media platforms, which can help in identifying public sentiment shifts and social trends.

There are various opportunities for personal, professional, and societal growth through the application of social media. There are some ethical considerations associated with it. It should be critically examined and evaluated. Social media should be used responsibly to reap its benefits. The underlying adverse effects of social media need to be addressed. The application of social media helps in customized understanding of the customer. It can also be leveraged for educational purposes.

2.2 METHODOLOGY

This study shows a structured literature review methodology that has examined the evolution, usage, limitations, and future of social media networks. The special focus is on the correlation of Social Network Analysis (SNA) and deep learning frameworks. Many peer-reviewed research articles, industry white papers, and case studies from various disciplines like computer science, information technology, the social sciences, and others have been critically reviewed.

One of the key challenges of this methodology lies in exploring the vast and interdisciplinary nature of the literature, which needs careful selection and formation of multiple sources to ensure comprehensive and stable coverage. In addition, the evolving nature of deep learning networks and their application in social media shows ambiguity and difficulty in maintaining relevance and coherence across different studies.

The novelty of this methodological approach lies in its interdisciplinary scope and its focus on integrating technical, social, and ethical perspectives. Unlike traditional reviews that often focus mainly on technical performance, this study also summarizes technological advancements, such as LSTM, transformers, Graphical Network Neurons (GNNs), and blockchain, with wider societal implications. This also includes misinformation, privacy, and mental health concerns. This study not only identifies emerging trends and limitations but also gives a future perspective and foundation for research and innovations in the field.

2.3 OVERVIEW OF SOCIAL NETWORKS

2.3.1 Evolution of Social Networks: From Early Platforms to Modern Giants

Revolutionary shifts in digital communication, connectivity, and technological advancement have marked the evolution of social networks. It was not until the early 2000s that platforms such as Friendster, MySpace, and LinkedIn gained prominence, each targeting distinct user demographics and networking needs. The launch of Facebook in 2004 transformed social networking by giving a structured news feed and personalized interactions, ultimately shaping the landscape of digital socialization. Twitter, founded in 2006, redefined real-time communication through microblogging, while later platforms like Instagram and TikTok further capitalized on visual content and short-form video engagement, respectively (Figure 2.1) (Edosomwan, 2011). Advancements in internet accessibility, mobile technology, and data-driven algorithms largely drove the transition from early networking sites to contemporary social media giants. The widespread adoption of smartphones and high-speed internet facilitated the exponential growth of social media usage, enabling seamless interaction across geographic boundaries. These technological shifts also influenced user behavior, with platforms evolving to incorporate AI, content recommendation systems, and real-time data analytics to optimize engagement.

Several studies have evaluated the historical growth of social networks, focusing on the key milestones that have shaped evolution. Boyd and Ellison (2007), in their study on foundational exploration of the development of social networking sites, have evaluated their usage and societal impacts. Another research by Hampton et al. (2011) stressed the role of mobile technology in increasing social media engagement. It showed how smartphone penetration can facilitate instant interconnectivity (Hampton & Goulet, 2011). Other studies have examined the structural dynamics of evolving networks. It has evaluated the link formation and evolution of user interactions. Alaa et al. (2015) made a micro-foundational model to examine the evolution of social networks. It focused on the interconnections between user behavior and network topology. Their results suggested that components such as homophily and social magnanimity influence the creation and sustainability of online communities (Alaa et al., 2015). Recent research conducted by Ubaldi et al. (2021) identified the

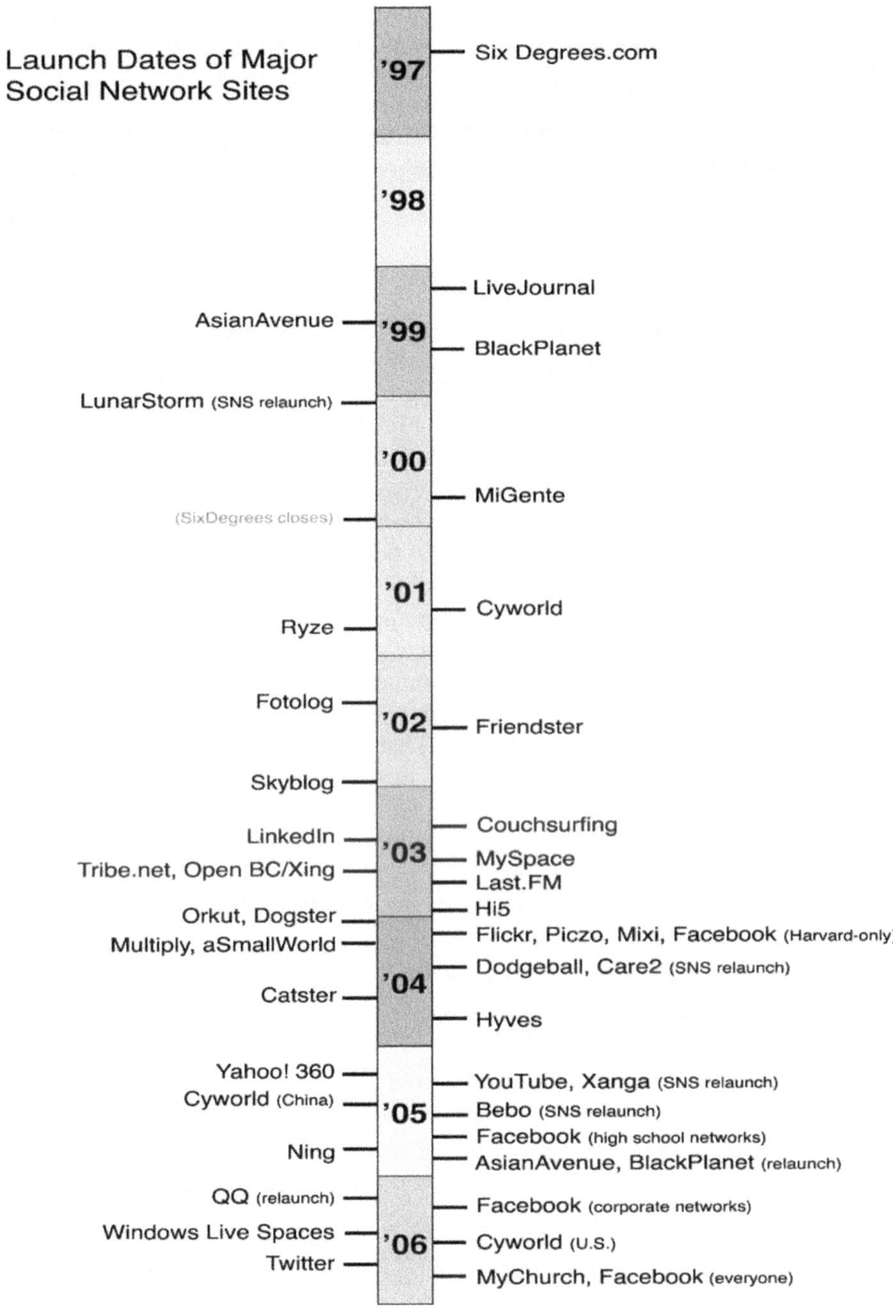

FIGURE 2.1 Timeline of the launch dates of many major Social Networking Sites (SNSs) and dates when community sites re-launched with SNS features (Boyd & Ellison, 2007).

concept of the Adjacent Possible space. It mainly focused on how social networks grow and evolve through a combination of exploration and reinforcement methods (Ubaldi et al., 2021).

As social networks continue to grow, new problems and opportunities come as well, including concerns related to privacy, disinformation, and digital wellbeing. The transformation of these platforms highlights the need for ongoing research into their technological, social, and economic considerations.

2.3.2 Current Trends in Social Network Usage Globally

Social media networks have become an integral part of global communication, with billions of users engaging and interacting on various platforms every day. Recent data trend indicates that as of 2025, there are over 5.24 billion social media users worldwide, with an average user engaging on 6.83 different platforms every month (Table 2.1). This enormous spread of social media has helped the rise of platforms like TikTok and Instagram, especially among the younger population who prefer short video content and interactive features. Meanwhile, social networks have increasingly integrated e-commerce, and there has been a surge in direct-to-consumer (D2C) channels of sales. Platforms like Facebook, Instagram, and TikTok are providing direct purchases through in-app shopping features.

AI and machine learning have also played a major role in shaping user experiences, enabling personalized content recommendations and targeted advertising. These tools use the most watched/performed contents based on user preferences, or contents with more engaging and customized behavior (Mariani et al., 2023; Vlačić et al., 2021). More so, regional differences in social media usage show cultural, economic, and technological variations. In China, platforms like WeChat dominate because of their multifunctional and multidimensional features that integrate

TABLE 2.1
Global Trend in Social Media Usage (2015–2024) with Year-on-Year Growth

Year	Active Social Media Users (Billions)	Year-on-Year Growth (%)	Sources
2015	2.08	—	Statista (2024)
2016	2.31	11.1	Statista (2024)
2017	2.8	21.2	Statista (2024)
2018	3.2	14.3	Statista (2024)
2019	3.48	8.8	Statista (2024)
2020	3.96	13.8	DataReportal (2024)
2021	4.48	13.1	DataReportal (2024)
2022	4.62	3.1	DataReportal (2024)
2023	4.95	7.1	Backlinko (2024)
2024	5.17	4.4	Backlinko (2024)

communication, payments, and services. While in India, WhatsApp is a primary tool for communication, as it is designed to be user-friendly and easily accessible to all.

To gather knowledge about current insights into social media involvement and usage patterns, there are reports like The Global Digital Reports by "We Are Social and Hootsuite." Their reports show the rapid growth in mobile-based platforms and the increasing shift toward video-based content consumption. Research done by Statista (2024) also supports this trend, showing that platforms providing visual and ephemeral content have experienced the highest engagement rates in recent years. Kaplan and Haenlein (2010) have explored the role of cultural and regional factors in social media adoption, showing how economic conditions and technological advancement influence platform choices (Kaplan & Haenlein, 2010). As digital platforms continue to evolve, understanding these trends is crucial for business managers, policymakers, and end users. The connection between AI, e-commerce, and regional platform choices will shape the future of social media networking, demonstrating how individuals and organizations interact in a connected world.

2.4 APPLICATIONS OF SOCIAL NETWORK ANALYSIS WITH DEEP LEARNING FRAMEWORKS

SNA has undergone considerable evolution in recent years, particularly with the growing use of deep learning approaches. These methods bring significant advantages in dealing with complex, high-dimensional, and dynamic social data by enabling automatic feature extraction and improving model generalization across a variety of tasks. For example, deep learning models are used frequently for sentiment analysis, to detect misinformation and fake news, unusual pattern identification, and to study underlying network structures. A major development in this area is the combination of techniques that are graph-based with deep learning architectures. This has led to applications that help researchers better understand user behavior, enhance personalization, and strengthen tools for mitigating harmful content online. Although these tasks have different objectives, they often share a common computational process that includes data preprocessing, representation learning, and task-specific deep model application.

To provide a unifying perspective, Figure 2.2 illustrates a general deep learning pipeline for SNA. This schematic traces the process from raw social media or interaction data, through representation learning, to output stages aligned with particular analytical goals. Representation like this offers a conceptual framework and also highlights the commonalities across diverse applications.

2.4.1 Sentiment Analysis: Understanding Public Opinion and User Behavior

Sentiment analysis, which is also known as opinion mining, uses advanced deep learning models to analyze and interpret the emotions or sentiments expressed in user-generated content on social media platforms like tweets, comments, and posts.

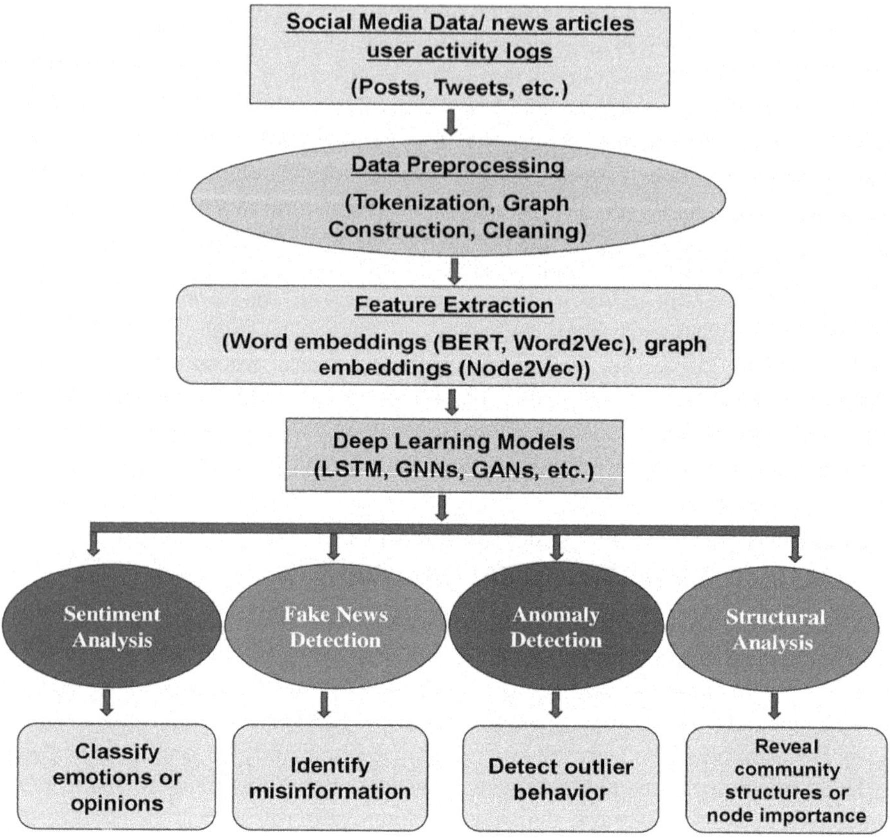

FIGURE 2.2 A unified deep learning pipeline illustrating key social network analysis tasks.

The main aim of sentiment analysis is to sort text into groups such as positive, negative, or neutral. This shows how people feel about a topic/product/brand. At the center of this work is Natural Language Processing (NLP). Moreover, NLP helps computers read and understand human language.

NLP steps include breaking text into tokens, highlighting parts of speech, and finding key names. These steps make complicated text easier to study. One of the common methods is the use of Recurrent Neural Networks (RNNs). They work well because text comes in order, like a sequence.

RNNs remember words that came before in a sentence. This memory helps in understanding the meaning of the whole text. RNNs often tend to ignore words in long text. That's why LSTM networks are more useful.

LSTMs are built to hold on to important details for longer. This helps them fix the problem that normal RNNs face. For example, take the review: "The camera is great, but the battery dies fast." A simple model may only see the good part, but an LSTM can see both good and bad at the same time.

TABLE 2.2
Sample Dataset Snapshot for LSTM-Based Sentiment Analysis

Raw Text Input	Preprocessed Text	Sentiment Label
"I love the new phone! Battery life is great."	Love the new phone battery life, great	Positive
"Terrible service. I'm never ordering again."	Terrible service, never ordering again	Negative
"The packaging was okay, nothing special."	Packaging okay, nothing special	Neutral
"Absolutely thrilled with the performance!"	Absolutely thrilled performance	Positive
"Worst update ever. Slowed my device down."	The worst update slowed the device down	Negative

Table 2.2 shows how raw text is cleaned before it is classified. It gives an example of tokenization and labeling. This makes it easier to connect the steps with real data. It shows how deep learning models actually work with text.

Research by Yin et al. (2023) highlights the efficiency of deep learning models (LSTM networks) in sentiment analysis. These models also show a strong ability to detect feelings and emotions in text from social media. By training on big sets of labeled data, LSTM networks can tell if a post is positive, negative, or neutral. They also detect deeper feelings like anger, joy, or sadness. This works even when the text has slang or emojis.

Companies use these insights to make better choices with data. The rise of user content online makes these tools even more useful. Deep learning models like LSTM keep improving over time. They give clear ideas about what people feel and how they behave.

2.4.2 Fake News Detection: Combating Misinformation Using AI

The spread of fake news is very common and easy in today's generation. This has become a big problem as it affects individuals, society, and politics in a negative way. Deep learning models, like CNNs (Convolutional Neural Networks) and transformer models such as Bidirectional Encoder Representations from Transformers (BERT), are used to find and sort fake news. These models look at different kinds of information, and they also study patterns in text, pictures, or videos.

BERT works a bit differently from older models. It looks at words both before and after. This helps it understand the meaning of a sentence more clearly. Its ability makes it good at finding misleading information. It studies word connections and hidden clues in the language.

BERT generally needs very large datasets to give an optimized result. It can only reach high accuracy after seeing lots of examples. Research by Mehta et al. (2021) has stressed this issue and also shown how strong transformer models can be more efficient. Their study shows that these models can find fake news by looking at language style, emotions, and credibility of the source. They also show that analyzing large amounts of news makes it easier to spot false stories (Mehta et al., 2021). Organizations and platforms may improve their ability to find and stop false information by using AI-driven models like BERT. This will make the digital information ecosystem more trustworthy. As deep learning techniques are getting better, so are fake news detection systems, which are an important way to stop the spread of false information.

2.4.3 Anomaly Detection: Identifying Unusual Patterns in Network Data

It is possible to spot anomalous patterns in network traffic that could indicate fraud, cyberattacks, or serious system failures. Anomaly detection has emerged as a key component of cybersecurity and large-scale data analytics. In simple terms, organizations use anomaly detection to find unusual patterns. These include strange login attempts, fraud in financial transactions, or weird packet flows in networks. You can see that this is really important because these things can cause big problems. With deep learning added in, analysts can monitor systems automatically. It helps spot strange activity faster. Sometimes way faster than a human could.

Recent models often mix traditional machine learning with NLP, especially when dealing with logs or text-based alerts, or even commands that users send with network data. These techniques help separate normal stuff from the weird or suspicious. Autoencoders, for example, learn normal traffic patterns, and they compress them. Anything that comes out with too high a reconstruction error gets flagged as abnormal.

Generative Adversarial Networks (GANs) are another approach that works really well. They have two neural networks, i.e., a generator and a discriminator, that "compete" with each other. The generator makes fake traffic that looks real. The discriminator tries to spot anything that doesn't fit. Over time, both get better. The generator improves, the discriminator improves, and the system can catch really subtle weirdness.

To show how this works, take the example in Figure 2.3. The generator learns normal traffic patterns. The discriminator slowly gets better at spotting stuff that doesn't match. You can see three traffic types on the plot: real normal traffic, GAN-made synthetic traffic, and traffic that has odd spikes and dips. Yeah, the weird spikes are usually easy to notice. Sometimes it's really subtle. Adding extra checks helps a lot. Analysts can look at metadata, like whether the news source is trustworthy. They can also study user behavior like shares and comments. All of this helps make anomaly detection more reliable. Often, it's still not perfect, but combining all these methods usually works pretty well.

The GAN-generated traffic closely follows the expected normal trend, while the anomalous traffic exhibits clear deviations, highlighting how GANs can model the baseline behavior and thus detect subtle anomalies by comparing real-time inputs against this learned distribution.

The plot compares normal network traffic. Synthetic data are used. It also shows GAN-generated synthetic traffic and anomalous traffic. The GAN-generated signal mimics the normal baseline closely. The anomalous traffic, on the other hand, shows

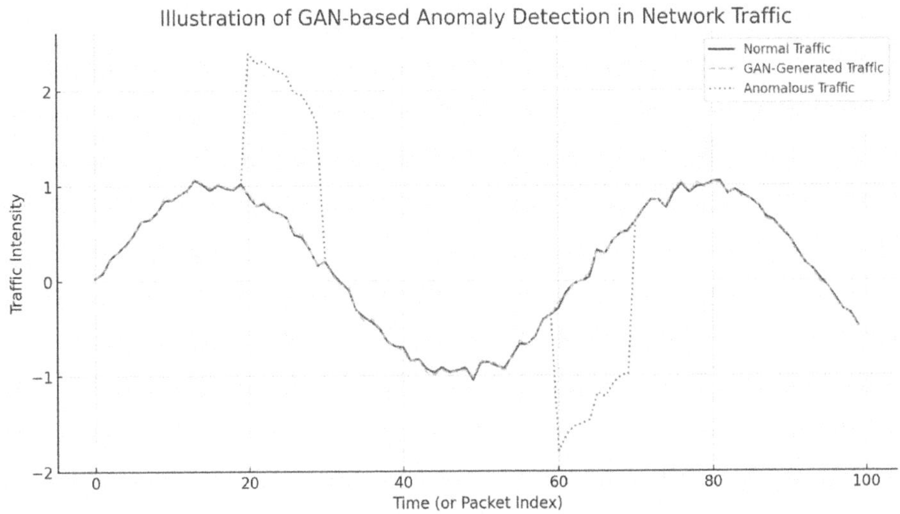

FIGURE 2.3 General illustration of GAN-based anomaly detection.

clear deviations. These include spikes and dips. This contrast helps the discriminator detect outliers more effectively.

Different research has shown that GAN-based training can improve the sensitivity of Network Intrusion Detection Systems (NIDSs) to such deviations. For example, Abdelaty et al. (2022) introduced GADoT, a GAN-based adversarial training framework. It is designed to make DDoS attack detection systems stronger. Their findings show that using adversarial samples during training really helps improve detection accuracy. This is true for machine learning–based NIDSs against tricky DDoS attacks (Abdelaty et al., 2022).

Guo (2023) reviewed machine learning–based zero-day attack detection methods. It also highlights the efficiency of GANs to find previously unknown shortcomings. GAN-based models offer a good way for proactive cybersecurity. It can also work for complex training with a lot of resources (Guo, 2023).

Cybersecurity not only detects mistakes but also helps prevent fraud. It can also do industrial monitoring, healthcare diagnostics, and financial risk checks. AI-powered models like GANs are helping organizations find and reduce/eliminate threats, thus making sure that critical systems stay safe and stable. With the improvement of deep learning models, anomaly detection methods would become more efficient. It can be scalable and adaptive. Also, they offer strong protection against new security challenges.

2.4.4 Structural Analysis: Insights from Graph-Based Models of Social Networks

The structural analysis of social networks depends on graph-based techniques. Basically, the techniques work on finding the patterns by which communication and community growth occur. It works upon graph-based analysis, where nodes and edges are used. Nodes help signify the people or entities, while edges show relationships or interactions. They also allow identification of influential users, network groups, and tightly knit communities. These are useful for understanding how information moves in a network, how communities grow, and how social influence develops.

GNNs are an important tool to understand complex relationships. It works on understanding the hidden patterns in broad-scaled networks more easily by gathering the information from neighboring nodes step by step. This provides a more dynamic and scalable way to study social networks. Another widely used approach is network embedding, which converts high-dimensional graph structures into lower-dimensional vector representations while preserving essential relationships (Zhou et al., 2020). It helps in understanding the patterns easily. Techniques like DeepWalk and Node2Vec make embeddings that can be used for tasks like classification, clustering, and showing social networks. Unlike handcrafted features, network embedding work on tools that automatically find meaningful patterns. This makes it easier to show emerging trends and user behaviors on social media platforms (Grover & Leskovec, 2016).

Graph-based models in SNA have led to advancements in various real-world applications, particularly in social media analytics, financial fraud detection, and biological network modeling. Major platforms such as Twitter and Facebook use such techniques to increase friend recommendations, detect coordinated misinformation, and identify trending influencers. Beyond digital spaces, structural analysis is instrumental in urban transportation planning, epidemic modeling, and supply chain optimization, highlighting its interdisciplinary impact. Scalability and interpretability remain key challenges, as real-world networks continue to grow in complexity and size. Future research should focus on integrating GNNs with reinforcement learning, hybrid models, and more specific network embedding techniques to increase computational accuracy and improve prediction efficiency. As these methods grow and evolve, graph-based analysis will continue to play a crucial role in interpreting the intricate web of connections that define human interactions in the digital era (Table 2.3).

2.5 CHALLENGES OF SOCIAL NETWORKS

The rapid growth of social networks has brought some challenges. In today's world, misinformation and fake news are big concerns (Figure 2.4). For example, the COVID-19 pandemic and political elections show how misinformation can change public opinion, support conspiracy theories, and reduce trust in institutions (Chen et al., 2020). Sensational content is psychologically appealing. Social media algorithms often promote it, which makes it spread faster than accurate information. To take care of this, algorithms make fact-checking initiatives that are AI-driven. It detects tools and gives the user a user-generated report (Lee et al., 2023; Tafur & Sarkar, 2023). Researchers also emphasize the need for a multilevel approach involving digital literacy programs. It also includes stricter regulatory frameworks. It has been collaborative efforts between technology companies and governments to stop the spread of fake news.

Social networks have a big issue with user privacy. It is a source of ethical and legal concern and debate. This is mostly about data collection, surveillance, and user consent. The Cambridge Analytica scandal, where personal information of millions

TABLE 2.3
Advancements in Deep Learning: Applications, Models, and Use Cases

Application	Deep Learning Models Used	Real-World Examples	Dataset Used	Key Benefits	Key Challenges
Sentiment analysis	RNNs, CNNs, transformers (BERT, GPT)	Twitter trend analysis, brand reputation monitoring	IMDb, Twitter Sentiment140, SST	Improves customer engagement and marketing strategies	Sarcasm detection, short text ambiguity
Fake news detection	GNNs, NLP-based classifiers, GANs	Google news verification, misinformation detection	LIAR, FakeNewsNet, BuzzFeed News	Helps in mitigating the spread of fake news	Domain adaptation, rapid content evolution
Anomaly detection	LSTMs, GANs, isolation forest, autoencoders	Fraud prevention on banking platforms, cybersecurity	NSL-KDD, CICIDS2017, NAB	Enhances security and prevents financial losses	Imbalanced data, evolving threat patterns
Structural analysis	DeepWalk, Node2Vec, GNN-based models	Community detection on LinkedIn, social network analysis	Facebook Social Circles, SNAP datasets	Improves network insights and recommendation systems	Scalability to large graphs, dynamic graph changes
Medical diagnosis	CNNs, transformers, GANs	AI-powered radiology (lung cancer detection), pathology AI	CheXpert, LIDC-IDRI, HAM10000	Enhances early disease detection and diagnostic accuracy	Data privacy, annotation scarcity, model interpretability
Autonomous driving	CNNs, RNNs, reinforcement learning, vision models	Tesla self-driving technology, ADAS systems	KITTI, Waymo Open, Udacity	Enables safer and more efficient transportation	Real-time inference, handling edge cases
Speech recognition	Deep speech, transformers (whisper), RNNs	Google assistant, Siri, Amazon Alexa	LibriSpeech, Common Voice, TIMIT	Enhances voice-driven user interfaces	Accents, background noise, multilingual recognition
Recommender systems	Matrix factorization, autoencoders, transformers	Netflix movie recommendations, Amazon product suggestions	MovieLens, Amazon Reviews, Yelp	Improves user experience and engagement	Cold start problem, dynamic user preferences

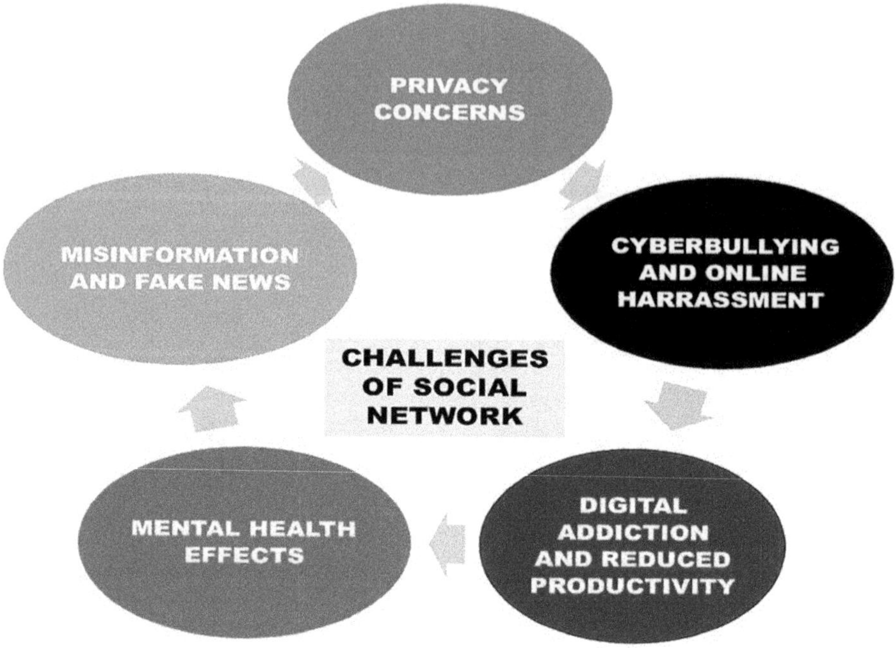

FIGURE 2.4 Challenges of social networks.

of Facebook users was used for political profiling, showed major weaknesses in data governance. It has also stressed the risk of sharing personal data in the public domain. Many platforms do make monetary benefits from this user data. They use this for customized ads. They often do this without fully explaining how data is collected, processed, and shared. Due to the reasons mentioned before, strict regulations like the General Data Protection Regulation (GDPR) and the California Consumer Privacy Act (CCPA) were introduced to protect privacy (Wong et al., 2023; Liu et al., 2022). Although challenges are ongoing, including evolving data mining techniques, the expansion of biometric surveillance, and the ethical issues surrounding AI-powered personalization. Researchers argue that having a balance between personalization and privacy protection requires robust encryption techniques, decentralized data storage solutions, and stronger enforcement of privacy laws.

The effect of social networks on mental health has been deeply studied, with concerns over increased anxiety, enhanced depression, and social comparison among each other. Research suggests that excess use of social media, specifically among adolescents or teens, correlates with decreased self-confidence and increased rates of cyberbullying, contributing to emotional stress (Patchin & Hinduja, 2010). Different factors like infinite scrolling, likes, and algorithmically curated content contribute to addictive behaviors, reinforcing compulsive usage patterns that affect sleep, productivity, and real-life interactions. Some of the efforts to address these issues include the introduction of screen time management tools, content moderation policies, and awareness campaigns promoting digital health. While platforms like Instagram and

TikTok have experimented with erasing visible counts to decrease social validation pressures, experts suggest that interventions, including mental wellbeing education and stricter design laws in digital platforms, are very important to reduce the adverse psychological effects of prolonged social media use. As social networks continue to grow, addressing these challenges will require a collective effort from technology companies, policymakers, and mental health professionals to provide a safer and more responsible digital environment.

2.6 OPPORTUNITIES FOR LEVERAGING SOCIAL NETWORKS FOR SOCIAL GOOD

Social media network off late has proved to be powerful tools for crisis management. It can enable real-time communication and coordination during emergencies. Platforms like Twitter and Facebook have played a vital role in spreading information during natural calamities. It may include hurricanes, flash floods, and earthquakes. It would enable the concerned victim to seek help in case of an emergency. Relief work can be coordinated through the platforms of social media. Crowdsourced mapping, abated by initiatives like Ushahidi, has been very useful in tracking disaster-affected areas. It helps in coordinating and giving required steps to be taken in disaster-affected areas (Duc et al., 2014). Recent research suggests that integrating AI and big data analytics with social networks can enhance disaster response. It can accomplish it by examining distress signals and predicting the affected areas.

The American Red Cross society's social media platform is a good example of a social media application. It has showed how it can be applied for the larger interest of the society.

During disasters, it responds quickly to the social media calls and requests for any help. It gives necessary information, such as safety tips and shelter locations. It also facilitates and coordinates blood donation opportunities. The society also uses social media to promote donation campaigns by encouraging followers to contribute to disaster relief efforts.

It has been reported that the society has seen significant engagement, with over three million followers on Twitter and over more than two million likes on Facebook. The organization has also improved its response times, with its social media team responding to inquiries within minutes. A case study titled "The American Red Cross Embraces Social Media" highlights its usages of social media in transforming its public relations and disaster response strategies. It has enabled direct communication with the public (Cass, n.d.).

The Ice Bucket Challenge during 2014 is an example of how social media can be used to raise awareness and funds for a social cause. The challenge that involves dumping a bucket of ice water over one's head or donating $100 to ALS (Amyotrophic Lateral Sclerosis) research was simple yet engaging. The campaign spread rapidly across various social media platforms. Participants shared videos and nominated their friends to take the challenge as well. Celebrities, athletes, and influencers also participated, giving a boost to the campaign's awareness and impact. As a result, the Ice Bucket Challenge successfully raised awareness about ALS, thus generating

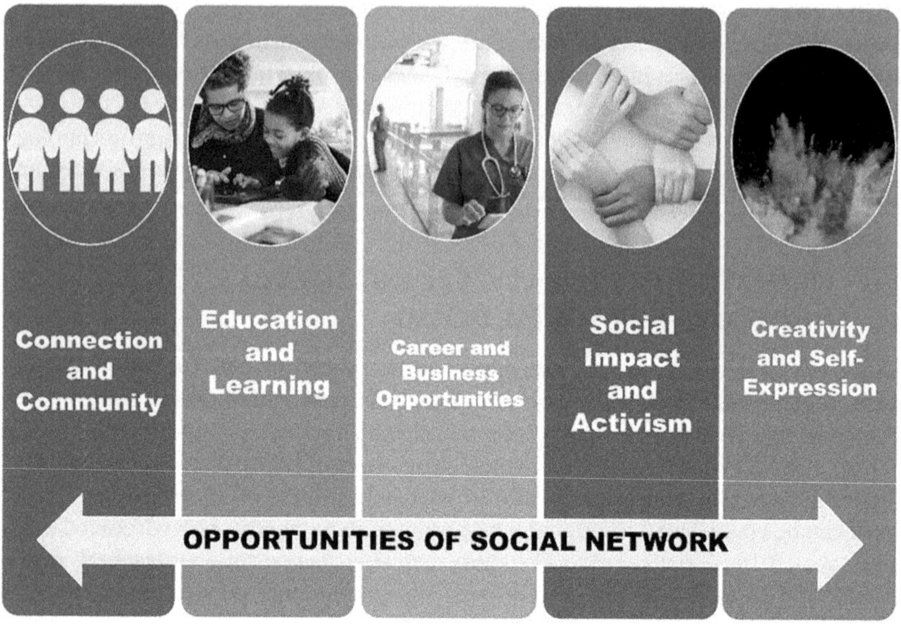

FIGURE 2.5 Different opportunities of social networks.

over 2.4 million tweets with the hashtag #IceBucketChallenge. The campaign also raised over $100 million for ALS research, with the ALS Association receiving over $115 million in donations (Bragazzi et al., 2017; Zhao et al., n.d.).

Social networks have provided us with tools and platforms for social help and growth. In terms of gathering funds, GoFundMe and Kickstarter have provided funding platforms for individuals and social groups by gathering funds. For legislative changes and corporate accountability, there are Websites like Change.org, which gather millions of signatures for policy reforms and social justice through online petitions. For career or job-related information and professional development, LinkedIn is a big platform. Moreover, platforms like YouTube and TikTok have become hubs for educational and entertainment content; along with this, they are used for earning money as well. These examples highlight the diverse ways in which social networks contribute to positive societal change, proving that when used effectively, they can be powerful instruments for empowerment and progress (Figure 2.5).

2.7 CASE STUDIES

Movements like #MeToo and Black Lives Matter too have gained fame and importance through social networks. In the business sector, companies can connect effectively with customers and other users through platforms like Instagram and Facebook. It can be used for targeted advertising and promotional campaigns. It can help with brand image management. It may lead to an increase in customer retention and help in making more revenue and sales. The above-mentioned examples clearly demonstrate how social networks help in business and other useful purposes. If it is used strategically, it can enable meaningful interactions and provide valuable insights. It can also be used to improve global connectivity.

Tackling these challenges requires a multidimensional approach. It involves technological advancements and policy interventions. It is also required that there be an increased public awareness. Governments and many organizations are increasingly investing in AI-enabled tools to combat fake news and hate speech. It also tackles and identifies harmful content while also ensuring transparency in its platform algorithms. Stringent data protection laws, such as the General Data Protection Regulation (GDPR), have been implemented to safeguard user privacy and limit data misuse. Some of the digital literacy programs aim to educate users on responsible social media engagement. It helps them in discerning credible information from misleading content. Social media networks continue to evolve, and their success would mainly be dependent on finding a balance between maximizing benefits and mitigating risks. It also ensures that it remains a positive and useful tool for mankind for the betterment of society.

2.8 FUTURE DIRECTIONS IN SOCIAL NETWORK RESEARCH

The future of social media networks will be dependent on technological advancements. It would also require a regulatory framework from the government. It would thus help monitor the evolving user behaviors. Many other promising research directions and innovations are expected to influence and reshape the way social networks operate now.

1. **Advancements in GNNs**: The application of GNNs optimizes SNA, especially with fake news detection. It also helps in detecting misinformation spread and hidden network events. Earlier models used data as independent samples, but GNNs utilize the relational form of social graphs. In this scenario, users, posts, and interactions work like nodes and edges. Future research would focus on heterogeneous groups of GNNs. That will consider multiple types of nodes, e.g., users, posts, and news sources. One very important discovery would be attention-based GNNs, which can use different weights to detect connections based on their influence. This would allow models to detect the propagation patterns of false formation and would help to assess the credibility of content. Techniques like graph streaming and continuous learning would play a major role in achieving this goal (Wu & Hooi, 2023).
2. **Privacy-Preserving Techniques**: The concern for data security and privacy is growing. The development of privacy-preserving methods like differential privacy, homomorphic encryption, and federated learning has become very useful. With these approaches, models can train without direct access to raw user data, which in turn can help in protecting user privacy while also maintaining model utility (Feretzakis et al., 2024).

3. **AI-Driven Solutions for Ethical Social Networking**: AI plays a major role in dealing with misinformation being spread on social media. It also creates hatred and animosity among the groups. AI tools like context-aware content moderation, deepfake detection systems, and sentiment analysis recommendation engines can be used. They will improve integrity by reducing harmful or false content. It would also promote inclusivity by creating balanced digital interactions. Future research may focus on making these models more robust and user-friendly. This would help in minimizing over-moderation and algorithm bias.
4. **Integration of Blockchain for Secure and Decentralized Networks**: The use of blockchain technology (a decentralized digital model) can transform social media. It also takes care of data ownership and its authentication process. Blockchain can be used to improve content integrity. It helps in storing unique hashes of digital material. It can now also trace the origin of the news and can make the necessary correction/alteration if required. It can also verify the authenticity of news by going through its roots. With these given applications, blockchain technology can become an important and reliable tool for accountability in the field of digital media. Decentralized social media platforms like Minds have greater autonomy and can prevent control over data and narratives. It plays an important role in fighting misinformation and censorship (Zhang et al., 2019).
5. **Metaverse and Immersive Social Experiences**: The application of virtual reality (VR) and augmented reality (AR) in social media will change the way users interact. These latest technologies will allow users to interact in simulated environments. On the flip side, this raises important questions about identity, representation, and behavioral rules. Ethical research will need to address the implications of misinformation and manipulation in virtual spaces, where traditional content verification methods may not work (Iqbal & Campbell, 2023).
6. **Regulatory Frameworks and Digital Ethics**: The rise in misinformation spread and privacy breaches is concerning. Technical institutions are now working with the government to create regulatory rules to ensure social platforms can be used responsibly and ethically.

2.9 CONCLUSION

Social networks have totally changed the way people, businesses, and organizations communicate, interact, and gather information from each other. This book chapter offers a comprehensive summary of the impact of social networks, exploring both the benefits and concerns associated with them. Social networks give connectivity, marketing, and the ease of information distribution. At the same time, it also poses various concerns related to data privacy, misinformation spread, and mental health. Nowadays, solutions provided by AI continue to shape the digital landscape, providing a better user experience. However, with the progress in technology, the need for ethical alignment grows strong. Future research should focus on improving AI content regulation, exploring privacy protection techniques, and enhancing the decentralized network. At the end, the future of social networks depends on collaboration between researchers, technology developers, and policymakers.

REFERENCES

Abdelaty, M., Scott-Hayward, S., Doriguzzi-Corin, R., & Siracusa, D. (2022). *GADoT: GAN-Based Adversarial Training for Robust DDoS Attack Detection*. https://arxiv.org/abs/2201.13102

Alaa, A. M., Ahuja, K., & van der Schaar, M. (2015). *Evolution of Social Networks: A Microfounded Model*. https://arxiv.org/abs/1508.00205

Backlinko. (2024). *Social Media Users — How Many People Use Social Media in 2024?* https://backlinko.com/social-media-users

Boyd, D. M., & Ellison, N. B. (2007). Social network sites: Definition, history, and scholarship. *Journal of Computer-Mediated Communication*, *13*(1), 210–230. https://doi.org/10.1111/j.1083-6101.2007.00393.x

Bragazzi, N. L., Martini, M., Igwe, S. C., Vecchio, I., Barberis, I., Tornali, C., Licata, M., Borromeo, F., Cardinale, A. E., Mohammadadawi, & Brigo, F. (2017). Has the ice bucket challenge really increased people's awareness of amyotrophic lateral sclerosis? Insights and ethical implications from Google Trends and wikipedia: A 2 years-follow up. *Acta Medica Mediterranea*, *33*(5), 875–878. https://doi.org/10.19193/0393-6384_2017_5_130

Cass, J. (n.d.). *CASE STUDY: The American Red Cross Embraces Social Media and Improves Its Image with Key Audiences* (Vol. 8, Issue 4). https://community.centredaily.com/

Chen, E., Chang, H., Rao, A., Lerman, K., Cowan, G., & Ferrara, E. (2020). COVID-19 misinformation and the 2020U.S. presidential election. *Harvard Kennedy School Misinformation Review*, *1*(7). https://doi.org/10.37016/mr-2020-57

DataReportal. (2024). *Digital 2024: Global overview report*. We Are Social & Meltwater. https://datareportal.com/reports/digital-2024-global-overview-report

Duc, K. N., Vu, T. T., & Ban, Y. (2014). Ushahidi and Sahana Eden open-source platforms to assist disaster relief: Geospatial components and capabilities. *Lecture Notes in Geoinformation and Cartography*, *0*, 163–174. https://doi.org/10.1007/978-3-319-03644-1_12

Edosomwan, S. O. (2011). The history of social media and its impact on business. *Journal of Applied Management and Entrepreneurship*. https://www.researchgate.net/publication/303216233

Feretzakis, G., Papaspyridis, K., Gkoulalas-Divanis, A., & Verykios, V. S. (2024). Privacy-preserving techniques in generative AI and large language models: A narrative review. *Information (Switzerland)*, *15*(11). https://doi.org/10.3390/info15110697

Grover, A., & Leskovec, J. (2016). Node2vec: Scalable feature learning for networks. *Proceedings of the ACM SIGKDD International Conference on Knowledge Discovery and Data Mining*, 13–17-August-2016, San Francisco, California, USA, 855–864. https://doi.org/10.1145/2939672.2939754

Guo, Y. (2023). A review of machine learning-based zero-day attack detection: Challenges and future directions. *Computer Communications*, *198*, 175–185. https://doi.org/10.1016/j.comcom.2022.11.001

Hampton, K. N., Goulet, L. S., Rainie, L., & Purcell, K. (2011, June 16). Social networking sites and our lives: How people's trust, personal relationships, and civic and political involvement are connected to their use of social networking sites and other technologies. *Pew Research Center*. http://pewinternet.org/Reports/2011/Technology-and-social-networks.aspx

Iqbal, M., & Campbell, A. (2023). Metaverse as tech for good: Current progress and emerging opportunities. *Virtual Worlds*, *2*(4), 326–342. https://doi.org/10.3390/virtualworlds2040019

Kaplan, A. M., & Haenlein, M. (2010). Users of the world, unite! The challenges and opportunities of Social Media. *Business Horizons*, *53*(1), 59–68. https://doi.org/10.1016/j.bushor.2009.09.003

Krishna, M. M., Midhunchakkaravarthy, & Vankara, J. (2023). Detection of sarcasm using bi-directional RNN based deep learning model in sentiment analysis. *Journal of Advanced Research in Applied Sciences and Engineering Technology*, *31*(2), 352–362. https://doi.org/10.37934/araset.31.2.352362

Lee, S., Xiong, A., Seo, H., & Lee, D. (2023). "Fact-checking" fact checkers: A data-driven approach. *Harvard Kennedy School Misinformation Review*, *4*(5). https://doi.org/10.37016/mr-2020-126

Liu, Z., Iqbal, U., & Saxena, N. (2022). *Opted Out, Yet Tracked: Are Regulations Enough to Protect Your Privacy?* https://arxiv.org/abs/2202.00885

Mariani, M. M., Hashemi, N., & Wirtz, J. (2023). Artificial intelligence empowered conversational agents: A systematic literature review and research agenda. *Journal of Business Research*, *161*. https://doi.org/10.1016/j.jbusres.2023.113838

Mehta, D., Dwivedi, A., Patra, A., & Anand Kumar, M. (2021). A transformer-based architecture for fake news classification. *Social Network Analysis and Mining*, *11*(1). https://doi.org/10.1007/s13278-021-00738-y

Olaniyan, D., Ogundokun, R. O., Bernard, O. P., Olaniyan, J., Maskeliūnas, R., & Akande, H. B. (2023). Utilizing an attention-based LSTM model for detecting sarcasm and irony in social media. *Computers*, *12*(11). https://doi.org/10.3390/computers12110231

Patchin, J. W., & Hinduja, S. (2010). Cyberbullying and self-esteem. *Journal of School Health*, *80*(12), 614–621. https://doi.org/10.1111/j.1746-1561.2010.00548.x

Singh, L. G., & Singh, S. R. (2024). Sentiment analysis of tweets using text and graph multi-views learning. *Knowledge and Information Systems*, *66*(5), 2965–2985. https://doi.org/10.1007/s10115-023-02053-8

Statista. (2024). *Number of social media users worldwide from 2015 to 2024* [Data set]. Statista. https://www.statista.com/

Tafur, B., & Sarkar, A. (2023). *User Perceptions of Automatic Fake News Detection: Can Algorithms Fight Online Misinformation?* https://arxiv.org/abs/2304.07926

Ubaldi, E., Burioni, R., Loreto, V., & Tria, F. (2021). Emergence and evolution of social networks through exploration of the adjacent possible space. *Communications Physics*, *4*(1). https://doi.org/10.1038/s42005-021-00527-1

Vlačić, B., Corbo, L., Costa e Silva, S., & Dabić, M. (2021). The evolving role of artificial intelligence in marketing: A review and research agenda. *Journal of Business Research*, *128*, 187–203. https://doi.org/10.1016/j.jbusres.2021.01.055

Wong, R. Y., Chong, A., & Cooper Aspegren, R. (2023). Privacy legislation as business risks: how GDPR and CCPA are represented in technology companies' investment risk disclosures. *Proceedings of the ACM on Human-Computer Interaction*, *7*(CSCW1). https://doi.org/10.1145/3579515

Wu, J., & Hooi, B. (2023). DECOR: degree-corrected social graph refinement for fake news detection. *Proceedings of the ACM SIGKDD International Conference on Knowledge Discovery and Data Mining*, Long Beach, California, USA, 2582–2593. https://doi.org/10.1145/3580305.3599298

Yin, Z., Shao, J., Hussain, M. J., Hao, Y., Chen, Y., Zhang, X., & Wang, L. (2023). DPG-LSTM: An Enhanced LSTM framework for sentiment analysis in social media text based on dependency parsing and GCN. *Applied Sciences (Switzerland)*, *13*(1). https://doi.org/10.3390/app13010354

Yue, Y., Peng, Y., & Wang, D. (2023). Deep learning short text sentiment analysis based on improved particle swarm optimization. *Electronics (Switzerland)*, *12*(19). https://doi.org/10.3390/electronics12194119

Zhang, R., Xue, R., & Liu, L. (2019). Security and privacy on blockchain. *ACM Computing Surveys*, *52*(3). https://doi.org/10.1145/3316481

Zhao, K., Wang, S., Vasi, I. B., & Zhang, Q. (n.d.). *Social Influence in the Concurrent Diffusion of Information and Behaviors in Online Social Networks*. PHBS.

Zhou, J., Cui, G., Hu, S., Zhang, Z., Yang, C., Liu, Z., Wang, L., Li, C., & Sun, M. (2020). Graph neural networks: A review of methods and applications. *AI Open*, *1*, 57–81. https://doi.org/10.1016/j.aiopen.2021.01.001

3 Understanding Factors Leading to Local and Global Spatial Spread in Social Media

Rimjhim

3.1 INTRODUCTION

As we know, the world today is a global village, and it takes no time to reach from one place to another. Any news, information, new technology, gadgets, and even diseases spread from one place to another with lightning speed. Similarly, real-world events (something associated with a time, location, and people) also unfurl to different regions[1] in no time. It is already a well-known fact that a few events spread to distant regions, and a few remain confined within a smaller region. For example, the event of COVID-19 spread globally and became a pandemic. However, the event of the death of Jiao Ruoyu,[2] a Chinese politician, remained confined within a region. Moreover, it is often required to manipulate the spatial spread of the event. For example, for any advertisement, they try to increase the spread in order to gather more and more audience. However, for many events, such as the leak of some private photos, there is an urgent call for dwarfing the spread. These spreading differences and manipulations require a critical understanding of the spatial spreading phenomena, which include the understanding of user participation, adoption of events, and propagation of events with respect to different regions.

The prior research has extensively explored the spreading mechanism and focuses on the diffusion mechanism from one user to another, which include the study of virality, cascades [1], influence [2], etc. However, as the information diffuses from one person to another, it also spreads from one location to another. But the phenomena of spatial spreading are still not explored much, leaving space for analysing spatial spreading. There are few works that highlight the spatial spreading of memes, hashtags, etc. [3–7]. They have found the spatial spreading phenomena similar to the "spray and diffuse" mechanism. As already explored in spreading among users, few pieces of information get attention from a smaller number of users, and few get attention from a very large number of users. Few information spreads for a longer time duration, and few fade within a small fraction of time. Thus, establishing the fact that different information spreads differently, following different pathways, user participation, adoption, etc. In spatial spreading also, little information gets attention from a smaller region (local), but few unravels across regions (global). Existing literature

 DOI: 10.1201/9781003611110-3

does not address the factors leading to local or global spatial spread. The "spray and diffuse" analogy for spatial spreading has been explored for generic information rather than local and global events. Information spreading within a region must have some particularity and peculiarity as compared to information that spreads across regions. To address these gaps, this research delves into the nuances of spatial spread mechanisms for local and global events. Three key research questions guide the investigation:

- Is the "Spray and Diffuse" phenomenon the same for local and global events?
- Is the user engagement similar for local and global events in terms of user participation and demographics?
- Does exposure to an event impact users similarly for local and global events?

We argue that this research lays the foundation for understanding spatial spread mechanisms, which can further be utilized for predicting geographical reach, next location, etc.

To answer our research questions, we considered one of the OSNs, i.e., Twitter, which is well known for reflecting real-world events and providing location information [8–10], thus creating a readily available platform for studying spatial spreading. Our experiments for understanding the spatial spreading of local and global events are for events of the country India.

The findings of this study, based on Twitter data from real-time events in India, reveal insightful observations:

- Local events tend to diffuse state by state, with adoption time increasing with distance, while global events exhibit a more random spread. The "spray and diffuse" phenomena are more evident in local events compared to global events.
- Local real-life events have a higher probability of propagating out of the network and enjoy denser user engagement than global ones. Demographically, local events involve a more homogeneous audience, while global events attract active participation from various segments of society.
- Local events are adopted quickly, and exposure to an event has a higher probability of influencing users and increasing their participation compared to global events.

Information spreading in social networks, often called as *Social Contagion* [11,12], undoubtedly travels by the media of network but is found to be affected by a number of additional factors, such as cognitive factors and the interest of the user. The social spread behaviour is also characterized by the environment of spread; for example, in the spread of product purchase environment, the user demands and needs come up as important factors. This is particularly significant in a pluralistic country like India, which stands 6th on the Cultural Diversity Index [13], 9th on the Linguistic Diversity Index [14], and 17th on the Ethnic Fractionalization Index [13] in the world. Most of the states of the country have different languages, cultures, etc., which make them distinct geographical units, but they still share the same country, thus creating a different spread scenario, unlike other research.

In this paper, we have studied the spread of real-time events extracted from geo-tagged tweets of India for a period of two months. The events are classified into two categories on the basis of the spread nature: local events and global events, with the aim of differentiating their spread mechanism. The spread is studied on the grounds of influence on users, correlation of distance and adoption, user engagement, and event propagation. The research not only addresses the spatial spreading phenomena but also explores the role of edge computing and its implications for different industries. Edge computing, with its decentralized computing infrastructure, aids in real-time data processing and analysis, which is particularly relevant for handling vast amounts of social media data.

3.2 RELATED WORK

This chapter analyses the differences in the spreading of local and global events in various regions. This study is closely related to research from four major areas, namely, (i) hashtags/events/memes, (ii) spreading mechanisms and underlying factors, and (iii) social contagion.

3.2.1 Events

The term *event* includes a broad section of definitions that are closely related. The broad definition of an event is "a significant thing that happens at some specific time and place" [15]. Nowadays, there is a huge participation of people in online media, which has emerged as new concepts very similar to events, i.e., *online events*, *real-time events*, *memes*, *fads*, etc. An *online event* is defined as a peak in the online activity [16]. With this definition, an online event can be an event, but not all events are online events. With the advent of online social media, all real-world phenomena are well reflected in online media as well [17]. In fact, it has been reported that 95% of the public tweets are composed of events [18], generating a concept of real-world events.

A real-time event is an *online event* that has happened in the physical world. So, in online media, a real-time event is defined as an online burst with a specific time period, location, or people [19]. These real-time events are also called breaking events. Another popular terminology is *meme*, which has been found to have multiple definitions in past literature. However, according to various definitions, meme is very similar to an online event except for the fact that it exists only in online media [20] and not in the real world, and it is also referred to as Internet memes [21] or ephemeral [22]. Wang et al. [1] define memes as "a piece of information that replicates among people". The major difference between a meme and an online event is that all memes are online events but not all online events are memes. Memes do not have any relevance to real-world happening; instead, they are evolving content that rapidly gains popularity or notoriety on the Internet [23].

Another close concept that emerges out of an event is the concept of local and global events. Local events are defined as "something that happens at some specific time and place and is limited both temporally and geographically" [24]. This definition lags behind proper quantification, which is properly quantified in a few works for memes [25] and has also been incorporated into events [4]. The study on events can primarily be categorized into four major categories: event detection, event tracking, event summarization, and event association [26]. The current work falls in the category of event tracking. All the past researches lag tracking of the spatial unfolding of local and global real-time events, which has been comprehensively studied in this research.

3.2.2 Spreading Mechanisms and Underlying Factors

With the advent of social media, a snapshot of information spread is now available. This has led to countless researches in understanding the spreading mechanism. In the spreading of information, there is a role of the information content (emotion/sentiment in information, topic, credibility, etc.), the users involved (hub users, underlying network, ego networks, etc.), and the environment (competing information, visibility) in which it is spreading. Here, we describe briefly the past works exploring these three factors.

3.2.2.1 Content

Researchers have found an impact of content type on spreading behaviour. Some of the popular aspects of content influencing spread are the topic of the information [27], the polarity of information [28], the credibility of information [29], etc. The authors in a study [27] have analysed the effect of exposure to different topics of content to understand the spreading differences in spread behaviour. They have found political content to be more persistent. The spreading also changes when the spread is taking on online social media as well as other media such as News Media. Many small-scale events, also called local events, that cannot make up to News Media and are just propagated through online networks will have different spread characteristics than a large-scale event, also called a global event, that captures sufficient media attention [4]. Thus, the available factors for different information differ, subsequently generating different spread characteristics.

Another study [30] has found 71% contribution of network diffusion and 29% contribution of external factors, i.e., Media outside the Social Network (such as News Media) in information spreading. In most of such large-scale studies, the understanding spread of different content types is on hashtags and memes. Though hashtags and memes cover events, the specific event spread has not been studied on a large scale. In this chapter, we study the spreading behaviour of events of two different natures, i.e., local and global, which are of two different content types.

3.2.2.2 User

The characteristics of engaged users also play a major role in determining spread. The major factors in user characteristics lie in the underlying network of engaged users. The influence of a user, clusters of the users, etc., has been established as one of the factors. The more connected the user is, the more will be his/her influence. Apart from network factors of a user, there are other factors that guide the spread and adoption, such as the activity of a user [31], interest [32], and homophily [33], thus originating the concept of complex contagion. In this paper, we study the spreading behaviour in the Indian context; India being a diverse country has States as different cultural units. State-wise spreading behaviour inculcates the impact of homophily and interests, which can be easily revealed by analyses of differences in local and global events.

3.2.2.3 Environment

Another factor that guides the spread is the environment in which information is spreading. For example, the visibility on the website, i.e., how a website displays the incoming flux, decides how a user will be exposed to information. Since there is a plethora of online content, the competition that information faces also decides the spread [34]. Adding to the environmental factor lies the effect of geography on the spread. Since geography is characterized by specific cultures, interests, etc., it strongly affects how information spreads. Inspired by these are few previous works [3,25], which have comprehensively studied the impact of geography. However, here again, the granularity of the considered geography is too broad to inculcate the unities and diversities within a country. In this paper, the event classification is done according to geographical spread to analyse the impact of distance on spreading behaviour in a unique environment of India.

3.2.3 Social Contagion

As explained before, the factors like *content, user homophily, user network, environment, etc.* play key roles in the spreading of information. The spreading in social media, commonly termed social contagion, involves several complex processes that are hardly explained by simple contagion [35]. The contagion process on social media adheres to the phenomena of complex contagion, which have been demonstrated by many researches [36,37]. In simple contagion, the probability of getting affected is directly proportional to the number of exposures [36]. While complex contagions, also known as threshold models, are explained as collective behaviour where an infection depends on the number of infected neighbours. There are several mechanisms at play while information spreads [38]. Past researchers have attempted to study the dominant mechanism, while in this study, we have explored several mechanisms at play in terms of spatial spreading.

3.3 DATASET

An overview of our proposed methodology is shown in Figure 3.1. Next, we explain each step of experiments in our proposed methodology. We collected geo-tagged tweets from the Twitter Location Filtering Streaming API with "India" as the

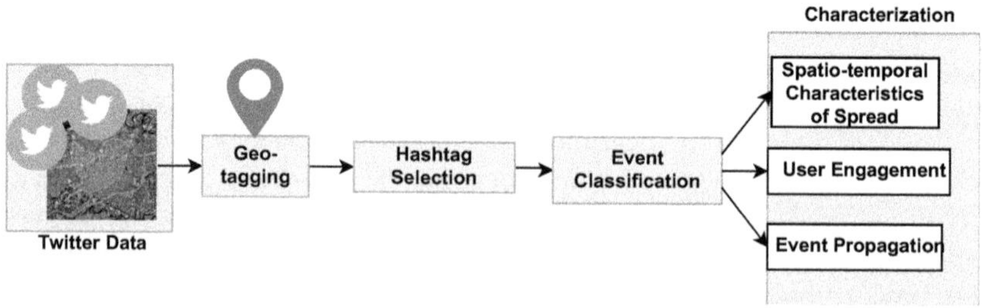

FIGURE 3.1 An overview of our proposed methodology.

required location for a period of around two months (*6 February–30 March*), which consists of 7,19,536 tweets, 1,26,430 unique users, and 93,718 hashtags. From the hashtags, we selected 500 according to the methodology described in the next section. For selected hashtags, the total number of tweets and unique users are 9,571 and 4,372, respectively. This accounts for a very less number of tweets and users due to the sparse availability of geo-tagged tweets (especially in India). So, we used "Get Old Tweets", a web-based crawler, to scrape all searchable tweets, irrespective of geotags, containing the required hashtags, which raised the total tweet count and unique user count to 15,92,184 and 6,76,627, respectively.

Here, we explicitly mention that both geo-tagged tweets and "Get Old Tweets" return only Original tweets for retweet information. Additional crawling is required for both cases. Also, it is worth mentioning that our analyses include temporal analyses where the time stamp of the tweets is important. Twitter gives different time stamps according to different time zones (streams have UTC, while geo-tagged have local time stamps). But here, for both of our data collection method, the time zone is local. Hence, there is no requirement for explicit conversion to ensure consistency. Since this crawler provides limited information, we used "tweet id" for crawling additional information, such as retweets and self-reported profile location, from the Twitter API [39].

3.3.1 Tagging Location with the Tweet

Our study includes state-level spatial analyses at the granularity of the "State" level. Tagging a "home location" [40] to the users is itself a challenging task. However, researchers have used various alternatives for tagging the "home location" such as using geo-tagged tweets, self-reported profile location, time zone, and even a combination of these. From the previous research, it has been found that the number of mappable users from self-reported locations is more than the number of geo-tagged tweets. Only 1%–2% [41] of tweets are geo-tagged, but around 75% self-reported locations are mappable locations [42]. The time-zone alternative cannot be used for our work as it cannot tag to "State" level granularity. So, we opt for using a self-reported profile location to tag the location.

It has been found in the literature that the maximum number of users mention their city-level location. For this, we created an Indian dictionary of locations containing the names of unique cities, places, and districts for each state. These names are collected from a Wikipedia list of places in each state. This dictionary is used for mapping the self-reported profile location to a "State" name. The popular alternative for mapping geographic information to structured locations, such as Yahoo Geocoder and Google Geocoder, is limited by rate limits. Our Indian dictionary provides a limitless mapping of Indian locations to a state. Since self-reported locations can be noisy and ambiguous, any geocoding doesn't guarantee the association of each reported location to a structured location [43].

3.3.2 Hashtag Selection

Often peaks in online activity are considered events. Hashtags are representative of events, but not all hashtags represent events. According to [19], hashtags mainly belong to three categories, i.e., continuous activity, periodic activity, and activity concentrated around a peak. The last one is considered representative of a unique event. For capturing such hashtags, we have used the method described in [44]. Firstly, we bin the hashtags by the number of their daily occurrences. Then, we found an activity peak by finding a significant increase in the maximum occurrence count from the median baseline count. An event can have multiple activity peaks; we have considered the day of maximum occurrence of hashtags as the peak day. Hence, the same is compared to the median baseline to detect a significant increase. Just to consider the events with a sufficient number of tweets, we have removed the hashtags with maximum occurrence lesser than a selected threshold. A median baseline is the median of days count of hashtags (m_b). The significant increase score is calculated by $s_i=(c_i-m_b)/max\ (m_b,\ 10)$, where c_i denotes the count of a hashtag on day i, as given in [19]. We selected hashtags with the top 500 significant increase scores for our experiments.

3.3.2.1 Event Classification

Different papers have classified events differently. One such classification is local and global events. This classification can be done on the basis of geography, the number of messages, the lifetime of the event, etc., since our objective is to study the difference in spread characteristics of events that have got limited geographic attention and event that has got unlimited geographic attention. So, we choose classification by geographic attention. We adopt the metric used by an earlier study [4] applied to the full life of events. The complete life of the event is considered in order to include the final temporal changes because some events can change from local to global with time. The metric used is called *Focus*, which is defined as the maximum probability of occurrence of an event at a single location and can be formulated as given in Equation 3.1, where C_i is the probability of occurrence of an event at location i and L denotes the set of locations where the hashtag has occurred. The same metric has been used by [4] to classify the events. We select a threshold of 0.5 to separate the local and global events, i.e., if 50% of the tweets have occurred from a single location, then the event is considered as a local event. From this classification, our definition of a local event is an event that has got at least 50% of its tweets from a single location, which denotes events with limited geographic attention. For global events, we select a threshold of 0.40; events having a focus less than the threshold are considered global events. We omit events having a focus in the range of 0.39–0.49, as these are mostly regional events, and their inclusion can generate average case results. After the division, we have 100 local events and 390 global events:

$$\text{Focus}(f_e) = \max\left[\frac{C_i}{\sum_{i\in L_e} C_i}\right] \tag{3.1}$$

3.4 SPREADING BEHAVIOUR

Since a spread is influenced by multiple factors, our analyses of spread behaviour include multiple paradigms to study spreading behaviour. We focus on two important paradigms, i.e., spatio-temporal properties of Spread and User engagement in spread. The main aim of this chapter is to study spreading behaviour so as to highlight the difference between the spreading properties of local and global events.

3.4.1 Spatio-temporal Properties of Spread

For analysing the spatial properties, we have well-defined metrics: *Focus* [4,25], *Entropy* [4,25], *Spread* [4,25], and *Adoption Lag* [25]. *Focus*, which is already defined in Equation 1, is used for event classification. Definitions of other metrics are elaborated as follows.

3.4.1.1 Entropy

Entropy is the measure of randomness in the geographical spread of an event, which is measured in terms of the number of bits required to represent the locations where the hashtag has appeared. This can be formulated as in Equation 3.2, where C_i is the probability of occurrence of an event at location i and L denotes the set of all locations where the hashtag has occurred. The larger the value, the more will be the geographical spread. An event present at only one location will give an entropy value of 0, which will increase as the number of locations increases:

$$\text{Entropy}(e_e) = \sum_{i \in l_e} - \frac{C_i}{\sum_{i \in L_e} C_i} \log \frac{C_i}{\sum_{i \in L_e} C_i} \tag{3.2}$$

The *Entropy* represents the number of the location where an event has travelled, thus failing to represent the actual distance the event travels. For example, an event occurs at two locations that are close to each other, while another event also occurs at two locations farther from each other. The *Entropy* will be the same for both events, thus overlooking the distance parameter. So, we go for another metric called *Spread*, which captures the distance parameter.

3.4.1.2 Spread

The *Spread* is the mean distance between a central location and all the locations where the event has appeared. The definition of this *Spread* can be adaptive according to the choice of central location. The study [25] has considered the geographic midpoint as the central location. We consider the *Focus Location* as the centre location for measuring the *Spread*. The *Focus Location* is the location that represents the *Focus* of the event is maximum, i.e., the location that represents the metric *Focus*, used to classify the events. For our analyses, we are measuring *Spread* of events as the mean geodesic distance between all the locations where the hashtag has appeared and the *Focus Location* of the event, as formulated in Equation 3.3, where l_{focus} is the *Focus Location* of the event:

$$\text{Spread}(S_e) = \frac{1}{|L_e|} \sum_{l_i \in L_e} \text{dist}(l_i - l_{\text{focus}}) \tag{3.3}$$

The above metrics explain the spatial distribution of events, which represents the concentration of events at a location, the locations covered by events, and the distance covered by the events. This misses out on the measurement of how fast the locations are covered. The time-lapse in the adoption of the events by different locations cannot be captured by the above metrics. So, we use the metric *Adoption Lag* [25].

3.4.1.3 Adoption Lag

Adoption Lag is defined as the difference in *Adoption Time* of an event at two different locations. The adoption time is considered as the first appearance of an event at any location. Henceforth, the *Average Adoption Lag* of an event is the average difference between the *Adoption Time* of each location where the event has appeared and the *Adoption Time* of the location where the event originated. This can be formulated as in Equation 3.4, where L_e is the set of all locations where the event occurred, t_i is the time stamp of the first appearance of the event at the location i, and t_o is the time of the first appearance of the event at originating location o:

$$\text{Adoption lag}(e) = \frac{\sum_{i \in L_e} |t_i - t_o|}{|L_e|} \tag{3.4}$$

These metrics represent the spatio-temporal spread of the events. For a finer understanding, we look into these metrics calculated overall for both local and global events. Table 3.1 summarizes these metrics by calculating the median of all metrics. For measuring the distance covered by an event, we have *Spread*. From this table, we see that global events spread around a median radius of 606 miles, which is almost double as compared to local events, i.e., 361 miles. As far as *Average Adoption Lag* is concerned, the local events are faster in being adopted by other locations, resulting in *Median Adoption Lag* of local events as 21 hours and for global events as 48 hours. We have also calculated the median *Focus*, which turns out to be 0.77 for local events and 0.24 for global events. For the understanding of the locations (State)

TABLE 3.1
Values of Different Metrics for Local and Global Events

Metric	Local	Global
Median spread	321 miles	606 miles
Median adoption lag	21 hours	48 hours
Median entropy	1.2 bits	3.4 bits
Median focus	0.77	0.24
States covered	2–7 States	3–16 States
Examples	*#HappyGudiPadwa*, *#VadaChennaiFirstLook*	*#FestivalOf Colours*, *#DeleteNaMoApp*

where an event has travelled, we have *Entropy*, which is 1.2 bits for local events and 3.4 for global events, i.e., more than double. Hence, the median number of states covered by a local event is 2–7 states, while for global events, it is 3–16 states. India has a total of 34 locations, i.e., states that include all states and union territories. The maximum spread is up to 16 states only, which shows that even a global event does not cover the whole country; few can be missed out due to a low Twitter population. A few examples of local events are *#HappyGudiPadwa* and *#VadaChennaiFirstLook*, which represent the local festival of the state Maharashtra and the local movie of the state Chennai, respectively. Similarly, in global events, we have *#FestivalOfColours* and *#DeleteNaMoApp*, which represent a country-wide celebrated festival, i.e., *Holi*, and a country-wide app launched by Prime Minister Narendra Modi, respectively.

3.4.2 Event Propagation

The above metrics characterize the spread of events as a whole. How these characteristics propagate with time and the difference in event propagation of local and global events need to be understood. This has been done by the analysis of *Focus*, *Entropy*, and *Adoption Lag* at different intervals of time. For *Focus* and *Entropy*, we have taken a time window of 10 minutes, and we are measuring the change in values of these metrics with these time windows during and after the peak time of the event. A time interval is considered as the peak interval, if the interval has a maximum number of the appearance of the event hashtag, i.e., the time window having a maximum frequency of the hashtags. The measure of *Entropy* and *Focus* over the interval of 10 minutes is termed as *Interval Entropy* and *Interval Focus*, respectively.

3.4.2.1 Interval Focus and Interval Entropy

The change in *Focus* for both local and global events during and after the peak hour has been shown in Figure 3.2. The median *Focus* value for global events is 0.24, as shown in Table 3.1. From Figure 3.2, we see that the *Focus* value of 10-minute window is more than the median *Focus* value. For local events, the median *Focus* is 0.77; the *interval focus* value is more than the median *Focus* value for local events

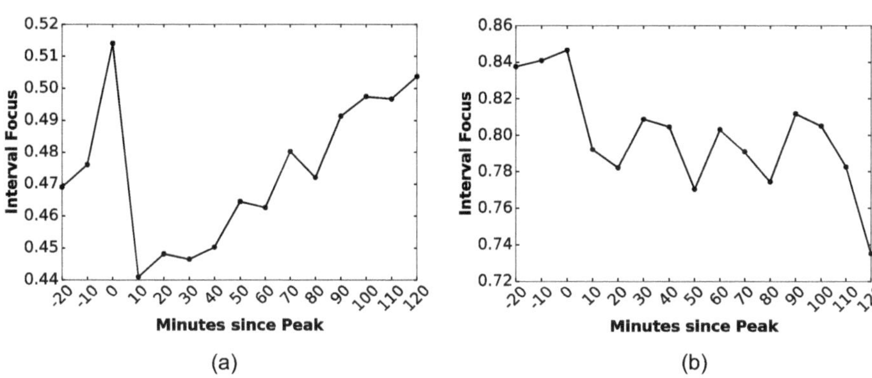

FIGURE 3.2 The interval focus with time for local and global events. (a) Global events. (b) Local events.

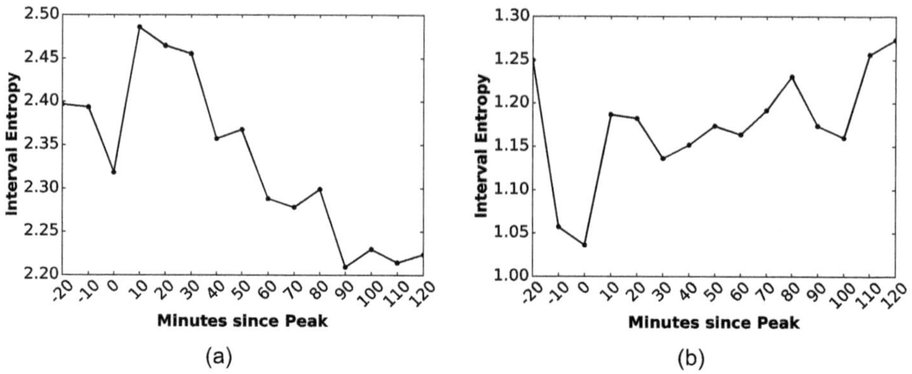

FIGURE 3.3 The interval entropy with time for local and global events. (a) Global events. (b) Local events.

also. This behaviour is supported by the *Entropy* values, as shown in Figure 3.3. The median *Entropy* value is 3.4 bits and 1.2 bits for global and local events, respectively, which again is larger than the *interval entropy* values for global events and local events, respectively.

As shown in Figures 3.2 and 3.3, the increased spike in *Focus* value and decreased spike in *Entropy* value at the peak for both local and global events show that events get most of the attention from a single location only. The sudden decrease in *Focus* value and the increase in *Entropy* value just after the peak show that events start getting attention from different locations. This pattern is the same for both local and global events, with local events having comparatively less steep increases and decreases. A similar pattern has been found for the hashtags considered by [25]. The major difference in the pattern of event propagation between local and global events is 10–20 minutes after the peak. For global events, the increasing *Focus* value and decreasing *Entropy* value after 10–20 minutes of the peak show that the attention gradually confines to the original most attended location. The 10–20 minute post-peak propagation of local events is different from global events. The *interval entropy* value for local events has a slightly increasing trend with minor deviations, and the *interval focus* value keeps deviating up and down. This represents that local events keep on spreading to other locations with time, while the maximum attention location remains the same.

With the metrics *Focus* and *Entropy* representing much of the event propagation, we correlate the *Focus* and *Entropy* for local and global events, as shown in Figure 3.4. We find a strong negative correlation (−0.948) between *Focus* and *Entropy* for local events. The correlation is however significantly less for global events (−0.638). For local events, the more the attention increase in the *Focus Location*, the more attention it receives from other participating locations as well, representing the narrowness of local events within a region in and around the *Focus Location*, while for global events, attention may increase in a particular location without affecting the participation from other locations.

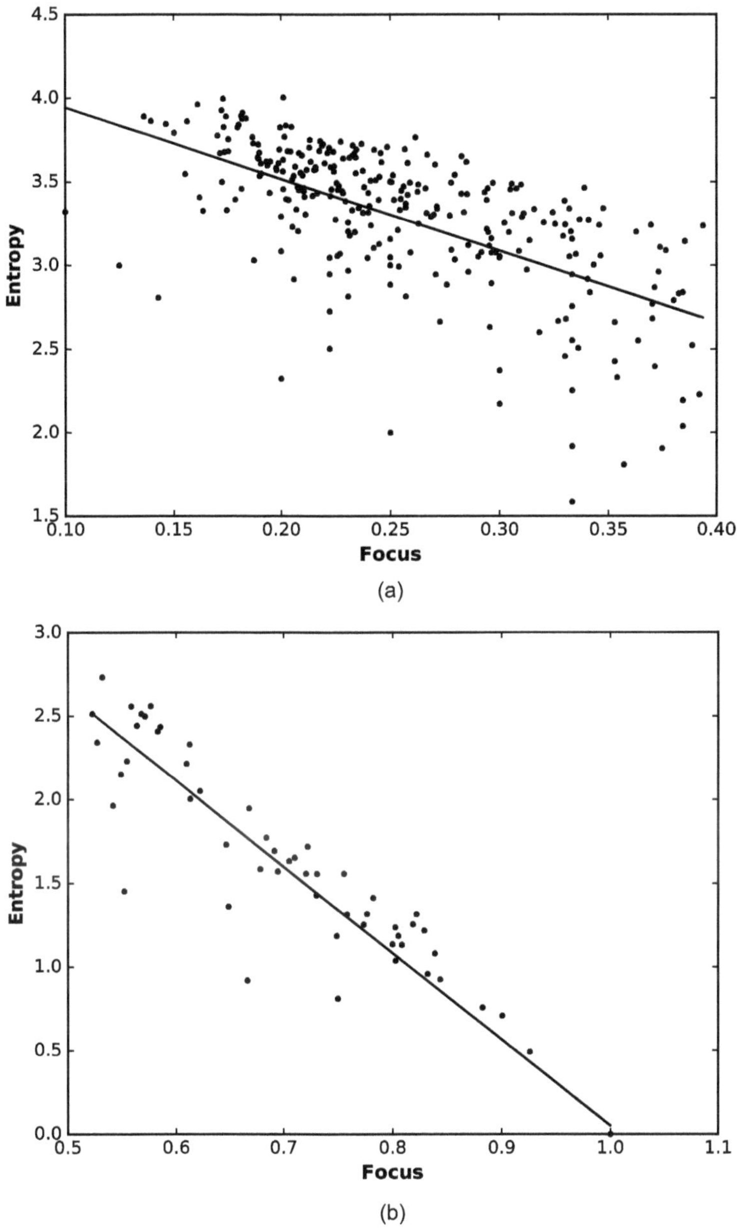

FIGURE 3.4 Correlation between focus and entropy. (a) Global events. (b) Local events.

3.4.2.2 Adoption Lag vs. Distance

The median adoption lag for global events is almost double that of local events, as shown in Table 3.1, but how the event is adopted with distance is unclear. To understand the correlation between distance and *Adoption Lag*, we calculate the Pearson Correlation between distance and *Adoption Lag* at different hours, as shown in

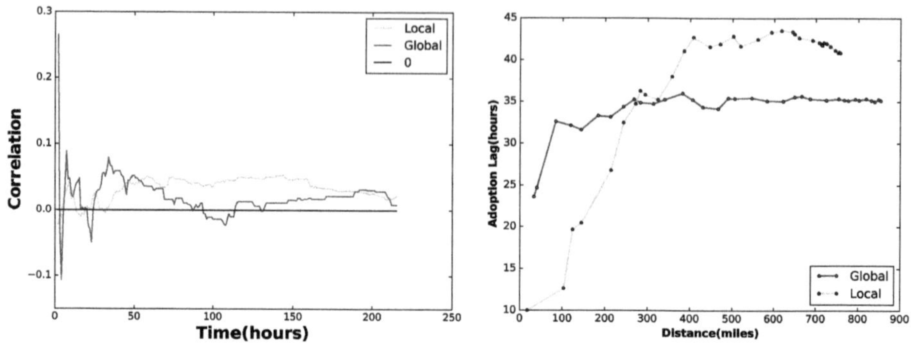

FIGURE 3.5 Adoption lag for local and global events. (a) Co-relation (adoption lag and distance) with hours. (b) Average distance vs average adoption lag.

Figure 3.5a. Global events show a mix of positive and negative correlation and the presence of non-diffusion patterns of spread. However, for local events, the correlation is always positive, indicating the adoption analogous to diffusion. Additionally, for more clarity on the relation with distance, we divided the distance into windows of 50 miles. We calculated the adoption lag between all the locations for all the events. Here, our location is the state of the country, India. For the distance between the two states, we consider the distance between the capital cities of the states. Averaging the distances in the respective windows and averaging the adoption lag for the corresponding distances, we draw a cumulative distance vs. adoption lag plot, as shown in Figure 3.5b. The plots here again show the steeper increase in *Adoption Lag* with distance for local events, while the same is not so prominent for global events.

3.4.3 User Engagement

Here, we find the differences in engagement patterns of users for local and global events. We measure engagements in terms of Twitter-specific features, i.e., retweet count and favourite count, as proposed by Elsherief et al. [45]. Since the retweet count and favourite count increase with the increase in follower count, they are normalized by follower count and termed as retweet rate and favourite rate, respectively. To test the distribution differences between retweet rate and favourite rate for local and global events, we perform the Kruskal–Wallis H test. The test statistic for the retweet rate is $H = 13655$ and p-value <0.001 and for the favourite rate is $H = 359.91$ and p-value <0.001. Other description statistics for user engagement are tabulated in Table 3.2. Global events, in spite of having more *spread*, have lower retweet rate and favourite rate. Local events are retweeted 8.4 times and favourited 1.6 times more than global events. Additionally, we calculate the probability of Retweets and Favourites extending beyond networks, i.e., P (Retweet rate > 1) and P (Favourite rate >1), respectively, for local and global events. The probabilities P (Retweet rate >1) and P (Favourite rate >1) are both greater for local events than global events.

TABLE 3.2
Descriptive Statistics for Engagement with Local and Global Events

Measures	Min	Max	Mean	Standard Deviation
Retweet rate (local)	0	107	0.16	1.10
Favourite rate (local)	0	48	0.032	0.30
Retweet count (local)	0	7,377	5.70	42.30
Favourite count (local)	0	20,198	6.22	80.12
Retweet rate (global)	0	101.5	0.019	0.33
Favourite rate (global)	0	106.5	0.02	0.21
Retweet count (global)	0	354,578	3.66	377.96
Favourite count (global)	0	754,440	8.66	858.94

TABLE 3.3
Averaged Percentage Distribution of Different Demographies for Local and Global Events

Event Type	Male (%)	Female (%)	Teenager (%)	Young (%)	Middle-Aged (%)	Old (%)
Local	88.4	11.11	2.07	78.3	15.2	0.2
Global	77.3	22.6	1.03	67.97	26.8	1.2

3.4.3.1 Demographic Differences

User engagement, as shown in the previous section, characterizes user participation, but the participation also varies with demography. So, we further study the demographic differences in users participating in local and global events. For this, we crawled the profile picture URL of each user, creating original tweets on the events. We use the Microsoft Azure Face API [46] to identify the gender and age demography of the involved users. For gender, we have male and female classes, and for age, we chose four classes, namely, Adolescent (13–19 years), Young (20–39 years), Middle-aged (40–64 years), and Old (65 years and above), as described in [47]. The Adolescent class represents teenagers, the Young class represents early adulthood, the Mid-Aged represents adulthood, and the old represents maturity. We find more female participation in global events. Additionally, global events have the majority of participants from Middle-Aged and Young, whereas local events have the majority participation from Young Ones, as shown in Table 3.3. We infer that local events are particular in user participation, resulting in participation only from particular demography. The local events are of interest to a particular locality, but all the demography of the locality doesn't show active participation. Global events have much-distributed participation, showing the involvement of all sections of society.

3.4.3.2 Influence and Exposure

Romero et al. [27] used the ordinal time estimate of exposure curves, i.e., $P(k)$ curves, to analyse the effect of exposure. $P(k)$ represents the fraction of users who are influenced by information after the kth exposure to it, given that they have not been

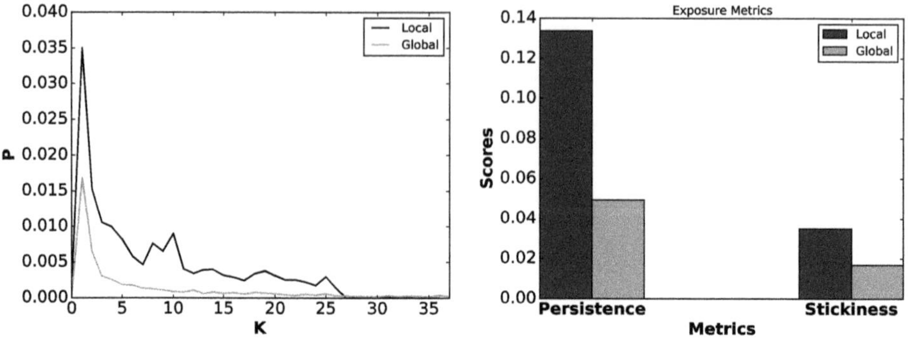

(a) (b)

FIGURE 3.6 Exposure curve and characteristics metrics. (a) Exposure curves. (b) Exposure curve metrics.

influenced yet. Thus, $P(k)$ is formulated as $P(k) = I(k)/E(k)$, where $E(k)$ represents the number of users who are k-exposed at some particular time and $I(k)$ represents the number of users who are influenced before being $K+1$-exposed. The influence is detected by the first tweet or retweet made by the user.

For measuring the exposure, we consider the *following* list of users crawled using Twitter API. So, exposure is calculated by the number of users whom a user is following and who has used the information before the user. The metrics, *Stickiness* and *Persistence*, are used to characterize the $P(k)$ curves. *Stickiness* is defined as the maximum $p(k)$ value (the maximum probability with which exposure is adopted). *Persistence* represents how rapidly the effect of exposure decays is calculated as we draw average $P(k)$ curves for local and global events to measure the affinity of users towards local and global events. From the plots in Figure 3.6, it is seen that both stickiness and persistence are more for local events as compared to global ones. The stickiness peak is at $K=1$, showing that the maximum users are adopting after only one exposure. The value decreases after the first exposure, showing the complex contagion in influence. The difference in the stickiness value of local and global events is not significant, but the persistence value differs significantly. This shows that the probability of getting influenced with increasing exposure is higher for a local event as compared to a global event.

3.5 CONCLUSION

In this chapter, we conducted an empirical analysis of hashtag spread in social media using Twitter data. We study the differences between the spreading patterns of local and global events. From our experiments, we find that the diffusion process, i.e., the movement from one place to another, is more evident in local events than in global events. In addition, local events also show a higher density of user engagement compared to global events. These also have a higher chance of propagating out of the network. In terms of the engaged demographics of participating users, local events are more likely to be attended by young people than by other age groups in society. In global events, participation is more diverse and involves all age groups in society. We also observe that local events are adopted more quickly than global events. Furthermore, the chances of a user engaging with a local event increase as the number of exhibitions increases. Thus, in this paper, we have observed several interesting observations about local and global events. Since the events in this paper are online entities, one can expect a similar pattern for other online entities, such as memes and news. In future work, we can design prediction models to predict whether an event will be local or global at an early stage. Additionally, exploring the role of edge computing in enhancing data analysis and prediction accuracy would advance our understanding of spreading phenomena and its potential applications in various industries.

NOTES

1 Here by unfurling to different regions, we refer to participation from different spatial regions.
2 https://simple.wikipedia.org/wiki/Jiao_Ruoy

REFERENCES

1. Weng, L., Menczer, F., Ahn, Y.-Y.: Predicting successful memes using network and community structure. In: *Eighth International AAAI Conference on Weblogs and Social Media*, pp. 535–544, Ann Arbor, Michigan USA (2014).
2. Bakshy, E., Hofman, J.M., Mason, W.A., Watts, D.J.: Everyone's an influencer: Quantifying influence on twitter. In: *Proceedings of the Fourth ACM International Conference on Web Search and Data Mining*, pp. 65–74, Hong Kong (2011).
3. Henry, D., Stattner, E., Collard, M.: Information propagation routes between countries in social media. In: *Companion of the Web Conference 2018 on The Web Conference 2018*, pp. 1295–1298 (2018). International World Wide Web Conferences Steering Committee, Lyon, France.
4. Mousset, P., Pitarch, Y., Tamine, L.: Studying the spatio-temporal dynamics of small-scale events in twitter. In: *Proceedings of the 29th on Hypertext and Social Media*, pp. 73–81, Baltimore, Maryland, USA (2018).
5. Kuo, H.-J., Fu, Y.-C.: Spatial effects on individual social capital: Differentiating the constraints of local occupational structures. *Social Networks* **64**, 194–211 (2021).
6. Yang, F., Qiao, Y., Qi, Y., Bo, J., Wang, X.: Bmp: A blockchain assisted meme prediction method through exploring contextual factors from social networks. *Information Sciences* **603**, 262–288 (2022).
7. Puura, A., Silm, S., Masso, A.: Identifying relationships between personal social networks and spatial mobility: A study using smartphone tracing and related surveys. *Social Networks* **68**, 306–317 (2022).
8. Rimjhim, C. R.: Characterizing user reactions towards twitter's 280 character limit. In: *Proceedings of the 10th Annual Meeting of the Forum for Information Retrieval Evaluation. FIRE'18*, pp. 48–51. Association for Computing Machinery, New York, NY, USA (2018). https://doi.org/10.1145/3293339.3293349.
9. Effrosynidis, D., Karasakalidis, A.I., Sylaios, G., Arampatzis, A.: The climate change twitter dataset. *Expert Systems with Applications* **204**, 117541 (2022).
10. Rimjhim, Dandapat, S.K.: Tagging multi-label categories to points of interest from check-in data. *IEEE Transactions on Emerging Topics in Computational Intelligence* **7**(4), 1191–1204 (2023) https://doi.org/10.1109/TETCI.2022.3229338.

11. Shin, H.: Social contagion of academic behavior: Comparing social networks of close friends and admired peers. *Plos One* **17**(3), 0265385 (2022).
12. Berry, G., Cameron, C.J., Park, P., Macy, M.: The opacity problem in social contagion. *Social Networks* **56**, 93–101 (2019).
13. Fearon, J.D.: Ethnic and cultural diversity by country. *Journal of Economic Growth* **8**(2), 195–222 (2003).
14. UNESCO: UNESCO World Report. https://unesdoc.unesco.org/images/0018/001852/185202E.pdf. Online Accessed 14-July-2022. (2009).
15. Fedoryszak, M., Frederick, B., Rajaram, V., Zhong, C.: Real-time event detection on social data streams. In: *Proceedings of the 25th ACM SIGKDD International Conference on Knowledge Discovery & Data Mining*, pp. 2774–2782, Alaska, USA (2019).
16. Afyouni, I., Al Aghbari, Z., Razack, R.A.: Multi-feature, multi-modal, and multi-source social event detection: A comprehensive survey. *Information Fusion* **79**, 279–308 (2022).
17. Zhou, D., Chen, L., He, Y.: An unsupervised framework of exploring events on twitter: Filtering, extraction and categorization. In: *Proceedings of the AAAI Conference on Artificial Intelligence*, pp. 2468–2474, Austin, Texas, USA (2015).
18. Petrovic, S., Osborne, M., McCreadie, R., Macdonald, C., Ounis, I., Shrimpton, L.: Can twitter replace newswire for breaking news? In: *Proceedings of the International AAAI Conference on Web and Social Media*, pp. 713–716, Cambridge, Massachusetts USA (2013).
19. Cui, A., Zhang, M., Liu, Y., Ma, S., Zhang, K.: Discover breaking events with popular hashtags in twitter. In: *Proceedings of the 21st ACM International Conference on Information and Knowledge Management*, pp. 1794–1798, Maui, Hawaii, USA (2012).
20. Carton, S., Park, S., Zeffer, N., Adar, E., Mei, Q., Resnick, P.: Audience analysis for competing memes in social media. In: *Proceedings of the International AAAI Conference on Web and Social Media*, pp. 41–50, Oxford, UK (2015).
21. Bauckhage, C.: Insights into internet memes. In: *Proceedings of the International AAAI Conference on Web and Social Media*, pp. 42–49, Barcelona, Spain (2011).
22. Kwak, H., Lee, C., Park, H., Moon, S.: What is twitter, a social network or a news media? In: *Proceedings of the 19th International Conference on World Wide Web*, pp. 591–600, North Carolina, USA (2010).
23. Kotsakos, D., Sakkos, P., Katakis, I., Gunopulos, D.: # tag: Meme or event? In: *2014 IEEE/ACM International Conference on Advances in Social Networks Analysis and Mining* $(_{ASONAM\ 2014})$, pp. 391–394, Beijing, China (2014).
24. Krumm, J., Horvitz, E.: Eyewitness: Identifying local events via space-time signals in twitter feeds. In: *Proceedings of the 23rd Sigspatial International Conference on Advances in Geographic Information Systems*, pp. 1–10, Washington, USA (2015).
25. Kamath, K.Y., Caverlee, J., Lee, K., Cheng, Z.: Spatio-temporal dynamics of online memes: a study of geo-tagged tweets. In: *Proceedings of the 22nd International Conference on World Wide Web*, pp. 667–678, Rio de Janeiro, Brazil (2013).
26. Dou, W., Wang, X., Ribarsky, W., Zhou, M.: Event detection in social media data. In: *IEEE VisWeek Workshop on Interactive Visual Text Analytics-Task Driven Analytics of Social Media Content*, pp. 971–980, Washington, USA (2012).
27. Romero, D.M., Meeder, B., Kleinberg, J.: Differences in the mechanics of information diffusion across topics: idioms, political hashtags, and complex contagion on twitter. In: *Proceedings of the 20th International Conference on World Wide Web*, pp. 695–704, Hyderabad, India (2011).
28. Ferrara, E., Yang, Z.: Quantifying the effect of sentiment on information diffusion in social media. *PeerJ Computer Science* **1**, 26 (2015).
29. Finn, S., Metaxas, P.T., Mustafaraj, E.: Spread and skepticism: Metrics of propagation on twitter. In: *Proceedings of the ACM Web Science Conference*, pp. 1–2, Oxford, United Kingdom (2015).

30. Myers, S.A., Zhu, C., Leskovec, J.: Information diffusion and external influence in networks. In: *Proceedings of the 18th ACM SIGKDD International Conference on Knowledge Discovery and Data Mining*, pp. 33–41, Beijing, China (2012).
31. Yardi, S., Boyd, D.: Tweeting from the town square: Measuring geographic local networks. In: *Fourth International AAAI Conference on Weblogs and Social Media*, pp. 194–201, Washington, DC, USA (2010).
32. Hu, Y., Farnham, S., Talamadupula, K.: Predicting user engagement on twitter with real-world events. In: *Proceedings of the International AAAI Conference on Web and Social Media*, pp. 168–177, Oxford, United Kingdom (2015).
33. Karsai, M., Iñiguez, G., Kikas, R., Kaski, K., Kertész, J.: Local cascades induced global contagion: How heterogeneous thresholds, exogenous effects, and unconcerned behaviour govern online adoption spreading. *Scientific Reports* **6**, 27178 (2016).
34. Min, B., San Miguel, M.: Competing contagion processes: Complex contagion triggered by simple contagion. *Scientific Reports* **8**(1), 10422 (2018).
35. Cheke, N., Chandra, J., Dandapat, S.K., Rimjhim: Understanding the impact of geographical distance on online discussions. *IEEE Transactions on Computational Social Systems* **7**(4), 858–872 (2020).
36. Hodas, N.O., Lerman, K.: The simple rules of social contagion. *Scientific Reports* **4**(1), 1–7 (2014).
37. Ternovski, J., Yasseri, T.: Social complex contagion in music listenership: A natural experiment with 1.3 million participants. *Social Networks* **61**, 144–152 (2020).
38. Dandapat, S.: Predicting spatial spread on social media. In: *Companion Proceedings of the Web Conference 2022*, pp. 656–659, Lyon, France (2022).
39. Twitter: Twitter API. https://developer.x.com/. Online; Accessed 7-June-2022.
40. Dandapat, S., Rimjhim: Is gender-based violence a confluence of culture? Empirical evidence from social media. *PeerJ Computer Science* **8**, 1051 (2022).
41. Paule, J.D.G., Sun, Y., Moshfeghi, Y.: On fine-grained geolocalisation of tweets and real-time traffic incident detection. *Information Processing & Management* **56**(3), 1119–1132 (2019).
42. Mahmud, J., Nichols, J., Drews, C.: Home location identification of twitter users. *ACM Transactions on Intelligent Systems and Technology (TIST)* **5**(3), 47 (2014).
43. Hecht, B., Hong, L., Suh, B., Chi, E.H.: Tweets from justin bieber's heart: The dynamics of the location field in user profiles. In: *Proceedings of the SIGCHI Conference on Human Factors in Computing Systems*, pp. 237–246, British Columbia, Canada (2011).
44. Lehmann, J., Gon¸calves, B., Ramasco, J.J., Cattuto, C.: Dynamical classes of collective attention in twitter. In: *Proceedings of the 21st International Conference on World Wide Web*, pp. 251–260, Lyon, France (2012).
45. ElSherief, M., Belding, E., Nguyen, D.: # notokay: Understanding gender-based violence in social media. In: *Eleventh International AAAI Conference on Web and Social Media*, pp. 52–61, Quebec, Canada (2017).
46. Microsoft: Microsoft Azure, Face API. https://docs.microsoft.com/en-in/azure/cognitive-services/face/overview. Online; Accessed 21-September-2022.
47. Chakraborty, A., Messias, J., Benevenuto, F., Ghosh, S., Ganguly, N., Gummadi, K.: Who makes trends? Understanding demographic biases in crowdsourced recommendations. In: *Proceedings of the International AAAI Conference on Web and Social Media*, pp. 22–31, Montreal, Canada (2017).

4 Understanding Deep Learning and LLMs for Detecting Depression in Social Media Posts

Piyal Roy, Rajat Pandit,
Amitava Podder, and Shivnath Ghosh

4.1 INTRODUCTION

Depression as a form of mental illness impacts millions of people across the globe. This condition leads patients to maintain feelings of unhappiness and demonstrates reduced interest in regular activities, along with multiple psychological and physical manifestations. Widespread depression goes largely untreated because people face prejudice in addition to having minimal understanding about depression and their inability to receive necessary mental healthcare. Through deep learning and large language models (LLMs), artificial intelligence shows promise for identifying depression by analyzing social media content. Social media data provides us with an opportunity to detect depression symptoms in real time by applying a scalable method to the abundant social media content, which can lead to early intervention.

4.1.1 Overview of Depression and Its Social Media Indicators

Users now heavily depend on social media channels, including Twitter, Facebook, and Instagram, for direct communication, where they can present their insights and personal characteristics. Users routinely produce digital behavioral patterns along with linguistic elements through their digital interactions, which later present possibilities for examining mental health indicators. The multifaceted disorder known as depression reveals itself through invisible patterns when people interact on social media through text messaging.

First-person pronoun abundance, when combined with ordinary words, along with feelings of loneliness and helplessness, might signal depressive symptoms. People who show depressive tendencies often show their depression openly through changes in their language style combined with tone. Depression indicators show differences between people as well as among different cultural patterns. This research executes an aggregated computational method analysis to find mental health issues from observed patterns despite these limitations [1]. Our ability to detect depression through linguistic cues remains limited to specific portions of this mental health condition.

DOI: 10.1201/9781003611110-4

Online behavior signs that indicate depression include posting less frequently and moving away from social activities, and erratic changes in how users interact with the platform. Social media data brings multiple dimensions to research, but artificial intelligence applications create their value for mental health studies. Combining the data described in detail in this chapter with AI algorithms enables a transformative approach to mental health solutions that impact a larger number of people.

4.1.2 Importance of Early Detection

The timely recognition of depression proves vital to decrease its widespread negative impact on individuals alongside communities. Untreated depression creates multiple serious results, such as reduced life quality and major social and cognitive limitations, as well as higher susceptibility to persistent physical conditions. The lack of treatment for depression can lead people to harm themselves and, in severe cases, result in suicide, thus requiring immediate medical attention [2]. Traditional diagnostic methods, which rely on self-reporting and clinical evaluation, have inherent limitations like stigma, underreporting, and limited access to mental health professionals. Social media tools provide an open-access view of people's ongoing emotional reactions at any time. This medium allows individuals to both notice and track depressive symptoms and access guidance that helps stop symptom progression. The method provides access to early detection intervention, enabling immediate treatment procedures. Social media delivers outstanding monitoring capacities for populations without service as it enhances both reach to new demographic groups and their engagement with technology interfaces.

Artificial intelligence systems improve the clinical value of social media data by integrating detection systems. Unstructured text analysis becomes practical alongside newly discovered information fields, thanks to deep learning–based algorithms, which reveal patterns beyond human reach. These models process individual user posts while linking insights across multiple social networks to create a unified scope of mental health awareness, tracking specific topics that influence users.

The integration of artificial intelligence in social media disease detection provides early-stage health feedback that aligns with preventive healthcare needs. The identification of at-risk individuals enables the launch of early health interventions that control symptoms, leading to improved long-term health outcomes. Public health initiatives gain insight into health conditions through early detection, allowing them to direct resources effectively and create targeted health reduction programs.

4.1.3 Role of AI in Mental Health Monitoring

Artificial intelligence serves as a primary research tool in mental health science, enabling the development of precise diagnostic methods that are both effective and affordable, and compatible with large-scale implementation for depression identification. Artificial intelligence empowers social media researchers to identify and interpret complex mental health patterns embedded within diverse datasets, revealing behaviors within the mental health system. Deep learning tools, specifically convolutional neural networks (CNNs) and recurrent neural networks (RNNs), demonstrate exceptional success rates when identifying slight behavioral and linguistic symptoms of depression in victims.

Artificial intelligence has reached new heights in mental health monitoring because of the development of LLMs, including Generative Pre-trained Transformer (GPT) and Bidirectional Encoder Representations from Transformers (BERT). These models achieve exceptional processing ability for complex textual information through their transformer foundation. Modern natural language processing (NLP) models successfully execute multiple text analysis operations, including sentiment analysis, emotion detection, and topic modeling, as research shows. Indeed, their training on huge datasets helps them understand the subtleties of context and language, which consequently enables them to recognize patterns of depression-related language present in social media content.

AI-driven methodologies address multiple practical challenges that exist with traditional diagnostic methods for mental health, in addition to their technical capabilities. The principal contributions include:

- **Scalability and Real-Time Monitoring**: It enables the real-time monitoring of large populations, which is very challenging with conventional methods, as AI systems are capable of working at a large scale and continuously.
- **Application in Resource-Constrained Environments**: The utility of AI-based assessment and treatment is most beneficial in areas where mental health professionals are scarce or nonexistent.
- **Reduction of Human Bias**: AI tools reduce subjective bias and inter-assay variability in evaluating mental health conditions.

Although these advantages exist, integrating AI into mental health monitoring is not easy. However, deployment must be done prudently and responsibly due to issues regarding privacy, ethical issues, and biases in algorithms. Additionally, many current AI models are also not very interpretable, a phenomenon known as the 'black-box' problem, which significantly undermines their trustworthiness and transparency, which are two fundamental values for any clinical AI model.

4.2 BACKGROUND AND LITERATURE REVIEW

The digital platform has become an increasingly important venue for understanding and recognizing mental health disorders using computational methods. In this section, a thorough analysis of psychological markers of depression embedded in text data is provided, along with a review of the literature on artificial intelligence and machine learning in the depiction of depression.

4.2.1 Psychological Markers of Depression in Text

It is the primary channel for communicating inner emotional states. Additionally, it has been shown that data extracted from social media, which is easily available at scale, stores information about depression-related psychological indicators through textual data. Some research finds that people who exhibit these characteristics tend to have a linguistic style with an overabundance of first-person singular pronouns ('I,' 'me,' and 'my') and an underabundance of second-person and plural pronouns. The implication is that this is a self-centered thought pattern associated with social withdrawal.

Depressive language may also show a high density of negative emotion words (i.e., sad, lonely, hopeless), accompanied by a lack of positive emotion words. (Studies have shown that depression is associated with distortions and dysregulation of this kind.) These linguistic tendencies may be correlated with symptoms of depression. Similarly, language markers of rumination and regret, as cognitive hallmarks of depression [3], are temporal markers; these forms of rumination and regret are frequent in the past tenses. Another dimension relates to the pragmatic aspect of communication, in which sentences are less complex and more variable. Linguistic entropy, as a measure of lexical diversity, is illustrated with an example: depressed individuals have low linguistic entropy, which means they are less attentive in producing varied expressions [4]. In addition, behavioral markers such as changes in online activity patterns and reduced posting of text further account for the person's mental state.

4.2.2 Previous Studies on Depression Detection Using AI and ML

Currently, there is an uptick in the application of artificial intelligence for monitoring mental health and using social media data to detect depression. Initial approaches largely focused on a feature engineering technique involving the extraction of linguistic or behavioral markers and then feeding those markers into classical machine learning algorithms, such as Support Vector Machines (SVMs) or logistic regression. Calvo and D'Mello [5] demonstrated the reasonable success of these models in identifying depressive states. However, these were limited in their scalability and generalizability.

Deep learning has provided a platform for artificial intelligence applications in depression detection. Both RNNs and CNNs have demonstrated a great ability to take advantage of contextual and sequential co-dependencies that are found in textual data [6]. Taking the example, RNNs, equipped with mechanisms like Long Short-Term Memory (LSTM), have been proposed to detect depressive symptoms from the sequences of tweets, where higher accuracy as well as sensitivity is reported [7]. Later, they became LLMs (BERT and GPT), which have transfigured this domain. These are pre-trained on large corpora to generate contextual embeddings that embed sensitive linguistic properties. The fine-tuned versions of these LLMs have significantly better performance in sentiment analysis and emotion detection, especially depression detection [8].

Despite these advancements, challenges remain. A significant amount of research has been conducted on imbalanced datasets, which comprise a majority of non-depressive samples and have an adverse impact on the performance of models. Furthermore, deep learning models are perceived as having issues, as they act as a 'black box,' making it difficult for clinicians to trust and therefore use these models [9]. Solving these challenges requires a multidisciplinary approach that combines artificial intelligence with psychology and ethics to create effective, fair, and achievable solutions for detecting depression.

4.3 DATA COLLECTION AND PREPROCESSING

The most significant factor influencing the effectiveness of computational models that aim to detect depression in social media posts is the quality and structure of the data used. Since such data is multidimensional, a complete methodology must be followed for the collection, cleaning, and preparation of the data, so that the final dataset is indicative and trustworthy enough to support the development of robust machine learning models. In this document, we describe our methods for obtaining social media data and preprocessing it to mitigate data quality issues, as well as our detailed feature engineering efforts to establish a relationship between phenomena reported in social media and depression indicators. At each stage of this pipeline's development, we seek to provide datasets that contribute to key advancements in computational mental health research.

4.3.1 Social Media Data Sources

In terms of social media platforms, user-generated content constitutes a dynamic reservoir of real-time user expressions and unparalleled access to user mental states. Research on depression detection has extensively utilized Twitter, Reddit, and Facebook as platforms. Because Twitter is so brief and immediate—emotions and thoughts fixed in textual forms—it is particularly valuable. While data access is limited on Facebook, its rich user narratives and interactional content provide greater insight into the makeup and conversations of each subreddit community [10].

Typically, data collection is executed via platform-specific Application Programming Interfaces (APIs). For example, Twitter's API allows researchers to pull out public tweets using customizable parameters, keywords, hashtags, or the ID of particular users. Throughout this process, ethical considerations remain relevant. Strict guidelines protect the acquisition of data to ensure that user privacy is protected and that informed consent is obtained from users. Additionally, Institutional Review Board (IRB) approval, in conjunction with compliance with jurisdiction-specific data privacy regulations, such as the General Data Protection Regulation (GDPR), is necessary to obtain ethical clearance [11].

To expedite research, datasets have been made available for those who are not directly involved in data collection. Notable examples include the eRisk dataset and the CLPsych Shared Task dataset, which were created specifically to identify linguistic patterns associated with mental health conditions. These datasets are valuable because they are pre-annotated and ethically sourced, supporting reproducibility and cross-study validation [12]. While there is a discussion about integrating multiple data sources, the authors argue that data diversity promotes robust model generalizability across various populations and contexts. Table 4.1 presents a summary of benchmark datasets used to perform studies on depression detection.

TABLE 4.1
Publicly Available Datasets for Depression Detection Research

Name of Dataset	Link (URL)
CLPsych Shared Task Dataset	https://clpsych.org/shared-task/
eRisk Dataset	https://erisk.irlab.org/
DAIC-WOZ (Distress Analysis Interview Corpus)	https://dcapswoz.ict.usc.edu/
Reddit Self-reported Depression Diagnoses (RSDD)	https://zenodo.org/record/1479354
DepSign-L Dataset	https://osf.io/m4frp/

4.3.2 Data Cleaning and Annotation

Direct analysis of a source of raw, unstructured, social media data is inherently heterogeneous and often noisy, making it infeasible. Preprocessing begins with removing obtrusive posts, such as advertisements, spam, or posts lacking useful content. Additional challenges exist, including typographical errors, non-standard abbreviations, emojis, and slang, which require a considered text normalization strategy to address these issues. Among the standard preprocessing techniques used to make the data linguistically consistent are tokenization, lemmatization, and removal of stopwords [13].

Labeled datasets are essential for the construction of supervised learning applications, and annotation is one of the main elements in their generation. In labeling, each post is assigned a label from a set of predefined labels based on a set of mental health indicators, such as 'depressed,' 'not depressed,' and 'off risk.' While labels obtained via manual annotation performed by human psychologists or domain experts are guaranteed to be highly faithful, this approach is resource-intensive and therefore slow. To tackle scalability challenges for annotation methods, we develop semi-automated annotation methodologies that incorporate pre-trained models to assist the human labeler. Moreover, these annotations are further improved with quality control protocols and crowdsourcing platforms (Amazon Mechanical Turk) [14], which can achieve a high level of standard (posterior checks and expert validation).

The classification is integrated with contextual metadata into the annotation process. For example, users' temporal patterns in posting behaviors or the evolution of language patterns in how a user expresses themselves over time may yield useful insights regarding the progression of a user's mental health. Since depression is dynamic on social media, we have adopted a dynamic approach to annotation.

4.3.3 Feature Engineering for Depression Indicators

The importance of feature engineering as part of the analytical pipeline cannot be overstated. It takes raw text and metadata and transforms it into quantifiable input for subsequently built machine learning models. Detecting depression using linguistic features has been based on lexical properties, namely word frequency, word sentiment polarities, and syntactic complexity, for years. Studies [1] have shown that individuals with depression are more dependent on the first-person singular pronoun, tend to use negative emotion words more, and are less diverse lexically. Additionally, we demonstrate that by integrating behavioral features derived from metadata, researchers can achieve greater analytic depth. Included in this analysis are metrics such as posting frequency, time of day, and user interaction, which can help reveal temporal variations in user engagement. For example, prolonged instances of inactivity or inconsistently frequent posts may be indicative of depressive episodes. In addition, interactional metrics, including the sentiment and engagement levels of responses to a user's posts, are considered as possible signs of social withdrawal or emotional distress [15]. Over the last few years, deep learning, especially through embeddings in very strong language models like BERT, GPT, Robustly Optimized BERT (RoBERTa), etc., has made feature extraction unbelievably fascinating. By representing these matrices as embeddings, we can capture the semantic and contextual relationships often lacking in standard methods, such as bag-of-words or term frequency-inverse document frequency (TF-IDF), and improve predictive accuracy. Even so, these features may not be interpretable. Researchers seek a synthesis combining interpretable models because these approaches represent essential requirements for mental health diagnostic systems [16]. Researchers employ textual together with behavioral data features at the same time. Social media platforms now offer photographic and audio content integrated with basic data to achieve comprehensive mental state assessments of users. Research into depression detection must handle complex mixtures of heterogeneous data sources because these methodologies lead to an increased requirement for successful feature engineering practices. A methodological approach to social media collection and preprocessing, as well as high-quality feature extraction, enables researchers to construct sophisticated, scalable depression modeling systems that demonstrate exceptional accuracy. The produced models serve as fundamental tools to understand the mental health-digital communication relationship, which enables early intervention applications.

4.4 DEEP LEARNING MODELS FOR DEPRESSION DETECTION

Deep learning is transforming NLP, providing powerful tools for detecting depression from textual data. This section presents three principal categories of deep learning models for detecting depression: CNNs, RNNs, and transformer-based models. Each model plays a unique role in feature representation, semantic understanding, and computational cost in addressing this problem, but they all share a common usage in mitigating this issue.

4.4.1 Convolutional Neural Networks

CNNs were primarily designed for image recognition. Still, for many NLP applications, such as text classification and sentiment analysis (Figure 4.1), they are quite effective. Pre-trained on various aspects of text, such as biomedical texts and news, these models are predominantly able to predict local patterns within text sequences using convolutional filters, which act as important linguistic markers to indicate the presence of depression. The extraction of these characteristics such as the overuse of negative sentiment words, self-referential pronouns (e.g., 'I,' 'me,' 'my'), and repeat

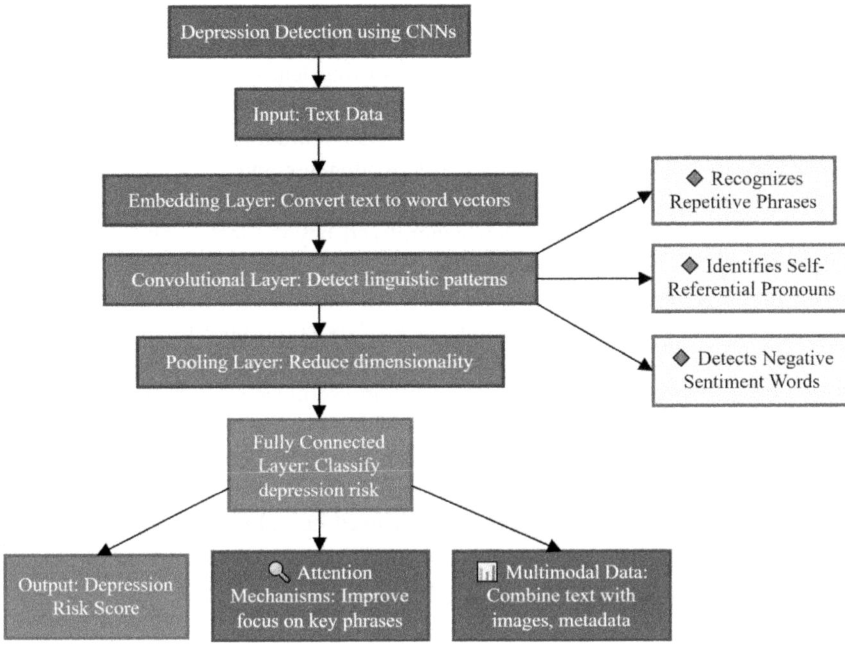

FIGURE 4.1 CNN for textual analysis.

phrasal units that may be associated with a depressive act are examples of these sorts of filters—although any combination of characteristics, not necessarily equivalent to these, is possible. In such a framework, CNNs can learn patterns and thus get insights regarding individuals' emotional and psychological states based on what they wrote or spoke about.

There are many components of a typical CNN architecture for text analysis. The first use of embedding layers is to generate dense vector representations of textual data, representing textual data as dense vectors that contain semantic meaning relationships between words. In these convolutional layers, these embeddings become the input, which the layers apply_filters learn to detect local patterns and features from the text. Next, we use pooling layers to downsample data by decreasing the dimensionality of the data, keeping only the most salient features. This process makes the computation efficient and reduces overfitting. Research has shown that CNNs with word embeddings are better than traditional machine learning methods in tasks based primarily on text [6]. These embeddings provide richer representations of words than bag-of-words representations, taking into account semantics and meaning, which helps sense the finer nuances of depressive text.

Despite their numerous useful properties that make them suitable for CNNs, they appear to have some shortcomings. A major drawback is their requirement for a fixed-size filter, which hinders their encoding of long-range dependencies and fine-grained contexts in text sequences. For example, the variety of depression often involves longer narratives, which can span multiple sentences or paragraphs within a single sentence. Despite this limitation, hybrid models that consist of CNNs along with other methodologies, such as hierarchical pooling or attention mechanisms, can overcome this limitation. This hierarchical pooling leads to the aggregation of the information across different granularities. Attention mechanisms, on the other hand, allow the model to pay attention to the appropriate textual parts and further improve its capability of modeling long-distance dependencies and fine-grained contextual specifics.

The CNN we developed has been generalized beyond text analysis and used as a feature extractor to analyze multimodal data that combines text with a wide spectrum of other data types (e.g., images, audio, or metadata from social media posts). For instance, in mental health monitoring, a CNN could take in various elements, such as the text of a social media post, an image, user engagement metrics, and other content from different timestamps over a temporal sequence. Multimodal approaches of the above greatly expand the level to which CNNs can be utilized in mental health research, enabling them to detect depression markers much more efficiently and accurately. By combining various data sources, CNNs enable a holistic view of an individual's mental state, allowing them to be used in real-world scenarios.

4.4.2 Recurrent Neural Networks

The recurrent nature of RNNs makes them a perfect fit for modeling sequential data (Figure 4.2), particularly text, as they can analyze both temporal and contextual dependencies. Unlike CNNs, which focus on finding local patterns in predefined text windows, RNNs maintain dynamic memory states and use this mechanism to monitor word sequence development across time. RNNs store information in a memory state to track how emotions and thoughts, as well as linguistic patterns, evolve

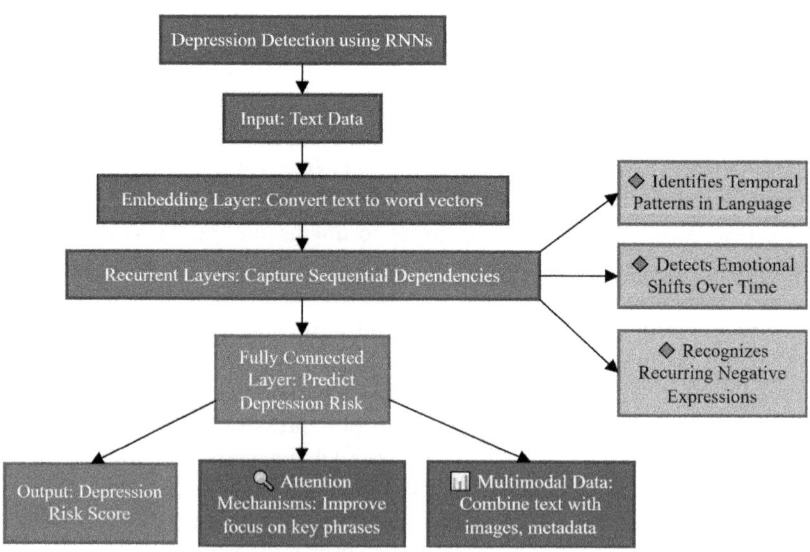

FIGURE 4.2 RNN for textual analysis.

across textual content, thus improving their ability to understand developmental patterns between elements. The ability to process sequences enables effective analysis of depression-related content because emotional tone and thematic elements evolve throughout the text, revealing concealed insights into user emotional states.

Researchers developed LSTM networks alongside Gated Recurrent Units (GRUs) as enhanced forms of RNNs to address the vanishing gradient challenge. These networks utilize special gating mechanisms to determine which information to sustain for longer periods and which data to discard based on their ability to assess relevance (i.e., identifying elements to discard). As a result, these networks exhibit excellent performance in recognizing long-range connections, thereby excelling at tasks that require such capabilities, including social media tone adjustment and written text sentiment analysis.

RNNs are exceptionally good at determining if depression is found within different types of data, such as social media posts or the contents of blogs or articles. For example, LSTM-based models cited in [7] are effectively correlated with an example of an individual gradually picking up a pessimistic outlook (as expressed through despair, hopelessness, or even self-deprecation). These models can detect changes that are very subtle in linguistic usage, such as an increase in negative sentiment words, reduction in positive words, and a change toward speech that is more self-referred, all of which point to depressive sentiment. In addition, RNNs excel at storing contextual subtleties spanning sentences and paragraphs—i.e., they capture the mood, the tone, or a particular style expressed over several posts or a span of a dialogue. As a result, RNNs are a powerful mechanism that can encode understanding of the wider context of language usage, leading to an understanding of the richness and dynamism of depression.

Still, RNNs have their drawbacks. A noteworthy factor is their computational intensity. Currently, processing extended text sequences is a tedious and resource-consuming task. Standard RNNs, including LSTMs and GRUs, demonstrate performance limitations with lengthy sequences when early sequence words ultimately lose their influence in the processing pipeline. Researchers counter these implementation problems by improving model functions through the addition of bidirectional processing, as well as the integration of attention mechanisms. These special RNNs process written content in both directions simultaneously, enabling deeper word comprehension and improving the model's understanding abilities.

These past couple of years have demonstrated the strong capabilities of attention-augmented RNNs as a valuable tool. The model utilizes attention mechanisms to determine which parts of a sequence require greater emphasis through weighted distributions, according to the task's significance. This functionality expands the model's capabilities by revealing where in the text the model prioritizes specific parts, leading to a simpler interpretation of the model's understanding. Through depression detection technology, important linguistic evidence, such as statements of sadness and worthlessness, as well as feelings of guilt, remains captured. The model can recognize precise, discreet, and meaningful health signals that help it detect mental health problems due to its special attention mechanism.

More recently, deep learning has evolved to incorporate RNNs alongside other architectures, such as CNNs and transformers, to leverage the benefits of both.

For example, the combination of CNNs, which are well suited for local pattern detection, with RNNs, which are experts in sequence analysis, has yielded good results for extracting fine-grained linguistic features while characterizing high-level dependencies in the context. Similarly, the integration of transformer-based models, which excel at accounting for long-range dependencies and global context, with RNNs is likely to enhance the capabilities of these models in analyzing complex sequences of text strings. By exploiting these hybrid approaches, detecting depression and other NLP tasks could be advanced in terms of providing more robust and diverse mental health monitoring.

4.4.3 Transformer-based Models

They have a revolutionary effect in the NLP domain, where they enable transformationally powerful modeling of local and global contexts in text data (Figure 4.3). Unlike RNNs, they process sequences simultaneously, rather than sequentially, and therefore circumvent many challenges associated with long-range dependencies. To do this, self-attention mechanisms are used, allowing the model to determine the importance of words relative to one another within a sequence, capturing subtle semantic relationships and dependencies across the text. Consequently, this advancement has led to the development of leading transformer-based models such as BERT, GPT, and RoBERTa, which have attained state-of-the-art status in numerous NLP tasks, including sentiment analysis, machine translation, and even depression detection.

In the case of depression detection, transformer-based models are very powerful as they can benefit from previously pre-trained embeddings, fine-tuned on domain-specific datasets. Excitingly, these kinds of models are well equipped to pull out extremely fine-grained patterns in text—the types of patterns that can

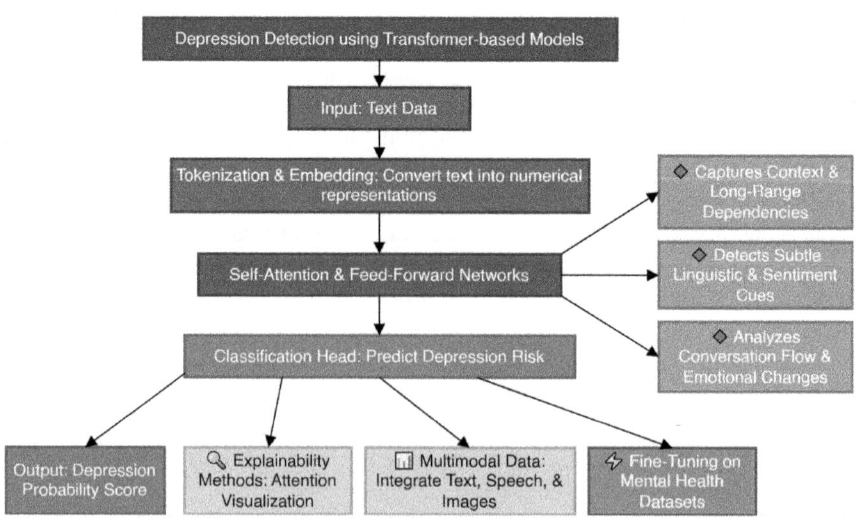

FIGURE 4.3 Transformer-based models for textual analysis.

discriminate between shifts in sentiment polarity, changes in lexical richness, and other small differences in syntax, all of which are indicators of mental health states. For instance, BERT has displayed excellent performance in finding fine-grained linguistic clues of depression, such as the use of negative self-referential language expressing hopelessness or a lack of future intentional thinking. Studies have also shown that BERT-based models outperform traditional methods such as CNNs and RNNs in terms of accuracy and robustness for this task [16]. Moreover, the transformers can handle the long-term dependency and multi-turn dialogues specific to the analysis of the extended social media conversations, where the context of an individual post depends on the previous interaction or a series of similar posts.

Another significant benefit of transformer-based models is their applicability to multimodal data, which involves aligning textual content with other forms of data, such as user interaction patterns, temporal activity, or visual content from social media posts. In particular, this capability has brought about novel multimodal depression detection, and models such as the Vision Transformer (ViT) are joined with text transformers to offer a more holistic way of discerning the psychological state of an individual. For instance, a social media post might include the post's text, the post's image, the time at which the post was created, and a user's history of engagement. Transformers also allow fusion of different diverse data sources, such as online behavior, to obtain a holistic view of an individual's mental health and to detect explicit and implicit cues of depression that may not be present in the text itself [17]. This multimodal approach has created new early detection and intervention methods, mainly for social media-based mental health monitoring.

Transformer-based models are not without their challenges. Another big problem is that they are non-interpretable. The power of their attention stems from complex self-attention mechanisms, which make it difficult to understand exactly how they make their prediction. To solve this, researchers made visualization techniques like attention heatmaps to infer how transformer models decide. These parts of the text are highlighted by these heatmaps so that we can have a better sense of the areas of the linguistic constructs or context that impact the model's predictions. In applications to mental health, in particular, this kind of interpretability is important. We need to be able to trust a model and understand its output; to do that, we need to know why a model outputs what it does. Transformers also have another problem: computing transformer-based models is expensive. The self-attention mechanism, while powerful, is very resource hungry, specifically with massive datasets or very long text sequences. In an effort to solve this problem, DistilBERT [18] and MobileBERT [18] have been developed as efficient transformer variants to lower the computational overhead without sacrificing performance. Lightweight models are expected to operate efficiently on feasible and constrained systems and in real-time applications. Additionally, there is research into applying model pruning, quantization, and knowledge distillation to get transformer-based models to perform better and more efficiently.

Table 4.2 presents a comparative overview of deep learning models used for detecting depression.

In the field of NLP, the rise of transformer models is increasingly driving innovation in the detection of depression and other mental health applications. These models

TABLE 4.2
Summary of Deep Learning Models for Depression Detection

Model Type	Key Characteristics	Strengths	Limitations
Convolutional Neural Networks (CNNs)	Extracts local text patterns using convolutional filters	Efficient in detecting linguistic markers (e.g., negative sentiment, self-referential language); good computational efficiency	Limited ability to capture long-range dependencies; needs hybrid methods for complex patterns
Recurrent Neural Networks (RNNs) (incl. LSTM and GRU)	Models sequential data through dynamic memory states	Captures temporal emotional evolution; handles sequence data better than CNNs	Computationally intensive; struggles with very long sequences without enhancements (e.g., attention, bidirectionality)
Transformer-based Models (e.g., BERT, GPT, RoBERTa)	Utilizes self-attention mechanisms for sequence modeling	Models both local and global dependencies; pre-trained models available; supports multimodal integration	High computational cost; interpretability challenges

are uniquely tailored to analyze the complex and nuanced language characteristic of mental health conditions because they can capture local and global context, long-range dependencies, historical data, and multimodal inputs. Model developers seek to boost interpretability alongside computational efficiency in transformers, yet these updates eliminate specific flaws that transformer models traditionally had in accuracy, scalability, and transparency levels. The intersection of transformer models with deep learning frameworks alongside newly developed multimodal data methods positions mental health detection and personalized care support at a transformative point.

4.5 ROLE OF LARGE LANGUAGE MODELS

The field of mental health analytics has undergone a radical change due to its adoption of NLP through LLMs. These models demonstrate a superior ability to interpret and produce human language, showing massive promise for future improvements in depression detection. The text generation capability and deep language pattern analysis abilities of GPT, together with BERT, have achieved high performance through extensive structured data processing using sophisticated algorithms. This section examines how LLMs support depression detection through architectural development alongside their potential for transfer learning and their performance evaluation against conventional deep learning methods.

4.5.1 Overview of GPT, BERT, and Other LLMs

GPT and BERT, along with other LLMs, serve as the peak language modeling tools today because they offer abilities that humans never possessed when processing human language. Through this model approach, machines gain a fresh and fundamental understanding of text content, helping humans better interpret language in its proper context. OpenAI's GPT is a model using a unidirectional transformer architecture, which is the architecture where text is ingested in only one direction (normally from left to right). GPT employs this design to output coherent and contextually rich text based on predicting the next sequence of words given the preceding input. Its strength comes in the generation of human-like text whose content retains both grammatical correctness and matches its context very well, making it extremely useful in tasks that include text generation, summarization, or conversational AI.

On the contrary, BERT by Devlin et al. relies on a bidirectional transformer, allowing it to understand contextual relationships of words in both preceding and following positions within a sentence. A bidirectional approach to this is better than simply the words before a word or phrase, because this is more comprehensive in understanding the text. In the case of a sentence like 'She went to the bank to deposit money,' BERT can understand 'bank' as a financial institution and not a riverbank from the context. Using this ability, BERT proves superior to any other structure on the tasks that require a deeper understanding of the language, such as question answering, sentiment analysis, and, most notably, depression detection [16].

GPT and BERT utilize an extensive corpus of textual data, comprising billions of words from various sources, including books, articles, and websites. One approach is through pre-training, which establishes a robust baseline of linguistic knowledge for the model, enabling it to learn general language patterns, grammar, and semantics. After pre-training these models, they can be fine-tuned on specific tasks like depression detection using only small domain-specific datasets. The models are then fine-tuned to fit the nuances of the desired target task via their general language understanding—for example, learning to identify depressive linguistic subtleties in social media posts or clinical texts. This is one of the key reasons why LLMs have become effectively ubiquitous in NLP applications.

Apart from GPT and BERT, multiple enhanced versions of those models have also been created to improve their capabilities. For example, RoBERTa improves its original BERT architecture by incorporating increased training dynamics, such as larger batch sizes, longer training times, and greater datasets. With these enhancements, RoBERTa can perform even better on a wide set of NLP tasks. T5 (Text-to-Text Transfer Transformer) also takes a unified approach to NLP by formulating all NLP tasks as text-to-text problems where both input and output are text sequences. This flexibility enables T5 to tackle functions such as translation, summarization, sentiment analysis, and depression detection using a single model architecture [19].

Aside from the fact that LLMs can interpret nuanced language markers, they are also perfectly suited for recognizing depression from textual data. For example, such models can detect slight emotional tone changes (from neutral or positive to emotional, sad, guilty, or hopeless). They can also sense self-referential language that points to depression tendencies; self-referential language involves things like an increased use of first-person pronouns such as 'I' or 'me.' Moreover, LLMs can take into account linguistic expressions that are indicative of hopelessness including phrases like 'nothing ever works out' or 'I can't see a way through.' LLMs can capture these fine-grained markers and help better understand the individual's mental

TABLE 4.3
Summary of Research on LLMs for Depression Detection

Study	Model Used	Dataset	Methodology	Key Findings
Devlin et al. [16]	BERT	Wikipedia, BookCorpus	Pre-trained BERT fine-tuned for depression detection on social media datasets	Achieved significant improvement over traditional methods in sentiment and depressive content analysis
Liu et al. [19]	RoBERTa	Reddit posts (mental health forums)	Used enhanced pre-training dynamics and fine-tuning	Outperformed BERT on depression detection tasks; better generalization to unseen posts
Raffel et al. [20,21]	T5	C4 dataset (Colossal Clean Crawled Corpus)	Unified text-to-text framework adapted for mental health prediction	Demonstrated flexibility in capturing depressive cues in varied text types

state, for detecting it early and taking necessary measures. To further highlight the progress and effectiveness of LLMs in depression detection, Table 4.3 summarizes key studies, models used, datasets involved, methodologies applied, and their major findings.

Despite this, challenges exist with their use. A far more significant problem is that these models are computationally wasteful, and training and fine-tuning them incur the expense of powerful GPUs and large-scale datasets.

4.5.2 Transfer Learning in Depression Detection

All LLMs employ the strategy of transfer learning. For specialized tasks such as depression detection, the utility of LLMs can be greatly enhanced. Due to the scarcity of labeled data, traditional machine learning approaches, which typically rely on a large amount of annotated data, often lead to unsatisfactory performance. However, transfer learning addresses this issue with LLMs, allowing them to learn to solve new tasks with minimal data fine-tuning, building on the generic language understanding they have acquired during pre-training.

Pre-trained models such as BERT can be fine-tuned on annotated sources of social media posts, clinical text, or any other relevant context to predict depression by learning patterns of sentences indicating depression and non-depression. It is possible that these patterns are related to subtler changes in sentiment (i.e., more negative sentiment overall, or less expression of positive sentiment). They may also be part of a long-standing pattern in the use of negative language, including routinely speaking about feelings of sadness, hopelessness, or of not being worthy, and making frequent use of first-person pronouns, including 'I,' 'me,' and 'my.' In addition, fine-tuned LLMs discover additional linguistic indicators of depression, such as a lack of forward thinking, low lexical diversity, and recurrent phrases that point toward rumination or obsession with negative thoughts. But fine-tuning does that by allowing you to capture these subtle patterns. It captures all the tiny indicators that provide you valuable insight into a person's mental state, and hopefully, early detection and intervention.

We all know that applying transfer learning to train LLMs results in achieving better accuracy and generalizability than using traditional supervised learning methods. However, conventional techniques may not perform well when being trained on small datasets because they do not possess the rich linguistic knowledge and contextual knowledge obtained by LLMs from their pre-training phase. In contrast, fine-tuning is extremely effective at generalizing to unseen data given a relatively small dataset to fine-tune on. They are particularly well suited to the task of depression detection, as labeled data is rarely available. Additionally, these models are scalable for deployment across a range of social media platforms, including Twitter, Reddit, and designated mental health forums. Within the realm of this problem, we may then leverage a fine-tuned BERT model to analyze the patients' Twitter posts for potential indications of depression, scan mental health forums for thought activity, and refine them in real time as we observe them, as well as comment on posts containing indications of difficulties and act as a support system to help those expressing distress on social media. Transferring learning to different tasks and other languages, dialects, and cultural contexts, LLMs are versatile. Linguistic markers of depression can differ among other cultures, specific language use, and individuals in the expression of the disease. But the varying sets of cultural practices, norms, and environments that we experience also vary wildly, and by drawing on datasets that reflect these variations, researchers and practitioners can fine-tune pre-trained models to create more culturally sensitive and culturally contextual mental health monitoring tools. In particular, this adaptability is critical for global applications, where a one-size-fits-all approach does not work.

However, there are obstacles to using transfer learning with LLMs. The most significant issue is that pre-trained models contain biases acquired during the training data collection. For instance, if the pre-training corpus language has such biases, the fine-tuned model's predictions can amplify these biases. This problem has drawn attention from researchers investigating debiasing algorithms, diverse dataset curation, and fairness-aware training methods. Another obstacle is that fine-tuning large models can be expensive, especially for an organization or researchers with limited resources. Transfer learning, however, model compression, distillation, and efficient fine-tuning have reduced the cost of transfer learning, and we are getting closer to only spending time along with truly new tasks.

4.5.3 Comparative Analysis of Deep Learning vs. LLMs

In this article, we describe the foundation of the technologies used to detect depression, which rely on traditional deep learning models, such as CNNs and RNNs. Both CNNs can extract features from localized text patterns using convolutional filters, and RNNs can capture dependencies in sequential data, making them very useful for language tasks. Unfortunately, these models tend to struggle with modeling long-range dependencies and grasping the intricate semantic structure needed to learn what constitutes human language [22].

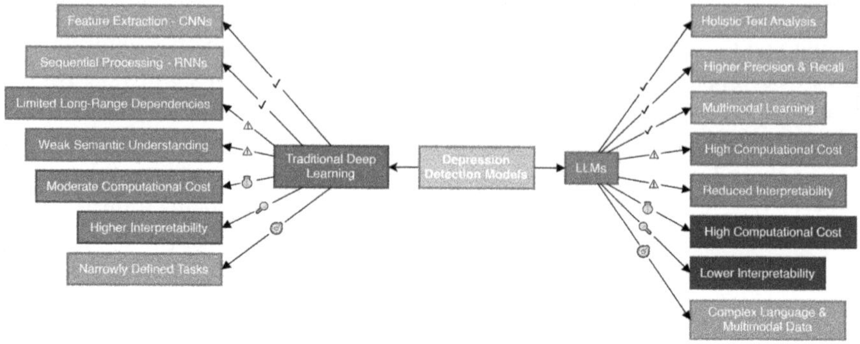

FIGURE 4.4 Analysis of deep learning vs. LLMs.

On the other hand, self-attention equipped LLMs are a transformative solution. In contrast, LLMs are designed to view each text sequence as a unified entity, which enables them to represent linguistic nuances better. Thanks to this capability, the precision, recall, and $F1$-scores of depression detection metrics show substantial improvement. Furthermore, the multi-task learning capabilities of the LLM allow it to analyze multidomain data sources, such as text and visual datasets extracted from social media posts [23].

However, as appealing as it might be, there are still challenges to the application of LLMs. Unfortunately, due to their computational costs, they sometimes suffer from a lack of interpretability. Training and deploying these models require a substantial amount of resources. However, this may mean that only larger organizations and research institutions with larger budgets can access. On top of that, LLMs inherently have a complex nature, which complicates the interpretation of the language used within them and, in turn, the understanding and validation of their decision making. Therefore, in response to these challenges, ongoing research is focused on mitigating them by developing more efficient and interpretable variants of LLMs. To solve these problems, we are trying to build lightweight model architectures and develop advanced explanatory techniques, such as attention visualization, to make LLMs accessible and reliable for practical usage [24].

Figure 4.4 illustrates a paradigm shift in the approach to depression detection techniques, comparing them to deep learning and LLMs. The former excels at executing precise, well-defined actions, while the latter excels at understanding and processing complex language constructions. Based on these findings, LLMs are currently the most versatile and, therefore, the most effective means to bring mental health diagnostics into the digital age.

4.6 CHALLENGES AND ETHICAL CONSIDERATIONS

Deep learning models working with LLMs encounter numerous ethical problems, along with complex detection challenges, when used to scan for depression indications across social media platforms. Core ethical issues related to this area form three components: privacy boundaries and diagnostic accuracy, with solutions to reduce racial bias and requirements for system transparency. By identifying these concerns, scientists create dependable systems that uphold ethical standards to support mental health initiatives. Both difficulties, their complex interrelationships, and their comprehensive solutions are discussed in this section.

4.6.1 Privacy and Consent Issues

Scientists run into an ethical issue with privacy breaches because they analyze depression-related content on social media platforms. Social media platforms maintain extensive mental health databases that require both strict privacy regulations and strict ethical standards for their protection. Users frequently post emotionally charged content on social media platforms without evaluating the mental health effects, so this practice creates uncertainties about how consent works [25].

Data anonymization stands out to numerous users as a practical way to safeguard their privacy. The study of data de-identification developed two contemporary approaches known as data masking and differential privacy, which eliminate individual identifiers from sources without compromising depression detection abilities. The approach combines both a complicated system for preserving privacy while enabling analysis effectiveness, with technical challenges that demand multiple equilibrium solutions. The GDPR demands complete transparency about data collection practices, while users must provide specific consent before the system can use their data [26]. Research developers have to develop data governance protocols that ensure user rights match ethical standards and legal obligations to gain public trust in artificial intelligence systems.

4.6.2 Risks of Misdiagnosis

AI models operate probabilistically, and this characteristic creates diagnostic uncertainty, which constitutes an essential problem in depression detection. Two distinct forms of misdiagnosis exist: false positive and false negative. A false positive detection where someone is labeled as depressed will lead to both unnecessary psychological harm and associated social stigma. False-negative diagnoses from depression detection systems produce missed opportunities for timely treatment that allow patient depression to remain undetected while leading to worsening mental health conditions [27].

The risks cannot be fully alleviated without having human experts oversee the system. AI technology should work in conjunction with the medical staff's analytical skills rather than function independently of them. AI systems should include mental health professionals to validate and contextually interpret their conclusions during output-based decision making. For robust outcomes, AI models must undergo strict training and validation procedures where data exists as both comprehensive and representative. The models require datasets that represent different cultural, linguistic, and demographic groups so they can operate reliably throughout all population groups.

Ongoing system performance checks represent a vital requirement for this process. AI systems require regular updates that incorporate modifications in social media language, as well as changes in user behavior. Error detection procedures, together with model calibration techniques, deployed after deployment, help decrease diagnostic uncertainties. An ongoing feedback cycle that involves artificial intelligence models interacting with mental health professionals enables precision improvement of these diagnostic systems through time [28].

4.6.3 Mitigating Model Bias and Interpretability Concerns

Artificial intelligence detection systems for depression face ongoing difficulties from interpretability shortcomings as well as detection bias. A model that receives biased training data will generate discriminatory results without intent. When datasets disproportionately represent particular demographic groups, it leads to bias because patients from those populations share social and cultural elements that affect how they report their depressive symptoms. These biases lead the models to become biased systems that lack fairness, targeting diverse populations [29]. A complete solution for bias reduction requires diversified efforts. The reduction of these disparities in unbalanced classification involves the implementation of adversarial training, together with resampling, along with other bias detection algorithms. A diverse set of training datasets that include every segment of society need to be carefully crafted because such data forms the basis for achieving fair outcomes. The process of selecting data for analysis alongside transparent data preprocessing helps identify bias sources before the model-building steps begin. AI systems require major trust-building through interpretable design features. Black-box models retain significant power but create difficulties for stakeholders who need to comprehend these systems' fundamental operational methods. SHapley Additive exPlanations (SHAP), as well as attention mechanisms and feature attribution methodologies through model-agnostic tools, explains how predictions form [30]. Through these methods, researchers plus medical staff can validate AI output while ensuring both clinical knowledge alignment and compliance with ethical guidelines. AI model interpretation directly affects a system's capacity to meet regulatory requirements. These systems demonstrate enhanced capability to comply with ethical review panels, together with regulatory bodies. The ongoing investigation into the explainable aspects of AI systems within mental health applications works simultaneously to both improve accountability and gain wider social acceptance of these technologies.

4.7 CONCLUSION AND FUTURE DIRECTIONS

Recent evidence from naive deep learning approaches and LLMs demonstrates their ability to detect depression from social media data, thus transforming mental health diagnostic practices. Neural network processing techniques, such as CNNs alongside RNNs and transformer-based models, deliver top performance in detecting depression markers in raw text data. Modern mental health monitoring technology produces flexible automated tracking solutions that provide real-time information because of its linguistic modeling capabilities. The implementation of these systems generates three major problems involving ethical challenges and privacy risks, along with diagnosis inaccuracies that appear when organizations deploy these platforms. Model interpretability limitations, together with bias issues, must be resolved to build fair and trustworthy diagnostic systems.

The discipline needs future investigations to optimize context analysis methods through a combination of textual data with information stored in biological indicators, together with images and acoustic data. LLMs continue to develop through new features that create potential pathways for customized mental health treatment solutions. To achieve universal availability in global mental health services, equitable access initiatives must build culturally specific models that adapt to regional language characteristics. These growth initiatives need technical infrastructure improvements to make secure data distribution systems that deliver reliability alongside control capabilities. A robust system of ethical rules for controlling data governance alongside clear policies and transparent operations will create reliable deployment practices. The future development of these fields aims to boost the effectiveness of AI-driven depression detection system and transform them into trusted, transformative mental healthcare solutions.

REFERENCES

1. Tausczik, Y. R., & Pennebaker, J. W. (2009). The Psychological Meaning of Words: LIWC and Computerized Text Analysis Methods. *Journal of Language and Social Psychology*, 29(1), 24–54. https://doi.org/10.1177/0261927x09351676
2. Cacheda, F., Fernandez, D., Novoa, F. J., & Carneiro, V. (2019). Early Detection of Depression: Social Network Analysis and Random Forest Techniques. *Journal of Medical Internet Research*, 21(6), e12554.
3. Nolen-Hoeksema, S. (2000). The Role of Rumination in Depressive Disorders and Mixed Anxiety/Depressive Symptoms. *Journal of Abnormal Psychology*, 109(3), 504–511. https://doi.org/10.1037/0021-843x.109.3.504
4. Schwartz, H. A., Eichstaedt, J. C., Kern, M. L., Dziurzynski, L., Ramones, S. M., Agrawal, M., Shah, A., Kosinski, M., Stillwell, D., Seligman, M. E. P., & Ungar, L. H. (2013). Personality, Gender, and Age in the Language of Social Media: The Open-Vocabulary Approach. *PLoS ONE,* 8(9), e73791. https://doi.org/10.1371/journal.pone.0073791
5. Calvo, R. A., & D'Mello, S. (2010). Affect Detection: An Interdisciplinary Review of Models, Methods, and Their Applications. *IEEE Transactions on Affective Computing*, 1(1), 18–37. https://doi.org/10.1109/t-affc.2010.1
6. Zhang, Y., & Wallace, B. (2015). A Sensitivity Analysis of (and Practitioners' Guide to) Convolutional Neural Networks for Sentence Classification. arXiv preprint arXiv:1510.03820.
7. Hochreiter, S., & Schmidhuber, J. (1997). Long Short-Term Memory. *Neural Computation*, 9(8), 1735–1780. https://doi.org/10.1162/neco.1997.9.8.1735
8. Wang, Y., Sun, Y., Fu, Y., Zhu, D., & Tian, Z. (2024). Spectrum-BERT: Pre-training of Deep Bidirectional Transformers for Spectral Classification of Chinese Liquors. *IEEE Transactions on Instrumentation and Measurement*, 73, 2516713.
9. Doshi-Velez, F., & Kim, B. (2018). Considerations for Evaluation and Generalization in Interpretable Machine Learning. In: Escalante, H.J., Escalera, S., Guyon, I., Baró, X., Güçlütürk, Y., Güçlü, U., & van Gerven, M. (eds.), *Explainable and Interpretable Models in Computer Vision and Machine Learning*, 3–17. Springer. https://doi.org/10.1007/978-3-319-98131-4_1
10. Al-Mosaiwi, M., & Johnstone, T. (2018). In an Absolute State: Elevated Use of Absolutist Words Is a Marker Specific to Anxiety, Depression, and Suicidal Ideation. *Clinical Psychological Science*, 6(4), 529–542. https://doi.org/10.1177/2167702617747074

11. Benton, A., Mitchell, M., & Hovy, D. (2017). Multitask Learning for Mental Health Conditions with Limited Social Media Data. *Proceedings of the 15th Conference of the European Chapter of the Association for Computational Linguistics*, Volume 1, Long Papers, 152–162. Valencia, Spain: Association for Computational Linguistics. https://doi.org/10.18653/v1/e17-1015
12. Losada, D. E., & Crestani, F. (2016). A Test Collection for Research on Depression and Language Use. In: Fuhr, N., Quaresma, P., Gonçalves, T., Larsen, B., Balog, K., Macdonald, C., Cappellato, L., & Ferro, N. (eds.), *Experimental IR Meets Multilinguality, Multimodality, and Interaction*, 28–39. Springer. https://doi.org/10.1007/978-3-319-44564-9_3
13. Klampanos, I. A. (2009). Manning Christopher, Prabhakar Raghavan, Hinrich Schütze: Introduction to information retrieval. *Information Retrieval*, 12(5), 609–612. https://doi.org/10.1007/s10791-009-9096-x
14. Kiritchenko, S., Zhu, X., & Mohammad, S. M. (2014). Sentiment Analysis of Short Informal Texts. *Journal of Artificial Intelligence Research*, 50, 723–762. https://doi.org/10.1613/jair.4272
15. De Choudhury, M., Gamon, M., Counts, S., & Horvitz, E. (2021). Predicting Depression via Social Media. *Proceedings of the International AAAI Conference on Web and Social Media*, 7(1), 128–137. https://doi.org/10.1609/icwsm.v7i1.14432
16. Devlin, J., Chang, M.-W., Lee, K., & Toutanova, K. (2019). BERT: Pre-training of Deep Bidirectional Transformers for Language Understanding. *Proceedings of the 2019 Conference of the North*, 4171–4186. USA. https://doi.org/10.18653/v1/n19-1423
17. Antsiperov, V. (2022). Generative Model for Autoencoders Learning by Image Sampling Representations. *Proceedings of the 11th International Conference on Pattern Recognition Applications and Methods*, 354–361. Lisbon, Portugal. https://doi.org/10.5220/0010915200003122
18. IEEE. (2019). Proceedings Fifth Workshop on Energy Efficient Machine Learning and Cognitive Computing. *2019 Fifth Workshop on Energy Efficient Machine Learning and Cognitive Computing - NeurIPS Edition (EMC2-NIPS)*, 1–1. Vancouver, BC, Canada. https://doi.org/10.1109/emc2-nips53020.2019.00001
19. Liu, Y., Ott, M., Goyal, N., Du, J., Joshi, M., Chen, D., … & Stoyanov, V. (2019). RoBERTa: A Robustly Optimized BERT Pretraining Approach. arXiv preprint, arXiv:1907.11692. https://doi.org/10.48550/arXiv.1907.11692
20. Raffel, C., Shazeer, N., Roberts, A., Lee, K., Narang, S., Matena, M., … & Liu, P. J. (2020). Exploring the Limits of Transfer Learning with a Unified Text-to-Text Transformer. *Journal of Machine Learning Research*, 21(140), 1–67.
21. Solanki, K., & Dalal, S. (2021). Detection of Intruder in Cloud Computing Environment using Swarm-Inspired Neural Network. *International Journal of Advanced Computer Science and Applications*, 12(9). https://doi.org/10.14569/IJACSA.2021.0120952
22. Chowdhury, A. K., Sujon, S. R., Shafi, M. S. S., Ahmmad, T., Ahmed, S., Hasib, K. M., & Shah, F. M. (2024). Harnessing Large Language Models over Transformer Models for Detecting Bengali Depressive Social Media Text: A Comprehensive Study. *Natural Language Processing Journal*, 7, 100075.
23. Ali, N., Zhang, C. C., Mayo, N., & Chancellor, S. (2024). Diverse Perspectives, Divergent Models: Cross-Cultural Evaluation of Depression Detection on Twitter. arXiv preprint arXiv:2406.15362.
24. Vaswani, A., Shazeer, N., Parmar, N., Uszkoreit, J., Jones, L., Gomez, A. N., … & Polosukhin, I. (2017). Attention Is All You Need. In: Koyejo, S., Mohamed, S., Agarwal, A., Belgrave, D., Cho, K., & Oh, A. (eds.), *Advances in Neural Information Processing Systems*, 30. NeurIPS.

25. Kosinski, M., Stillwell, D., & Graepel, T. (2013). Private Traits and Attributes Are Predictable from Digital Records of Human Behavior. *Proceedings of the National Academy of Sciences*, 110(15), 5802–5805.
26. Feretzakis, G., Vagena, E., Kalodanis, K., Peristera, P., Kalles, D., & Anastasiou, A. (2025). GDPR and Large Language Models: Technical and Legal Obstacles. *Future Internet*, 17(4), 151.
27. DeVylder, J. E. (2022). Suicide Risk Prediction in Clinical Settings—Additional Considerations for Face-to-Face Screening and Machine Learning Approaches. *JAMA Network Open*, 5(5), e2212106.
28. Chouldechova, A., & Roth, A. (2020). A Group of Industry, Academic, and Government Experts Convenes in Philadelphia to Explore the Roots of Algorithmic Bias. *Communications of the ACM*, 63(5), 82–89.
29. Hutchinson, B., & Mitchell, M. (2019). 50 Years of Test (Un)fairness: Lessons for Machine Learning. *Proceedings of the Conference on Fairness, Accountability, and Transparency*, 49–58. Atlanta, GA, USA.
30. Murugamoorthy, G. (2023). Interpreting Uncertainty in Model Predictions in Bayesian Neural Networks for COVID-19 Diagnosis (Doctoral dissertation, Toronto Metropolitan University).

5 Deep Learning and Large Language Models for Detecting Depression in Social Media Posts – An Indian Context

Ruchi Kumari, Kirti Kumari, and Upkar Kedia

5.1 INTRODUCTION

Major Depressive Disorder (MDD), generally referred to as depression, is one of the most widespread and exhausting mental health conditions worldwide (Gutiérrez-Rojas et al., 2020). It impacts emotional, cognitive, and physical wellbeing and is a leading cause of worldwide disability across all ages, genders, and socioeconomic groups. In India, the obstacle is a particular hurdle due to low levels of mental health awareness, severe disapproval, and inadequate provision of professional psychiatric services, particularly in rural areas. Consequently, millions of individuals remain undiagnosed and untreated, emphasizing the urgent requirement for scalable, technology-driven measures.

With over 800 million internet users, India is home to one of the world's largest digital communities (DataReportal, 2025). Digital platforms such as WhatsApp, Facebook, Instagram, and Twitter and domestic platforms like ShareChat and Koo have become fundamental to daily communication and self-expression. These digital platforms not only deliver spaces for exchanging thoughts and emotions but also serve as informal outlets where psychological distress, sadness, and even suicidal ideation are often expressed. This builds social media as an indispensable yet underutilized asset for early mental health monitoring.

Recent innovations in Artificial Intelligence (AI) and Machine Learning (ML), especially Deep Learning (DL) and Large Language Models (LLMs), have enabled the evaluation of huge amounts of user-generated text to identify structures of depressive expression. Unlike traditional clinical methods, which rely on structured interviews and self-report questionnaires that are time consuming and resource intensive, AI-driven systems can provide real-time, scalable, and non-intrusive monitoring. DL models such as Convolutional Neural Networks (CNNs), Long Short-Term Memory (LSTM), and Bidirectional LSTMs (BiLSTMs) have already shown effectiveness in learning emotional and contextual features from social media data,

 DOI: 10.1201/9781003611110-5

offering an improvement over lexicon- and rule-based methods. However, these classical models are limited in their ability to capture nuanced semantics, figurative language, and long-range dependencies. Transformer-based models such as BERT, RoBERTa, ALBERT, and XLNet represent a major advancement. By leveraging self-attention mechanisms and large-scale pre-training, they excel at contextual interpretation, sarcasm recognition, and multilingual adaptability, capabilities essential for India's linguistically diverse environment. Essentially, multilingual and code-mixed variants of these models now enable the analysis of cognitive emotional expression across major Indian languages such as Hindi, Bengali, Tamil, Telugu, and Marathi, thereby increasing comprehensiveness and cultural inclusivity.

Despite these innovations, clinical validation is still crucial. AI systems may identify at-risk individuals, but diagnosis and assistance still require medical knowledge and suggestions. Thus, the most effective procedure lies in incorporating AI-based depression detection with clinical techniques, combining adaptability with clinical consistency. This chapter addresses the critical gap by positioning AI-driven depression identification within India's socio-cultural and linguistic landscape. Particularly, it investigates how LLMs like RoBERTa, DistilBERT, and others can be employed to analyse social media information for early detection of depression and how their integration with existing clinical frameworks can develop scalable, ethical, and context perceptive mental health guidance systems.

This chapter explores the convergence of social media analytics, advanced AI models, particularly transformers and DL, and their role in understanding and detecting depression, with a distinct focus on depression detection in the Indian context. It begins by highlighting the connection between depression and self-expression, particularly online, followed by a summary of clinical diagnostic methods currently used in India. It then evaluates computational methods, starting with lexicon- and rule-based methods, followed by DL methods, and then specific emphasis on Transformer-based LLMs like RoBERTa and DistilBERT and their multilingual proficiencies. A synthesis of literature studies is compiled to highlight the results and methods of these approaches. The chapter further investigates the potential for integrating AI-driven systems and clinical practice, while emphasizing ethical elements such as privacy, authorization, and algorithmic bias. Finally, it identifies future directions, including the development of culturally adapted LLMs for Indian languages, AI-enabled mental health screening in schools and workplaces, and hybrid clinical–AI frameworks for rural populations.

5.2 DEPRESSION AND SOCIAL MEDIA

5.2.1 Symptoms of Depression

Depression manifests differently among individuals; however, several symptoms are commonly observed (see Figure 5.1).

According to the Diagnostic and Statistical Manual of Mental Disorders, Fifth Edition (DSM 5), these symptoms should persist for at least two weeks and cause clinically significant distress or impairment in social, occupational, or other important areas of functioning to meet the criteria for MDD (5th ed., text rev.; American Psychiatric Association (2022)).

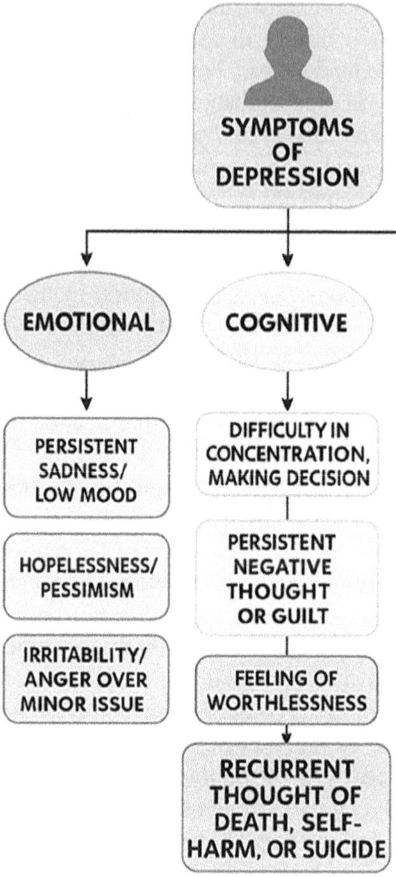

FIGURE 5.1 Common symptoms of depression.

Depression manifests through a combination of emotional, cognitive, and physical symptoms that can significantly impair an individual's daily functioning. Emotional symptoms often include persistent sadness, hopelessness, irritability, and a loss of interest or pleasure in previously enjoyable activities. Difficulty in concentrating, poor memory, indecisiveness, and recurring negative thoughts, including feelings of worthlessness or suicidal ideation, are the common symptoms of cognition. Fatigue, changes in weight or appetite, sleep disturbances such as insomnia or hypersomnia, and undefined aches or pains are parts of physical symptoms. Therefore, careful assessment and timely intervention are required to erase the seriousness, duration, and integration of these symptoms.

5.2.2 Depression and Social Media in India

5.2.2.1 Role of Social Media in Expressing Mental Distress

In contrast to many Western societies, where treatment is more commonly accepted, in India, people are scared of sharing their mental illness due to their emotional struggles of fear of criticism or punishment from friends, family, or society in general. Because of this, social media platforms provide a somewhat secure and indirect avenue for self-expression.

Social media penetration is still rising as a result of more people using the internet, especially young people and adults living in cities. Commonly, distressed people leave behind faint digital footprints that could provide a focus for declining mental health. Typically, these patterns include:

- Text-based posts such as tweets, WhatsApp statuses, and Instagram captions containing expressions of sadness or hopelessness.
- Hashtags and emojis conveying low mood (e.g., #FeelingLow, #TiredOfLife).
- Memes and self-deprecating humour, often masking emotional pain with humour.
- Creative expressions such as poetry, song lyrics, or cryptic statements that hint at personal struggle.
- Changes in posting behaviour, including sudden withdrawal or an unusual surge in activity.

These behaviours, when analysed collectively, can provide early warning signs of emotional distress.

5.2.2.2 Suicide and the Mental Health Crisis in India

Such online expressions sometimes precede severe mental health crises, including suicide. According to the National Crime Records Bureau (NCRB), more than 1.6 lakh suicides were reported in 2022, with a significant proportion linked to academic stress, unemployment, and family-related problems (see Figure 5.2). States such as Maharashtra, Tamil Nadu, and Madhya Pradesh report the highest suicide rates, with rising cases among students and young professionals (Accidental Deaths & Suicides in India 2022 National Crime Records Bureau, n.d.).

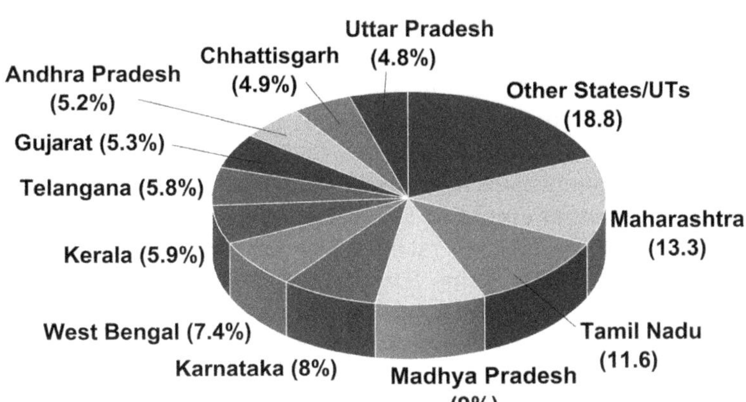

FIGURE 5.2 State/UT-wise percentage share of suicides during 2022. (Accidental Deaths & Suicides in India 2022 National Crime Records Bureau, n.d.)

Research indicates that social media activity in the days or weeks preceding suicide often contains depressive cues, such as farewell-like messages, withdrawal from interactions, or posting of dark or fatalistic content. Identifying and analysing these patterns using AI-based detection models can help enable timely intervention, potentially preventing loss of life.

5.3 CLINICAL METHODS OF DEPRESSION DETECTION IN INDIA

Although international diagnostic standards form the cornerstone of mental health evaluation, the identification of depression in India requires adaptation to local healthcare realities, cultural perceptions, and resource availability.

5.3.1 Diagnostic Criteria (DSM-5 and ICD-11)

DSM-5 (Diagnostic and Statistical Manual of Mental Disorders, Fifth Edition): It defines depression as the appearance of at least five depressive symptoms during a two-week duration, with at least one symptom being present, which could be either depressive mood or loss of interest/pleasure.

ICD-11 (International Classification of Diseases, Eleventh Revision): It follows similar symptom and duration instructions but places supplementary emphasis on cultural understandings of mental health symptoms, acknowledging that the expression and identification of depression may vary across various cultural settings.

5.3.2 Screening Tools and Questionnaires Used in India

In India, different screening tools have been used to assess depressive symptoms and overall psychological depression. These techniques are not diagnostic in themselves but assist as valuable aids in identifying individuals who may need further clinical evaluation. Widely used illustrations include the Patient Health Questionnaire-9 (PHQ-9), a brief self-report scale synchronized with DSM criteria and translated into numerous Indian languages for broader availability; the Beck Depression Inventory (BDI), a prolonged measure assessing symptom severity, commonly used in urban clinical and counselling contexts; and the General Health Questionnaire-12 (GHQ-12), which screens for general mental anxiety in both community and research scenarios. These tools can be administered by trained mental health professionals, general clinicians, social workers, or even used as self-assessment instruments in community health initiatives. Additionally, several other tools are used in certain contexts, such as the Hamilton Depression Rating Scale (HAM-D) for clinical assessments, the Geriatric Depression Scale (GDS) for adults, the Center for Epidemiologic Studies Depression Scale (CES-D) for community studies, and the Kessler Psychological Distress Scale (K10/K6) for public health screenings (Table 5.1). The acclimatization of these implements into regional languages such as Hindi, Tamil, Bengali, and Kannada secures cultural and linguistic inclusivity, making it more efficient in varied Indian populations.

TABLE 5.1
Comparisons of Clinical Tools for Depression Detection in India

Tool	Description	Usage in India	Languages Available	Who Can Administer
PHQ-9 (Patient Health Questionnaire-9)	9-item self-report questionnaire aligned with DSM criteria, used to assess depression severity	Widely applied in clinics and community health programmes	Hindi, Tamil, Bengali, Kannada, Malayalam, and others	Self-administered; general practitioners; mental health professionals
BDI (Beck Depression Inventory)	21-item self-report tool measuring intensity of depressive symptoms	Common in urban clinical and counselling settings	English, selected regional translations	Self-administered; psychologists; psychiatrists
GHQ-12 (General Health Questionnaire-12)	Brief screening tool for general psychological distress; not depression specific	Frequently used in academic research and large-scale surveys	Multiple Indian languages	Self-administered; researchers; community health workers
HAM-D (Hamilton Depression Rating Scale)	Clinician administered tool for assessing depression severity in adults	Used in psychiatric hospitals and clinical studies	English (clinician administered)	Psychiatrists, clinical psychologists
CES-D (Center for Epidemiologic Studies Depression Scale)	20-item self-report scale for depressive symptoms in the general population	Applied in epidemiological and community-based studies	English, Hindi, and adapted regional versions	Self-administered; researchers; trained health workers
GDS (Geriatric Depression Scale)	Screening tool designed for detecting depression in older adults	Used in geriatric clinics and elder care settings	English, Hindi, and other regional versions	Self-administered (for literate older adults); geriatric specialists; nurses
Kessler Psychological Distress Scale (K10/K6)	Measures non-specific psychological distress	Used in public health screenings and population surveys	English, Hindi, Tamil, Telugu, and others	Self-administered; public health workers; general practitioners
ICD-11 Diagnostic Guidelines	WHO's classification system for depression symptoms and severity	Used by psychiatrists and clinical psychologists across India	Standardized nationally; culturally adapted	Psychiatrists, clinical psychologists
DSM-5 Criteria (Clinical Interview)	Gold standard diagnostic framework for Major Depressive Disorder (MDD)	Used in hospitals and psychiatric consultations	English (clinician administered with translation)	Psychiatrists, clinical psychologists

5.4 DEEP LEARNING APPROACHES FOR DETECTING DEPRESSION FROM SOCIAL MEDIA POSTS

Social media platforms are developed by people to demonstrate their ideas, emotions, and daily experiences, frequently giving an insight into their emotional health. Due to this, these platforms are turning into a useful tool for identifying early indicators of mental health concerns like depression. Researchers and developers can identify signs of emotional distress and potential mental health concerns by analysing users' language patterns, tone, and content on social media through advanced DL methods and LLMs. DL architectures, such as CNNs and Recurrent Neural Networks (RNNs), have been widely applied for sentiment analysis, emotion recognition, and text classification in detecting depressive tendencies. Recently, transformer-based LLMs like BERT, RoBERTa, and GPT-based models have demonstrated better results in capturing nuanced linguistic cues, context, and semantic relationships that often signal depression. Intelligent systems can use these models to track online activity in real time and provide resources, interventions, or alerts on time. At last, the development of intelligent systems that can identify online behaviour and provide timely support or intervention when needed helps advance mental wellbeing and care.

5.4.1 Lexicon- and Rule-Based Approaches for Depression Detection from Social Media Posts

Lexicon- and rule-based is the oldest method among different depression detection techniques. These methods basically work on the NRC Emotion Lexicon and Linguistic Inquiry Word Count (LIWC), which understand words, sentences, and phrases related to fear, sadness, hopelessness, anxiety, and other emotional states. To analyse the mental health of individual from social media posts, their content is compared to these lexicons, and several factors like word frequency, sentiment polarity, and co-occurrence patterns are used for its identification. For example, "I am worthless," "exhausted," or "tired of life," these phrases were mostly found as Depressive behaviour

Using specific depression like lexicon- and rule-based approach, which assign a sentiment or severity rating to terms associated with depression symptoms, the technique has been discussed. Rule-based systems improve these lexicons by recognizing specific linguistic patterns, such as an increase in the use of first-person pronouns, negative self-references, absolute terms ("always," "never"), and indicators of social disengagement. Time-based analysis can further enhance detection by tracking language changes over time and detecting progressive increases in words that convey negative emotions or decreases in socially engaging language. Emoji–emotion mapping lexicons, for example, enable detection of depressive states through visual symbols, while hybrid lexicon–topic modelling approaches identify thematic contexts in which depressive language occurs (Kusal et al., 2025). In some studies, writing style metrics, such as reduced sentence complexity or limited vocabulary, have also been linked to depressive expression. In view of the above, Table 5.2 summarizes several studies of lexicon-based approaches for depression detection across multiple social media platforms.

TABLE 5.2
Summary of Lexicon-Based Approaches for Depression Detection Across Multiple Social Media Platforms, Detailing Data Sources, Methodologies, Evaluation Metrics, Key Findings, Limitations, and References

Platform/Data Source	Approach Type	Lexicon/Rule Source	Key Methodology	Key Findings/Accuracy	Limitations	Ref.
Twitter (Korean, English, Japanese) and Everytime forum	Lexicon-based labelling + deep learning (CNN, BiLSTM, BERT)	Multilingual depression lexicons verified by experts	POS tagging + lexicon match → label → classification; SMOTE and undersampling for balance	BERT, $F1$: 0.9912; multilingual improves practicality	Ambiguity of terms, poor cross-domain performance, and no medically diagnosed data	Cha et al. (2022)
Twitter and depression blogs	Lexicon-based sentiment classification	Depression lexicons from prior studies + hate speech lexicon; validated by psychologists	Keyword expansion (thesaurus), RAKE extraction, manual validation, and rule formula for classification	Proposed formula: $P = 77.43\%$, $R = 70.66\%$, $F1 = 73.89\%$; offensive words improved detection	Limited to English; only public tweets; no medical diagnosis confirmation	Ziwei and Chua (2022)
Weibo microblogs (Chinese)	Automatic lexicon construction + ML classifiers	Custom depression lexicon (2,000+ words) built via W2V LPA	Seed terms → W2V expansion → Label Propagation; features + ML models (LR, SVM)	W2V LPA $F1 = 0.893$; improved accuracy by 2%–9% over baselines	Small corpus; cultural/language specificity; performance drop with imbalance	Li et al. (2020)
Facebook and Twitter	Lexicon-based emotion dynamics analysis	LIWC 2007 emotion dictionaries	Measured instability/variability of emotion word use; correlated with PHQ-9	FB: higher negative emotion instability → greater depression severity; Twitter: opposite trend	Small sample; content unavailable; retweets excluded	Seabrook et al. (2018)
Twitter (COVID 19 period)	Regex-based depression user ID + fusion model (DL + lexicon features)	Regex keyword rules: LIWC, VADER for features	Regex to label users; transformer models + psycholinguistic and demographic features fused with ML	Fusion model Accuracy = 78.9%, $F1 = 79.2\%$; identified linguistic and personality predictors	Possible control group contamination; limited to English	Zhang et al. (2021)

Despite the interpretability and low computational cost of lexicon- and rule-based approaches, they face certain limitations. They may skip culturally specific or context-dependent expressions, struggle with sarcasm and figurative language, and require ongoing updates to remain relevant in evolving online discourse. To tackle these issues, recent work integrates lexicon/rule-based systems with machine learning classifiers, utilizing the interpretability of lexicons with the adaptability of data-driven models. In summary, while lexicon- and rule-based methods have made a substantial contribution to early depression detection research, particularly in resource-limited settings, their effectiveness is enhanced considerably when combined into hybrid frameworks that adapt to various linguistic and cultural frameworks.

5.4.2 Classical Deep Learning Models

For recognizing depression in social media posts, traditional DL models like CNNs, LSTM networks, BiLSTMs, and Gated Recurrent Units (GRUs) have been extensively employed. These architectures are especially useful because they can reduce the need for manually created linguistic or lexicon-based features by automatically learning rich semantic and syntactic representations of features simply from raw text or already trained embeddings. In order to detect subtle depressive prompts dispersed throughout different posts, recurrent models such as LSTM and BiLSTM are particularly well suited for capturing long-range associations and sequential structures in language. GRUs, a condensed form of LSTMs, are computationally smaller and offer comparable efficiency. CNNs are compelling for capturing important signals of depressive expression within brief social media messages because they are adept at recognizing local n gram patterns and emotionally charged terms. By acquiring latent linguistic, contextual, and emotional descriptions that can be difficult to manually design, these models collectively show the ability to extend across a variety of social media datasets.

In view of the above, Orabi et al. (2018) worked on CNN and BiLSTM architectures with optimized word embeddings, on the CLPsych 2015 Twitter dataset (1,145 users labelled as control, depression, or PTSD), with an external Bell Let's Talk dataset (154 users) to explore depression-related posts. On the CLPsych dataset, a CNN with global max pooling achieved an accuracy of 87.96%, an $F1$-score of 86.97, and an AUC of 0.951. When applied to the Bell Let's Talk dataset, the highest achieving model got an accuracy of 83.12% and an AUC of 0.923, underscoring its relevance beyond the original training domain. The study also showcased the advantage of optimized and adaptable word embeddings that captured domain-specific language patterns suitable for depressive representation on social media (Orabi et al., 2018). Similarly, in a study summarizing techniques from 2017 to 2021, Babu and Kanaga (2022) discovered that LSTM and BiGRU models consistently worked on depression identification datasets.

Ren et al. (2021) developed a BiLSTM model that uses an emotion-based attention mechanism (EAN) and successfully employed it to identify depression in Reddit text with a high accuracy of about 0.9 (Ren et al., 2021). Furthermore, Zogan et al. (2021) used a multimodal hybrid deep learning model (MDHAN) that combined hierarchical attention methods with behavioural and textual features. Using attention-based

TABLE 5.3
Summary of a Few Classical Deep Learning Models for Depression Detection from Social Media

Models Used	Dataset/Platform	Performance Highlights	Ref.
BiGRU	Reddit (suicide classification)	Stacked BiGRU: Acc/$F1$ ~92.6%	Rizky Febriansyah et al. (2024)
BiLSTM and BERT	Twitter and Reddit social media platforms	BiLSTM- and BERT-based knowledge distillation scheme achieved an accuracy of 96% and 98%	Intelligence and Neuroscience (2023)
BERT (B) + Emotion Detector (E, CNN-based) + Attentive BiGRU, with late fusion of Profanity features (P) and Morality features (M)	Reddit Pirina dataset (post level), Reddit Self-reported Depression Diagnosis (RSDD) dataset (user level)	RSDD: $F1 = 62.73\%$ (+2.65% absolute over baseline BERT); Pirina: Accuracy = 93.87%, $F1 = 95.65\%$ (+6.73% absolute $F1$ over baseline BERT).	Triantafyllopoulos et al. (2023)
BERT, ALBERT, SVM (TF IDF, Word Embeddings, TF IDF + Word Embeddings), Naïve baseline	DATD (Depression and Anxiety in Twitter Dataset), compiled from English tweets collected via Twitter Stream API (May 2018–August 2019).	On the balanced DATD dataset, fine-tuned BERT achieved 74.9% accuracy, 71.3% precision, 85.6% recall, and 77.4% $F1$-score, closely matching inter-annotator agreement.	Owen et al. (2020)

interpretability, their model produced predictions that could be understood with improved accuracy (Zogan et al., 2021) (Table 5.3).

As discussed above, DL techniques like LSTMs, BiLSTMs, GRUs, and CNNs offer specific benefits over lexicon- and rule-based methods, having automatically learned meaningful features from raw text or embeddings, enabling them to capture wider semantic, syntactic, and psychological trends in social media posts. These features make the techniques more accurate and reliable than handcrafted lexicons, which rely on predefined dictionaries and struggle with setting. Even so, DL models are also not without their limitations; they struggle with figurative speech like metaphor and sarcasm, are less adept at managing long-range dependencies, and require a lot of labelled data often to function repeatedly. On the other hand, transformer-based architectures use self-attention to model complex contextual relationships, identify subtle depressive cues, and adapt more effectively to diverse and noisy social media environments, which makes it worthy for use over classical DL models.

5.4.3 Transformer-Based Large Language Models (LLMs)

Transformer-based LLMs have made significant contribution to the detection of depression on social media as it works upon using the power of self-attention and limiting the drawbacks of previous DL techniques. Transformers get subtle linguistic cues that are mostly separated by a large amount of time in a user's timeline. It recognizes long-range dependencies across entire documents. This capability is compared with traditional approaches that process text sequentially and are less effective at capturing long-range dependencies across entire documents. Although finding a depression rarely depends on a single post, it might be detected by multiple posts, and this ability is important for mental health analysis. Furthermore, transformers are trained for interpreting complex contextual meanings, which enables them to tell sentiment even if it is expressed indirectly like through sarcasm text, metaphor, or tone shifts. Another advantage is their ability to adapt across multiple languages, making it possible to analyse informal, code-mixed, and culturally diverse social media language with high accuracy, an area where traditional lexicon-based and DL methods often fall short. Overall, these improvements turned Transformer-based LLM models into a groundbreaking technology that provides robustness and scalability for detecting intricate depressive markers in online discussions.

In view of the above, several studies have shown their efficacy in terms of depression detection through social media. For mental health monitoring or depression detection tasks, models like DistilBERT and RoBERTa have been successfully improved. Owen et al. (2020) developed a refined BERT model that demonstrated a strong ability to recognize subtle psychological cues in text, achieving 74.9% accuracy, 71.3% precision, 85.6% recall, and a 77.4% $F1$-score for depression and anxiety identification, using the DATD Twitter dataset (Owen et al., 2020). Further, Patil et al. (2023) showed that multilingual and code-mixed adapted BERT variants, such as mBERT and HingBERT, achieved outstanding results on Hindi-English code-mixed social media datasets, demonstrating their adaptability to informal and linguistically diverse content (Patil et al., 2023).

It has been observed that transformers are also very good at sarcasm detection and contextual understanding, which are crucial for recognizing depressed expressions that might not involve explicitly negative language. To classify the level of depression in social media posts, Poświata and Perełkiewicz (2022) worked on the RoBERT model, which effectively differentiated between the categories of "not depressed," "moderately depressed," and "severely depressed". Such multi-class classification enabled these techniques to detect masked depressive language, distinct expressions, and emotional shifts with high accuracy. In a study by Dubey et al., the experimental results demonstrate that RoBERTa achieves 98.5% accuracy with metadata for Sarcasm detection (Dubey et al., 2025). With their strengths in multilingual adaptability, nuanced context modelling, and the detection of implicit or indirect depressive signals, Transformer-based LLMs have grown as a cornerstone technology for next-generation depression detection systems on social media platforms. Given the above, Table 5.4 summarizes different literature studies based on Transformer-Based LLMs with their performance highlights.

Although the reviewed studies demonstrate promising accuracy and robust results in detecting depression from social media data using DL models, it is important to acknowledge that such approaches cannot serve as standalone diagnostic tools. Clinical evaluation by mental health professionals remains essential for ensuring reliability, contextual understanding, and ethical application in real-world scenarios. Automated systems may effectively flag at-risk individuals or reveal patterns

TABLE 5.4
Summary of Transformer-Based Large Language Models (LLMs) for Depression Detection from Social Media

Transformer Model(s) Used	Dataset/Platform and Domain	Key Methodology	Performance Highlights	Ref.
BERT Base (12 layers, 110M parameters) combined with CNN	Custom Instagram multimodal dataset (10,295 posts: 3,431 depressive, 6,863 non-depressive; text + images; psychiatrist validated) and Instagram posts	Multimodal fusion: BERT for contextual text embeddings; CNN for image features; emoticons converted to text; 70% text + 30% image weighted soft voting; extensive preprocessing for text and images	Hybrid BERT CNN: Accuracy = 99%, Recall = 97%, Precision = 100%, *F*1-score = 99%, significantly outperforming text only BERT (97% acc.) and image only CNN (89% acc.); Friedman's Rank Test confirmed statistical significance	Beniwal and Saraswat (2024)
DistilBERT base uncased (last four layers, weighted average), compared with BERT base uncased	Depression Severity Dataset (Reddit posts, four severity levels: Minimum, Mild, Moderate, Severe; augmented to 4,353 posts) and Reddit mental health posts	Hybrid model: DistilBERT embeddings + auxiliary features (medication mentions, EmoRoBERTa emotion features)	DistilBERT (last 4 layers) + auxiliary features + MLP head (512 hidden units), Best model achieved 84.26% Precision, 84.18% Recall, 84.15% F1	Kerasiotis et al. (2024)
Fine-tuned GPT 3.5 Turbo 1106 (300B tokens, context 16,385), Fine-tuned LLaMA2 7B (7B parameters, LoRA fine-tuning)	"Depression Detection via Harvesting Social Media" (Shen et al., IJCAI 2017) – Twitter posts; 20k train, 20k test, and Mental health, depression detection from social media	Fine-tuned GPT 3.5 Turbo with 4 epochs, batch size 4, LR multiplier 1.57; Fine-tuned LLaMA2 7B using LoRA; Binary classification (depressive vs. non-depressive); compared with GPT 3.5 Turbo (vanilla), GPT 4, GPT 4 Turbo, GPT 4 Omni, Gemini	Fine-tuned GPT 3.5 Turbo: 96% Acc, $P = 0.954$, $R = 0.968$, $F1 = 0.960$ (outperformed all baselines, exceeding best prior accuracy ≈86.8%); Fine-tuned LLaMA2 7B: 84% Acc, $P = 0.852$, $R = 0.840$, $F1 = 0.846$; Baselines: GPT 3.5 Turbo (68% Acc), GPT 4 (74% Acc), GPT 4 Turbo (74% Acc), GPT 4 Omni (72% Acc), Gemini (62% Acc)	Shah et al. (2024)

(*Continued*)

TABLE 5.4 (*Continued*)
Summary of Transformer-Based Large Language Models (LLMs) for Depression Detection from Social Media

Transformer Model(s) Used	Dataset/Platform and Domain	Key Methodology	Performance Highlights	Ref.
BERT base uncased, MentalBERT base uncased; Modified with Multimodal Adaptation Gate: M BERT, M MentalBERT	Depression_Mixed (Reddit + forums, binary depression vs. non-depression), Dreaddit (Reddit, binary stress vs. non-stress), Depression_Severity (Reddit, 4 severity levels), and Depression and stress detection from social media text	Extracted linguistic features (NRC Emotion Lexicon, LIWC, LDA GOSS, Top2Vec); Integrated via Multimodal Adaptation Gate and attention control; Applied label smoothing for calibration; Compared base vs. feature injected models	Depression_Mixed: M MentalBERT (Top2Vec) + label smoothing: $P=96.12\%$, $R=90.18\%$, $F1=93.06\%$, Acc = 93.45%, ECE = 0.033, ACE = 0.043 (+1.89% $F1$ over base) Dreaddit: M MentalBERT (LIWC) + label smoothing: $F1=83.40\%$, Acc = 81.96%, ECE = 0.116, ACE = 0.112 (+3.36% $F1$ over base) Depression_Severity: M MentalBERT (LDA topics) + label smoothing: WF1 = 73.16%, WP = 73.74, WR = 73.23 (+1.49% $F1$ over base) Feature injection + label smoothing improved accuracy, $F1$, and calibration across all tasks	Ilias et al. (2023)
RoBERTa base (final choice; outperformed BERT)	CLEF 2021 eRisk Task 3 dataset – Social media posts + Beck Depression Inventory (BDI) questionnaire responses (21 questions, 4–7 severity levels) and Depression severity estimation from social media	Preprocessed text; trained 21 independent RoBERTa classifiers (one per BDI question); extracted last four hidden layers, concatenated into linear classification head; sentence-level predictions aggregated by majority voting; post-processing weighting strategies to push towards higher severity (Run2 best)	AHR = 32.62%, ACR = 69.46%, ADODL = 83.59%, DCHR = 41.25% – highest ADODL in 2021 and improved over prior years; weighting towards higher severity boosted DCHR and ADODL; RoBERTa outperformed BERT in development accuracy	Wu and Qiu (n.d.)

(*Continued*)

TABLE 5.4 (*Continued*)
Summary of Transformer-Based Large Language Models (LLMs) for Depression Detection from Social Media

Transformer Model(s) Used	Dataset/Platform and Domain	Key Methodology	Performance Highlights	Ref.
RoBERTa base (fine-tuned); DistilBERT (fine-tuned for comparison)	Custom dataset (ShreyaR/ DepressionDetection, Hugging Face) – Depressive posts from Twitter and Reddit; Non-depressive from Sentiment140; Severity labels via Burns Depression Checklist and Depression detection and severity prediction from social media	Collected and merged Twitter/Reddit depressive posts with Sentiment 140 non-depressive tweets; severity labels from Burns Checklist; preprocessing and split 70/30; fine-tuned RoBERTa and DistilBERT using Hugging Face Trainer API; cross-entropy loss	RoBERTa: Val Loss = 0.1385, Acc = 97.45%; DistilBERT: Val Loss = 0.1495, Acc = 94.45%; RoBERTa outperformed DistilBERT by ~3% accuracy; public dataset and models released for reproducibility	Rani et al. (2022)

of depressive expression, but without professional oversight, there is a risk of misclassification or over-reliance on algorithmic predictions. Therefore, an integrated approach, combining the strengths of data-driven machine learning models with clinical expertise, offers the most balanced and responsible pathway for advancing depression detection and support.

5.5 INTEGRATION OF CLINICAL AND DEEP LEARNING MODELS FOR DEPRESSION DETECTION FROM SOCIAL MEDIA

Integrating clinical screening tools such as the PHQ-9, BDI, and DSM-5 criteria with AI-based DL models for depression detection from social media posts offers significant advantages. Traditional clinical tools provide validated, standardized methods for assessing depression severity and diagnosis, but their utility is often limited by dependence on patient self-reporting, willingness to participate, and access to healthcare providers. On the other hand, AI models analysing social media enable passive, large-scale monitoring by identifying linguistic, emotional, and behavioural cues indicative of depression in real time. However, AI models alone sometimes lack direct clinical grounding or standardized severity validation and can suffer from interpretability and precision challenges due to language variability and noise in social media data. By combining these two approaches, systems can leverage the strengths of both: AI provides early warnings and scalable screening through automated analysis of vast digital footprints, while clinical tools confirm diagnosis and reliably quantify symptom severity, enhancing overall detection accuracy and clinical relevance (Figure 5.3).

Several key studies exemplify this integration. One study used NLP and machine learning classifiers trained on social media posts alongside user PHQ-9 questionnaire scores to classify sentences corresponding to depression symptoms, demonstrating that depression likelihood can be predicted without requiring explicit user input, thus enabling early identification based on clinical criteria (Kim et al., 2022). An AI-powered multimodal system combined transformer-based text analysis with linguistic behavioural markers and temporal posting patterns, validated against expert clinical assessments aligned with DSM-5 diagnostic criteria, achieving high accuracy and lead time for predicting mental health crises across different languages and platforms (Mansoor & Ansari, 2024). Additionally, studies confirmed that integrating PHQ-9 with machine learning methods on mobile and digital platforms can maintain clinical screening sensitivity and specificity comparable to traditional in person administration, allowing for scalable and remote depression assessment (Kim & Lee, 2021). Finally, research on transformer models enhanced with auxiliary clinical, linguistic, and sentiment features from Reddit posts showed improved depression severity classification consistent with clinical scales, proving that adding metadata and emotional markers enhances model validity (Ilias et al., 2023).

While DL models applied to social media data have shown promising accuracy in detecting depression, they cannot replace professional diagnosis. Clinical evaluation remains essential to ensure reliability, contextual understanding, and ethical use. The combination of clinical tools with AI models is used to enhance the accuracy

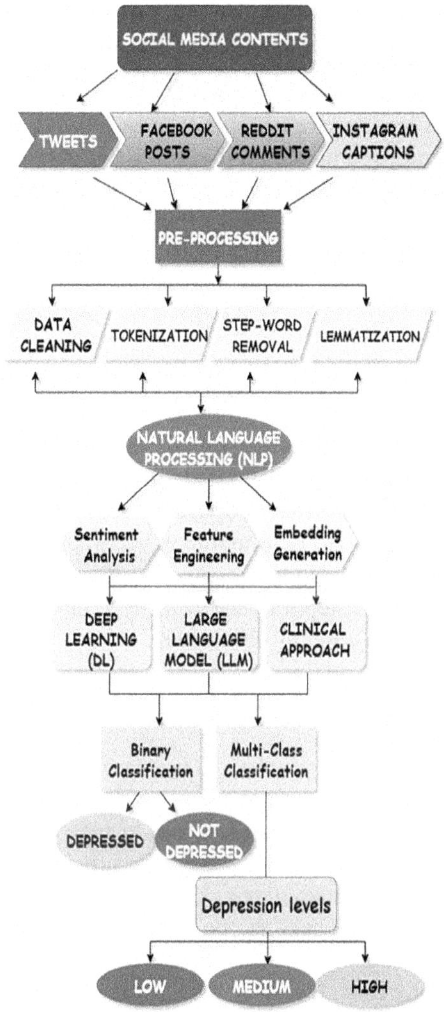

FIGURE 5.3 Workflow for depression detection using social media content through natural language processing (NLP), deep learning, and clinical approaches.

and clinical relevance of detection systems. It can also provide early, continuous, and generalized mental health monitoring. With this, we can reduce dependencies on self-reporting and frequent clinical visits. This combination can be used to interpret and standardize the quantification of the depression severity scale, thereby supporting mental healthcare experts in making decisions. However, important limitations are patient privacy compromise, user consent, and the potential difference between one's online behaviour and their offline mental state. When using AI in medicine, it's important to follow ethical rules. Non-consented social media data should not be used. When used together, AI and clinical practice hold great potential for advanced depression detection and management.

5.6 ETHICAL AND PRACTICAL CONSIDERATIONS IN AI-BASED DEPRESSION DETECTION

Using AI tools for depression detection sounds very good. In a country like India, where access to mental health support is still very limited, it sounds hopeful. But people should be very careful ethically before using any AI tool. These tools use personal and sensitive information. If it is not handled properly, it can do harm instead of benefits. The major concerns are patient privacy, wrong predictions, and whether people understand what they are engaging in.

5.6.1 Respecting Data Privacy

Although people share more of their thoughts and expressions more on social media, no one wants their post to be analysed or judged by anyone else till they permit for it. AI systems should be prompt to find the signs of depression, only when their consent or approval is gained. In India, like general education, digital literacy should also be widespread across all regions, so that people may realize when their digital data is being used (Khalil et al., 2024). These methods become more crucial when we are working with something as important as mental health. India's new Digital Personal Data Protection Act (2023) is a step forward towards it, but ensuring practical protections on the ground is still an ongoing challenge.

5.6.2 Reducing Misclassification and Bias

AI models are very powerful, but they have a few imperfections. One major problem is misclassification, like false positives or negatives. For example, any person posting sad song lyrics in Tamil/Telugu or using sarcasm in mixed language, Hindi English slang, can be wrongly detected as depressed. At the same time, a person truly in distress might go unnoticed if their language isn't well represented in the training data. This happens because many models are built on Western or English-centric data. Without diverse Indian languages and cultural contexts, the models can't always "understand" what's being said. One way forward is through explainable AI (XAI) tools like SHAP or LIME that help researchers and clinicians understand why the model flagged a post. This makes the system more transparent and helps catch errors before they cause harm. "AI systems might inherit prejudices from training data… making it critical to develop fair and unbiased AI systems."

5.6.3 Ensuring Informed Consent and Clarity

AI tools that analyse emotional content rely heavily on trust. In India, where stigma around mental health is still high, people need clear and respectful communication about what's happening with their data. Getting real consent means more than just a checkbox. Users should be told, in simple and local language, what kind of analysis is being done, why it matters, and how they can opt out. Some AI tools, such as Replica, are trying to include consent-based models, but they still have a long way to go in terms of clarity and cultural fit.

5.7 CONCLUSION

Depression is a serious mental health concern, especially in India, where various social judgements and stigma, with a lack of mental health resources, make it tough to get help on time. Even the rapid growth of social media brings chances and challenges together, as people often share signs of their emotional struggles without even knowing the consequences of uploading personal and professional information. Therefore, the use of advanced AI, such as DL and LLMs, makes people to identify and help with depression in real time. By observing language changes, emotional signals, and behavioural differences, AI may offer a reliable and respectful way to identify those who might be at risk and help them to seek early clinical and emotional support. Combining AI with mental health resources, such as chatbots, and counselling provided online, could be a revolutionary step in filling the mental health treatment gap in India. Also, keeping the rural areas in consideration, multilingual LLMs can pick up distress signals in several regional/local languages. That being said, ethical considerations are very important, such as patient data privacy, consent, and potential misdiagnoses by AI. However, professional psychiatric treatment and assessments cannot be replaced by any AI tool or technology. At the end, it is mental health/clinical experts who must interpret and validate the insights provided by DL- and LLM-based tools. As these hybrid systems work efficiently, their integration into mental healthcare can enable a more proactive, complete, and flexible support system.

5.8 FUTURE DIRECTIONS

Early detection of mental health problems is crucial, especially among working adults and students who frequently suffer from stress, anxiety, and depression. Early identification of at-risk individuals can be facilitated by integrating DL-based screening tools into corporate and educational settings. Together, strategies like wearable behavioural monitoring, sentiment analysis of online interactions, and LLM-driven wellness initiatives can promote prompt intervention and stop mental health issues from getting worse.

Though mostly DL tools and LLM models are trained on Western datasets, they fail to capture the linguistic diversity, dialectal variations, and cultural nuances of India. The development of domain-specific LLMs for Indian languages like Hindi, Tamil, Bengali, Marathi, and Telugu should be the main goal of future developments. In order to enable more accurate sentiment analysis, chatbot-based counselling, and psychological evaluations in native languages, these models must take into account the cultural and social factors that affect mental health.

In the case of rural India, where mental health experts are limited in number, DL provides immense solutions in terms of early identification of mental health or depression with a comfortable and specified language. Early detection of anxiety and depression can be assisted by a hybrid approach that utilizes human professionals with digital tools. Access to mental healthcare in underserved areas can be greatly increased by voice-based assistants in regional languages, self-assessment equipped apps for smartphones, and referral systems that link patients to online psychiatrists in cities.

Tools based on DL and LLM can provide individualized therapeutic support in addition to diagnosing depression. These systems can offer clinical recommendations, relaxation techniques, and personalized treatment plans by examining a person's emotional and behavioural patterns. When combined with a clinical approach, such a digital suggestion guarantees mental health while addressing each person's particular needs.

REFERENCES

Accidental Deaths & Suicides in India 2022 National Crime Records Bureau. (n.d.). https://data.opencity.in/dataset/accidental-deaths-and-suicides-in-india-2022

American Psychiatric Association. (2022). *Diagnostic and Statistical Manual of Mental Disorders* (5th ed., text rev.) [DSM 5 TR]. American Psychiatric Association Publishing. https://doi.org/10.1176/appi.books.9780890425787

Babu, N. V., & Kanaga, E. G. M. (2022). Sentiment Analysis in Social Media Data for Depression Detection Using Artificial Intelligence: A Review. *SN Computer Science*, 3(1), 74. https://doi.org/10.1007/s42979-021-00958-1

Beniwal, R., & Saraswat, P. (2024). A Hybrid BERT CNN Approach for Depression Detection on Social Media Using Multimodal Data. *Computer Journal*, 67(7), 2453–2472. https://doi.org/10.1093/comjnl/bxae018

Cha, J., Kim, S., & Park, E. (2022). A Lexicon Based Approach to Examine Depression Detection in Social Media: The Case of Twitter and University Community. *Humanities and Social Sciences Communications*, 9(1). https://doi.org/10.1057/s41599-022-01313-2

DataReportal. (2025, February 25). Digital 2025: *India* [DataReportal – Global Digital Insights]. Retrieved August 23, 2025, from https://datareportal.com/reports/digital-2025-india

Dubey, P., Dubey, P., & Bokoro, P. N. (2025). *Unpacking Sarcasm: A Contextual and Transformer Based Approach for Improved Detection*. https://doi.org/10.3390/computers

Gutiérrez-Rojas, L., Porras-Segovia, A., Dunne, H., Andrade-González, N., & Cervilla, J.A. (2020). Prevalence and Correlates of Major Depressive Disorder: A Systematic Review. *Brazilian Journal of Psychiatry*, *42*(6), 657–672. https://doi.org/10.1590/1516-4446-2020-0650

Ilias, L., Mouzakitis, S., & Askounis, D. (2023). Calibration of Transformer Based Models for Identifying Stress and Depression in Social Media. *IEEE Transactions on Computational Social Systems*, *11*(2), 1979–1990. https://doi.org/10.1109/TCSS.2023.3283009

Intelligence and Neuroscience, C. (2023). Retracted: A Novel Text Mining Approach for Mental Health Prediction Using Bi-LSTM and BERT Model. *Computational Intelligence and Neuroscience*, *2023*(1). https://doi.org/10.1155/2023/9872487

Kerasiotis, M., Ilias, L., & Askounis, D. (2024). Depression Detection in Social Media Posts Using Transformer Based Models and Auxiliary Features. *Social Network Analysis and Mining*, *14*, 196. https://doi.org/10.1007/s13278-024-01360-4

Khalil, S. S., Tawfik, N. S., & Spruit, M. (2024). Federated Learning for Privacy Preserving Depression Detection with Multilingual Language Models in Social Media Posts. *Patterns*, *5*(7). https://doi.org/10.1016/j.patter.2024.100990

Kim, N. H., Kim, J. M., Park, D. M., Ji, S. R., & Kim, J. W. (2022). Analysis of Depression in Social Media Texts through the Patient Health Questionnaire 9 and Natural Language Processing. *Digital Health*, *8*. https://doi.org/10.1177/20552076221114204

Kim, S., & Lee, K. (2021). Screening for Depression in Mobile Devices Using Patient Health Questionnaire 9 (Phq 9) Data: A Diagnostic Meta Analysis via Machine Learning Methods. *Neuropsychiatric Disease and Treatment*, 17, 3415–3430. https://doi.org/10.2147/NDT.S339412

Kusal, S., Patil, S., & Kotecha, K. (2025). Multimodal Text Emoji Fusion Using Deep Neural Networks for Text Based Emotion Detection in Online Communication. *Journal of Big Data*, 12(1). https://doi.org/10.1186/s40537-025-01062-4

Li, G., Li, B., Huang, L., & Hou, S. (2020). Automatic Construction of a Depression Domain Lexicon Based on Microblogs: Text Mining Study. *JMIR Medical Informatics*, *8*(6). https://doi.org/10.2196/17650

Mansoor, M. A., & Ansari, K. H. (2024). Early Detection of Mental Health Crises through Artificial Intelligence Powered Social Media Analysis: A Prospective Observational Study. *Journal of Personalized Medicine*, *14*(9). https://doi.org/10.3390/jpm14090958

Orabi, A. H., Buddhitha, P., Orabi, M. H., & Inkpen, D. (2018). Deep Learning for Depression Detection of Twitter Users. *Proceedings of the Fifth Workshop on Computational Linguistics and Clinical Psychology: From Keyboard to Clinic*, New Orleans, LA, https://doi.org/10.18653/v1/W18-0609

Owen, D., Collados, J. C., & Espinosa Anke, L. (2020). *Towards Preemptive Detection of Depression and Anxiety in Twitter*. https://arxiv.org/abs/2011.05249

Patil, A., Patwardhan, V., Phaltankar, A., Takawane, G., & Joshi, R. (2023). Comparative Study of Pre Trained BERT Models for Code Mixed Hindi English Data. *2023 IEEE 8th International Conference for Convergence in Technology (I2CT)*, Lonavla, India. https://doi.org/10.1109/I2CT57861.2023.10126273

Poświata, R., & Perełkiewicz, M. (2022). *OPI@LT EDI ACL2022: Detecting Signs of Depression from Social Media Text using RoBERTa Pre trained Language Models*. https://aclanthology.org/2022.ltedi-1.40/

Rani, S., Patil, V., Katawala, F., Dsouza, A., & Paswan, R. (2022). Use of RoBERTa Model To Analyze Depressive Texts. *JETIR*. www.jetir.orgd348

Ren, L., Lin, H., Xu, B., Zhang, S., Yang, L., & Sun, S. (2021). Depression Detection on Reddit with an Emotion Based Attention Network: Algorithm Development and Validation. *JMIR Medical Informatics*, *9*(7). https://doi.org/10.2196/28754

Rizky Febriansyah, M., Nicholas, Achmad, S., & Suhartono, D. (2024). Depression Detection System for Social Media Users. In *The 18th IMT GT International Conference on Mathematics, Statistics and their Applications* (pp. 12–16). Banda Aceh, Indonesia, Sciendo. https://doi.org/10.2478/9788367405713-003

Seabrook, E. M., Kern, M. L., Fulcher, B. D., & Rickard, N. S. (2018). Predicting Depression from Language Based Emotion Dynamics: Longitudinal Analysis of Facebook and Twitter Status Updates. *Journal of Medical Internet Research*, 20(5). https://doi.org/10.2196/jmir.9267

Shah, S. M., Gillani, S. A., Baig, M. S. A., Saleem, M. A., & Siddiqui, M. H. (2024). *Advancing Depression Detection on Social Media Platforms through Fine Tuned Large Language Models*. https://arxiv.org/abs/2409.14794

Triantafyllopoulos, I., Paraskevopoulos, G., & Potamianos, A. (2023). *Depression Detection in Social Media Posts Using Affective and Social Norm Features*. https://arxiv.org/abs/2303.14279

Wu, S. H., & Qiu, Z. J. (n.d.). *A RoBERTa Based Model on Measuring the Severity of the Signs of Depression*. https://ceur ws.org/Vol 2936/paper 86.pdf

Zhang, Y., Lyu, H., Liu, Y., Zhang, X., Wang, Y., & Luo, J. (2021). Monitoring Depression Trends on Twitter During the COVID 19 Pandemic: Observational Study. *JMIR Infodemiology*, *1*(1). https://doi.org/10.2196/26769

Ziwei, B. Y., & Chua, H. N. (2022). A Depression Diagnostic System using Lexicon based Text Sentiment Analysis. *International Journal on Perceptive and Cognitive Computing (IJPCC)*, 8(1). https://journals.iium.edu.my/kict/index.php/IJPCC/article/view/250

Zogan, H., Razzak, I., Wang, X., Jameel, S., & Xu, G. (2021). *Explainable Depression Detection with Multi Modalities Using a Hybrid Deep Learning Model on Social Media*. https://arxiv.org/abs/2007.02847

6 Identifying Hate and Offensive Content Using Multimodal Deep Learning

Ashish Kumar Dwivedi,
Rajendra Shivaji Patil, and Ankit Jha

6.1 INTRODUCTION

The fast evolution of digital platforms enables rapid transmission and information sharing. Digital transformation also promotes the hate speech and offensive content, which presents challenges to keep safe and comprehensive online environments. To mitigate this, powerful detection techniques can assist in preventing harmful interactions while protecting freedom of expression. Traditionally, identification of hate speech relies on linguistic analysis and rule-based systems. These methods use predefined dictionaries, syntactic structures, and manually curated rules to identify offensive content [1]. While they offer precision in controlled environments, they struggle to adapt to evolving language patterns, nuanced expressions, and implicit hate speech. Moreover, rule-based techniques are inherently rigid and cannot learn from contextual variations, making them less effective in handling the dynamic nature of hate content.

Machine and Deep learning (ML and DL) approaches are mostly employed to reduce the aforementioned limitations. Early ML-based models, such as Decision Trees, Support Vector Machines (SVM), and K-Nearest Neighbours (KNN) classifiers, utilized handcrafted linguistic features to detect offensive content [2]. Although these models improved adaptability compared to rule-based approaches, their effectiveness depended heavily on feature engineering and data quality. They also struggled with generalization when exposed to unseen or ambiguous expressions of hate speech. Figure 6.1 shows unimodal learning, where image and text are used separately, with multimodal learning, where features are combined to improve learning outcomes by leveraging cross-modal interactions.

DL has significantly enhanced hate speech detection by enabling models to learn intricate patterns from large-scale textual and multimodal data. Architectures based on Transformer like BERT [3], Recurrent Neural Networks (RNNs) [4], and Long Short-Term Memory (LSTM) [5] have gained new benchmarks in the classification of textual hate speech [3]. These models help to capture contextual dependencies and semantic nuances, thereby enhancing detection performance. However, while

DOI: 10.1201/9781003611110-6

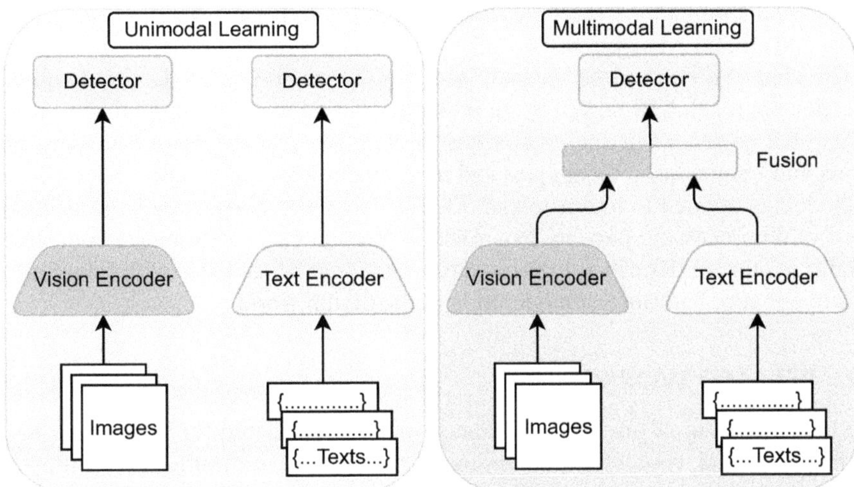

FIGURE 6.1 Generic overview of unimodal and multimodal learning for identifying hate and offensive content.

text-based DL models have shown promise, they often fail to detect implicit hate speech that relies on sarcasm, slang, or multimodal content.

Beyond text, multimodal DL integrates multiple data modalities, including images, videos, and audio, to enhance classification performance. Due to the evolution in social media, vision-language models like CLIP [6] and multimodal transformers have gained prominence, allowing for the simultaneous analysis of textual and visual cues [6]. These advancements are crucial for identifying multimodal hate speech, where offensive content is embedded within images, memes, and videos. Multimodal models solve the problem of compatibility between image and textual interpretation, providing a more comprehensive technique to detect hate speeches. Alongside established ML and DL models, hybrid and graph-oriented architectures are considered as accepted solutions. Graph Neural Network (GNN) models are a type of neural network proposed to handle data structured as graphs that support social network structures to determine hate speech campaigns. Hybrid models aggregate rule-based features using DL approach to enhance robustness and interpretability of a system. Moreover, adversarial attacks pose a significant challenge to automated hate speech detection. Attackers can manipulate text, images, or both to evade detection models. Therefore, developing adversarially robust detection systems remains an active area of research. Ensuring fairness and reducing bias in hate speech detection models is also critical, as automated moderation can inadvertently discriminate against specific communities [7].

This chapter explores the evolution of hate speech detection from traditional linguistic methods to advanced DL approaches, with a focus on multimodal DL. Models integrating text, images, and videos, such as CLIP and multimodal transformers, have become crucial for effective detection. Key challenges are discussed, including cross-modal ambiguity, dataset biases, and interpretability, emphasizing the need for robust and ethical AI systems.

The chapter is organized into six sections. First, an overview of hate content detection approaches, followed by an in-depth discussion of multimodal approaches. Section 6.2 presents existing approaches in the area of hate content detection, such as text and image-based techniques and multimodal learning. Section 6.3 shows the methodology applied to find hate and offensive contents. Subsequently, Data collection and preprocessing part are examined in Section 6.4. Performance comparison and discussion are described in Section 6.5. Section 6.6 concludes with future directions to enhance hate speech moderation in the digital world.

6.2 RELATED WORKS

The understanding of unimodal content is mainly considered for various purposes; on the other hand, content understanding of multimodal has limited scope [8,9] and has inherent challenges [10–14]. Nowadays, more research efforts are observed in the area of offensive language [15–18] detection in other languages. Recent studies have also explored multimodal consistency and semantic alignment for fake news detection [19–21]. In this section, a multimodal-based existing approaches are presented for text data and image data. A brief summary of existing approaches is shown in Table 6.1.

TABLE 6.1
Summary of Related Work

Study	Main Focus	Modalities Used	Approach	Description
Adebayo et al. [10]	Fake news, hate speech, offensive language	Text + image (unified modality)	Inter-modal attention-based deep learning framework	Joint detection across multiple tasks using shared representations
Alam et al. [11]	Disinformation detection	Multimodal (general)	Survey of models	Covers datasets, models, and challenges in multimodal disinformation detection
Alonso-Bartolome et al. [8]	Fake news detection	Text + image	Survey of deep learning methods	Analysis of datasets and model strategies in multimodal settings
Alzu'bi et al. [15]	Offensive memes detection	Text + image	Discriminant deep learning with handcrafted descriptors	Focus on detecting offensive content in memes using multimodal deep learning

(Continued)

TABLE 6.1 (*Continued*)
Summary of Related Work

Study	Main Focus	Modalities Used	Approach	Description
Ayetiran et al. [12]	Fake news, harmful language	Multimodal (text, image, video)	Review of deep learning techniques	Broad review with the emphasis on architecture comparison and performance
Bozarth et al. [9]	Fake news evaluation	Text (primarily)	Evaluation framework	Proposal of robust metrics for fake news classifiers
Hossain et al. [13]	Hate speech detection	Text + speech + vision	Transformer with cross-modal attention	Integration of multiple modalities for hate speech detection
Husain et al. [16]	Offensive language (Arabic)	Text (low-resource language)	Survey	Focused on Arabic language with insights into resources and challenges

6.2.1 Text-Based Approach

Text-oriented hate detection is the initial step, which accepts textual data as input and processes it by conventional ML techniques such as SVM, decision tree, and KNN [22]. The traditional ML models are applied at the surface-based attributes such as term frequency-inverse document frequency (TF-IDF), character n-grams, and sentiment scores. The major challenge with these techniques is lacking to capture semantic meaning and implicit hate speech. Due to the advancement of DL models such as CNN models and LSTM models, lots of aforementioned challenges can be mitigated. CNN model is mostly effective in detecting patterns such as offensive content combinations and syntactic constructs by using the filters employed on word embeddings. Whereas, the LSTM [5] model tackles the other issues such as sequential dependencies, which handle the context of ordering of words. The LSTM-based approach is robust in nature for modelling of long-range dependencies in a sentence. A Transformer-based analysis is considered as a paradigm in text understanding. Models such as BERT [3], RoBERTa [23], and, more recently, HateBERT [24] and Detoxify [25] leverage self-attention mechanisms to capture complex dependencies between all tokens in a sequence simultaneously, rather than incrementally like RNNs. This allows for better handling of nuanced language, sarcasm, and coded hate speech. These pre-trained models, which are fine-tuned on domain-specific corpora for hate and offensive content detection, have demonstrated superior performance due to their rich contextual representations and transfer learning capabilities.

6.2.2 Vision-Based Approach

An image-based technique has attempted to identify offensive content and hate speech by examining images, especially in social media settings where image-based memes often show disrespectful or coded messages [26,27]. Offensive language detection has also been studied in multilingual contexts including Greek datasets [28]. Initial works used CNN-based architectures such as VGGNet [29], ResNet [30], and InceptionNet [31] for classifying vision based on offensive visual cues such as violent imagery, intolerant symbols, and contextually inappropriate content. CNNs excel at capturing spatial hierarchies in image data from identifying lower level edges and textures to higher level object parts and semantics. The aforementioned representations help to learn features that may be a form of hate such as specific logos, gestures, or visual metaphors. However, the major limitation of vision-only approaches lies in their lack of contextual grounding. Hate speeches in images are mainly tenuous or require accompanying text such as captions or overlays to be fully understood. For the use case, a benign image might become a hate speech when associated with offensive language or sarcastic narration. Recent advances show weakly supervised learning, domain-specific fine-tuning, and adversarial training to adapt image-based models to the hate detection task. Regardless of these attempts, standalone visual models often underperform on real-world data, motivating the shift toward multimodal learning.

6.2.3 Multimodal Learning

The integration of textual and visual modalities has proven to be a powerful strategy for detecting hate and offensive content, particularly in contexts like memes, where both image and text are key to understanding the meaning [32]. Early fusion techniques combine features from both modalities early in the model pipeline, offering a model to learn joint representations from text and image. This approach works well when both modalities contribute equally to understanding the content, but it may struggle in cases where one modality is more informative than the other. On the other hand, in late fusion, individual modalities are processed independently, with their outputs integrated at a subsequent point in the model, often through ensemble methods or learned weighting. This strategy is more flexible but may not capture the fine-grained interactions between the text and image as well as early fusion methods. Recent progress has seen the rise of multimodal transformer models such as ViLBERT [33], VisualBERT [34], and UNITER [34], which are specifically designed to handle text–image pairs [35]. These models use shared attention mechanisms to learn the relationships between text and image, improving the model's ability to understand complex content, including sarcasm, where meaning is often derived from the interaction between both modalities. Facebook's Hateful Memes Challenge [36] has been a significant milestone in multimodal hate detection, with leading solutions using these transformer-based approaches to tackle nuanced content that would be difficult for either modality to address independently.

Regardless of the advancements in multimodal hate identification, various challenges remain. Sarcasm and irony present significant hurdles, as hateful content may be implicit or subtle, often looking for both the text and image to be interpreted in context. Multilingualism and code-switched content are also critical challenges, as many models and datasets are limited to English, which restrict their applicability to diverse linguistic contexts. Bias and fairness issues persist, with models potentially reinforcing societal biases if trained on skewed data, leading to unfair targeting of certain groups. Finally, generalization across platforms and domains remains an open problem, as models often struggle to adapt to new environments without further fine-tuning, especially given the rapid evolution of online content.

6.3 METHODOLOGY

6.3.1 PRELIMINARIES

In this section, mathematical notations are used in the methodology to describe the detection of multimodal offensive content. Let the dataset D consist of pairs of image-text data $D = \{(I_1, T_1), (I_2, T_2), \ldots, (I_N, T_N)\}$, where $I_i \in \mathbb{R}^{H \times W \times C}$ represents the ith image, with H being the height, W the width, and C the number of channels, and T_i represents the textual description corresponding to the ith image, which is a sequence of tokens $T_i = \{t_1, t_2, \ldots, t_{L_i}\}$, where t_j denotes the jth token and L_i is the length of the textual sequence. Each data pair (I_i, T_i) is associated with a label $y_i \in \{0,1\}$, where 1 indicates that the content is hateful or offensive and 0 indicates that it is not.

This section of the chapter discusses both unimodal and multimodal learning approaches for hate speech detection. Different fusion strategies are also discussed, and optimization functions are used to train the multimodal architecture, along with the model's inference process.

6.3.2 TEXTUAL AND VISUAL FEATURE EMBEDDINGS

Text feature embedding: Generally, BERT [3] and RoBERTa [23], which are pre-trained transformer-based language models, are capable of extracting rich textual features that capture deep semantic and contextual information. Let the textual feature extractor be denoted as f_t. Given a textual input T_i, the model first tokenizes the text using the tokenizer associated with f_t, converting the raw input into a sequence of subword tokens, which are passed through the transformer encoder to generate contextualized embeddings, $\mathbf{T}_i = f_t(T_i) \in \mathbb{R}^{n \times d}$. Here, n represents the token numbers (padded or truncated to a maximum length), and d is the hidden dimension of transformer model. To obtain a fixed-size representation for downstream processing, the embedding corresponding to the special [CLS] token is typically used, $\mathbf{t}_i = \mathbf{T}_i^{[\mathrm{CLS}]} \in \mathbb{R}^d$. Alternatively, mean pooling or attention-based aggregation over token embeddings can be employed to enhance robustness against noise in the textual input, which is particularly useful in scenarios involving informal language, sarcasm, or multilingual data.

DL techniques using Convolutional Neural Networks (CNNs), such as ResNet-50 or EfficientNet, are employed to extract distinctive visual features from the image modality. These architectures are effective in capturing hierarchical image representations—ranging from low-level textures to high-level semantic regions. Let f_v

denote the visual feature extractor and I_i represent the ith input image. The CNN processes the image to generate a spatial feature map $\mathbf{V}_i = f_v(I_i) \in \mathbb{R}^{h \times w \times c}$, where h and w denote the spatial dimensions of features, and c denotes the number of channels in the final convolutional layer.

While CNNs are effective, they often struggle with modelling long-range dependencies due to their localized receptive fields. To overcome this limitation, Vision Transformer (ViT)–based architectures have been proposed as an alternative for visual representation learning. In contrast to CNNs, ViTs divide the image into a sequence of fixed-size patches, which are then linearly embedded and passed through standard transformer blocks. The global image representation is derived either from the [CLS] token or by aggregating the patch embeddings, akin to the mechanism used in transformer-based language models. This design allows ViTs to capture global context and long-range dependencies more effectively, making them highly suitable for vision-language tasks.

6.3.3 Multimodal Feature Embedding

Once the unimodal features are extracted from the text and image modalities, the next step is to effectively combine these representations into a unified multimodal embedding for downstream classification.

In Section 3.2, the textual feature embedding is denoted as $\mathbf{T}_i = f_t(T_i) \in \mathbb{R}^{d_t}$ generated from the pre-trained transformer-based model, and the visual features embedding with $\mathbf{V}_i = f_v(I_i) \in \mathbb{R}^{d_v}$ are extracted via a CNN or ViT-based backbone. Here, d_t and d_v represent the dimensionalities of the textual and visual feature spaces, respectively. Since both of these modalities capture different properties, direct fusion is not going to be useful. In order to align and fuse these modality-specific features, first project them into a common embedding space. This is typically achieved using linear projection layers or fully connected networks $\hat{\mathbf{T}}_i = W_t \mathbf{T}_i + b_t$, $\hat{\mathbf{V}}_i = W_v \mathbf{V}_i + b_v$, where $W_t \in \mathbb{R}^{d \times d_t}$, $W_v \in \mathbb{R}^{d \times d_v}$, and $b_t, b_v \in \mathbb{R}^{d}$ are learnable parameters, and d is the common embedding dimension. The projected embeddings $\hat{\mathbf{T}}_i$ and $\hat{\mathbf{V}}_i$ are then fused using a suitable fusion strategy and provide the fused feature denoted as $\mathbf{F}_i = \left[\hat{\mathbf{T}}_i; \hat{\mathbf{V}}_i\right]$, where $[;]$ refers to the concatenation operator.

As the main goal of *multimodal learning* is to bridge the gap between modalities and exploit complementary cues that unimodal models often fail to capture, various fusion strategies have been shown in Figure 6.2. These include:

- **Early-level fusion**, where features from various modalities are integrated early in the process of the network;
- **Mid-level fusion**, where fusion occurs at intermediate layers; and
- **End-level fusion**, where the modality-specific features are integrated toward the end of the network.

The selection of fusion strategy is typically based on the task requirements and the complexity of the underlying architecture. In addition to these conventional approaches, more sophisticated methods such as *Gated Multimodal Units (GMUs)*,

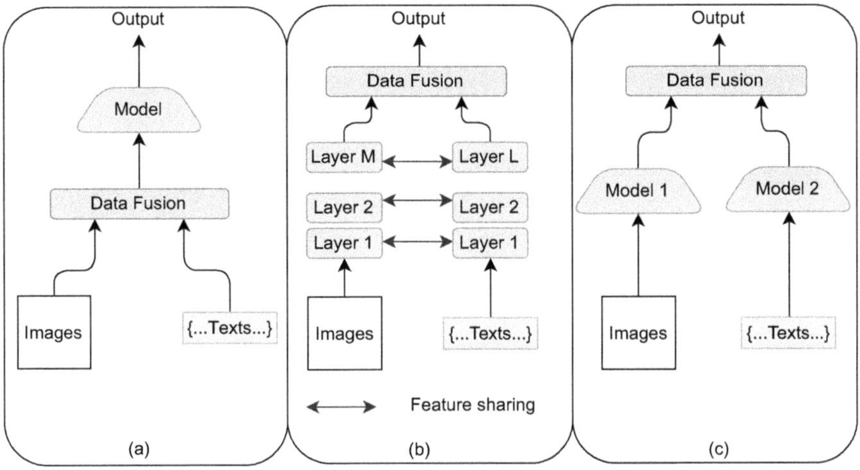

FIGURE 6.2 The different types of fusion mechanism. (a), (b), and (c) denote the early-level fusion, the mid- or intermediate-level fusion, and the end-level fusion, respectively.

cross-attention mechanisms, and *bilinear pooling* have been employed to learn richer and more informative representations by explicitly modeling cross-modal interactions. The resulting fused representation $\mathbf{F}_i \in \mathbb{R}^{2d}$ is then passed to a classification head to predict whether the given image–text pair contains hate or offensive content. This joint embedding enables the model to capture fine-grained contextual dependencies across modalities, which is crucial for the nuanced understanding required in multimodal hate and offensive content detection tasks.

6.3.3.1 Attention-Based Multimodal Feature Learning

Attention mechanisms are considered as a useful tool in multimodal learning, allowing models to dynamically concentrate on the key elements of the input from each modality. In contrast to simple concatenation-based fusion strategies, attention enables more fine-grained and context-aware interaction between the features of text and image. A commonly employed strategy is *cross-attention*, where features from single modality attend over features from another. Let $\hat{\mathbf{T}}_i \in \mathbb{R}^{n\times d}$ denote the sequence of projected textual token embeddings and $\hat{V}_i \in \mathbb{R}^{m\times d}$ denote the sequence of projected visual patch or region features. Cross-attention mechanisms compute a representation of one modality that adapts based on the context of another, implemented through scaled dot-product attention:

$$\text{Attention}(\mathbf{Q},\mathbf{K},\mathbf{V}) = \text{softmax}\left(\frac{\mathbf{Q}\cdot\mathbf{K}^{\top}}{\sqrt{d}}\right)\mathbf{V}$$

where **Q** denotes queries, **K** denotes keys, and **V** denotes values that trained projections of input features. For instance, text attending to image features would involve setting $\mathbf{Q} = \hat{\mathbf{T}}_i \cdot W_Q$, $\mathbf{K} = \hat{\mathbf{V}}_i \cdot W_K$, and $\mathbf{V} = \hat{\mathbf{V}}_i \cdot W_V$, where $W_Q, W_K, W_V \in \mathbb{R}^{d\times d}$ are trainable matrices.

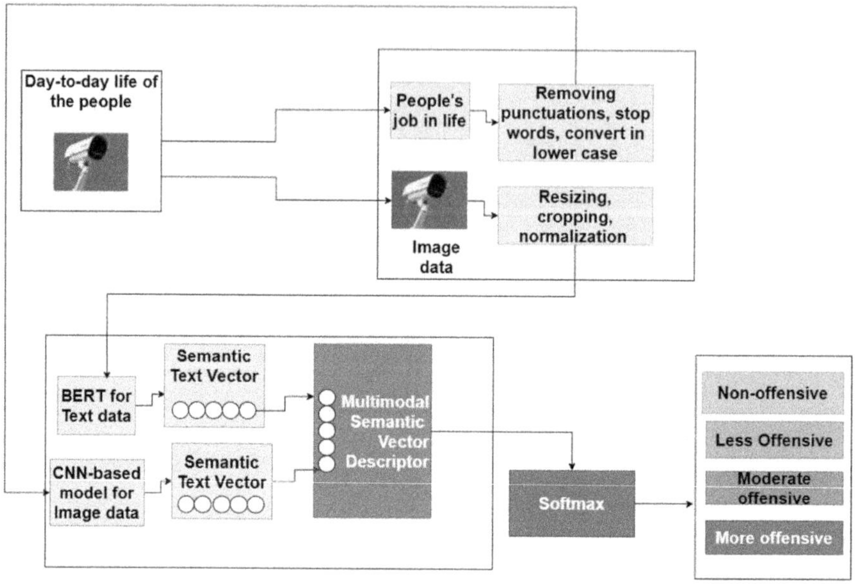

FIGURE 6.3 Process pipeline of the multimodal architecture for hate and offensive content identification [15].

In addition to cross-attention, *self-attention* within each modality can be employed to capture intra-modal relationships before fusion. The use of *multi-head attention* (MHA) further allows the model to learn interactions across multiple representation subspaces, enriching the learned joint representation. Transformer-based multimodal models such as ViLBERT, LXMERT, and VisualBERT utilize stacked layers of self-attention and cross-attention to enable deep and bidirectional interactions between modalities. Overall, attention-based mechanisms play a critical role in enabling flexible and effective fusion of multimodal information by allowing the model to focus on modality-specific or cross-modal cues that are most relevant to the downstream task.

In Figure 6.3, the process pipeline of multimodal architecture is presented for hate content detection, as proposed in [15]. The text and image features are extracted from the respective text and image encoders and are later fused to obtain a multimodal semantic vector descriptor that possesses high discriminating semantic information. The fused features are processed by attention approach to generate attention weights, which are used to find useful features before aggregating to generate new feature that shows memes. In general, the contents are classified into the level of offensiveness such as non-offensive, less offensive, moderate offensive and more offensive, as shown in Figure 6.3.

6.3.4 Loss Function

This section discusses the optimization functions used in training the multimodal network designed for hate and offensive content identification. First, the binary

cross-entropy loss and the contrastive loss are introduced. Once the fused representation $\mathbf{F}_i$ is obtained, it is passed through the learnable classifier f_c to produce a prediction $\hat{y}_i = f_c(\mathbf{F}_i)$. Training of model is carried out using the following loss functions:
Binary Cross Entropy (BCE): It is defined as follows:

$$\mathcal{L}_{\text{BCE}} = -\sum_{i=1}^{N}\left[y_i \log(\hat{y}_i) + (1 - y_i)\log(1 - \hat{y}_i)\right] \tag{6.1}$$

Contrastive Loss: In order to fix text and image embeddings in a joint latent space, the model learns the embedding using the contrastive loss, defined as follows:

$$\mathcal{L}_{\text{contrast}} = \sum_{i} \log \frac{\exp(\text{sim}(T_i, V_i)/\tau)}{\sum_{j} \exp(\text{sim}(T_i, V_j)/\tau)} \tag{6.2}$$

where $\text{sim}(\cdot,\cdot)$ denotes a similarity function and the temperature parameter is τ.

Total Loss: The multimodal network jointly optimizes $\mathcal{L}_{\text{BCE}}$ and $\mathcal{L}_{\text{contrast}}$ using Equation 6.3, where λ denotes the weighting parameter to adjust the loss terms.

$$\mathcal{L}_{\text{Total}} = \mathcal{L}_{\text{BCE}} + \lambda \cdot \mathcal{L}_{\text{contrast}} \tag{6.3}$$

6.4 DATASET COLLECTION AND PREPROCESSING

The process of dataset collection and preprocessing is crucial for training robust models in the detection of offensive content using multimodal DL. The details are described in the following.

6.4.1 Dataset Collection

Hate speech and offensive content can manifest across different modalities, such as text, images, audio, and video. However, in this chapter, two most prevalent and accessible modalities are focused such as text and images. The multimodal nature of such content necessitates the development of datasets that incorporate both modalities to enable effective detection and moderation systems. A number of multimodal datasets are available in the literature [37–43]. These datasets differ in their scope, sources, annotation strategies, and modalities covered. The process of dataset collection largely depends on the source of data. Major sources include social media platforms, hate speech repositories, and crowdsourcing sites. Social networks including Facebook, Twitter, and LinkedIn serve as massive digital storehouses of user-generated content, which can be accessed through their respective APIs. These platforms serve as a rich source of both textual and visual content. Hate speech repositories like Hatebase[1] and the Stormfront dataset[2] offer structured textual data, whereas resources such as the Hateful Memes Challenge [44] and Memotion [45] datasets provide multimodal examples that combine visual and textual information in

TABLE 6.2
Statistics of PolitiFact and MHS150K Datasets

Dataset	Category/Label	Train	Validation	Test
PolitiFact	News contents	624 (real)/432 (fake)/1056 (total)	—	—
	• With text	528 (real)/420 (fake)/948 (total)	—	—
	• With image	447 (real)/336 (fake)/783 (total)	—	—
MHS150K	Hate	29,447	2,500	5,001
	Not Hate	105,346	2,500	4,999
	Total	134,823	5,000	10,000

memes. Crowdsourcing is also widely used for annotating datasets, wherein human annotators, either domain experts or crowd workers, label content based on predefined categories of offensiveness or hatefulness. Platforms like Amazon Mechanical Turk facilitate large-scale annotation through structured guidelines.

Types of data collected:

- **Text Data**: Includes tweets, comments, and forum posts, which may contain slurs, sarcasm, coded language, or hate speech embedded in everyday language.
- **Image Data**: Includes hateful memes, offensive symbols, or manipulated visuals. These often require OCR techniques to extract embedded or overlaid text to fully understand the message.

While multiple modalities exist for expressing hate and offensive content, this chapter emphasizes text and image-based datasets due to their availability and prominence in current research. We consider two benchmark datasets, i.e., PolitiFact [46] and MMHS150K [47], for the study of multimodal learning in the given paradigm. The PolitiFact dataset consists of 2,037 positive pairs made by 2,026 tweets and 467 FC-articles. The MMHS150K dataset contains 150,000 tweet samples combining text and visual content, which are manually annotated for hate speech classification. The dataset splits are provided in Table 6.2. Curating high-quality, representative, and ethically sourced multimodal datasets is crucial for developing reliable detection systems. Collecting high quality of dataset for offensive content is an essential task for training DL models. The challenges are bias in collection, legal and platform restriction, lack of quality labelled data, and ethical and privacy concern. Collecting social media data may violate privacy laws.

6.5 PERFORMANCE COMPARISON AND DISCUSSION

A comparative analysis of multimodal learning approaches is presented against unimodal learning setups for hate and offensive content detection. Multimodal models combine text and image information and often demonstrate improved performance over unimodal counterparts by leveraging complementary cues present in different modalities. However, the integration of multiple modalities also introduces new challenges such as modality imbalance, noise in one modality affecting the overall prediction, increased computational complexity, and difficulties in aligning heterogeneous data representations. These challenges in context of hate content identification are presented, emphasizing the trade-offs between performance gains and the complexities involved in designing robust multimodal systems.

6.5.1 Multimodal vs. Unimodal Learning

First, a comparison of the performance of multimodal network with other baseline methods for classification is done. Second, a comparison of the impact of multimodal learning against the unimodal learning for hate and offensive content identification is discussed. Table 6.3 showcases performance of individual modalities, i.e., text and image, against the joint multiple modalities text+image. We refer BiLSTM-CNN [12] for the experimental results and discussion.

From Tables 6.3 and 6.4, we can observe that the inter-modal attention model (BiLSTM-CNN) [12] demonstrates significant improvements over literature methods on both PolitiFact and MMHS150K datasets. On PolitiFact, it obtains notable gains in accuracy and $F1$-score, outperforming the strongest baseline (MCNN)

TABLE 6.3
Comparative Analysis between the Inter-modal Attention Approach and Cutting-edge Models Using the PolitiFact Dataset

Model	Accuracy	Precision	Recall	*F*1
LBP-sim	—	—	—	0.925
SAFE	0.874	0.889	0.903	0.896
MCNN	0.884	**0.973**	0.867	0.917
BiLSTM-CNN	**0.940**	0.939	**0.940**	**0.939**

Bold values indicate the best-performing results among the compared models for each evaluation metric

TABLE 6.4
Benchmarking the Inter-modal Attention Framework against Leading Models Using the MMHS150K Dataset

Model	Acc	Precision	Recall	*F*1	AUC
Feature concatenation model (FCM) [47]	0.684	–	–	0.704	**0.734**
Spatial concatenation model (SCM) [47]	0.685	–	–	0.702	0.732
Textual concatenation model (TKM) [47]	0.682	–	–	0.701	0.731
BiLSTM-CNN [12]	**0.687**	0.659	**0.761**	**0.706**	0.687

Bold values indicate the best-performing results among the compared models for each evaluation metric by approximately 5.6% in accuracy and 2.2% in *F*1-score. This improvement reflects the model's ability to better align multimodal cues for fake news detection. Similarly, on MMHS150K, BiLSTM-CNN [12] model yields a higher *F*1-score and recall compared to existing models like Feature-Concatenation-Model (FCM), Spatial-Concatenation-Model (SCM), and Textual-Kernel-Model (TKM), [47] with around a 0.5% increase in accuracy and over 6% improvement in recall. While some prior methods show slightly higher AUC values, BiLSTM-CNN model provides a more balanced performance for metrics that represents its effectiveness in modeling complex inter-modal dependencies.

The performance comparisons in Tables 6.5 and 6.6 demonstrate the effectiveness of incorporating all available modalities in a unified multimodal learning framework. On both the PolitiFact and MMHS150K datasets, the model utilizing all three modalities—i.e., text, image, and image–text—consistently outperforms other modality combinations across all evaluation metrics. Specifically, on the PolitiFact dataset, the tri-modal setup achieves an *F*1-score improvement of over

TABLE 6.5
The Performance Comparison of Inter-modal Attention Models with Different Combinations of Modalities on the PolitiFact Dataset

Modality	Accuracy	Precision	Recall	*F*1
Text & image	0.893	0.898	0.894	0.896
Text & image-text	0.893	0.893	0.903	0.898
Image & image-text	0.570	0.568	0.546	0.557
Text & image & image-text	**0.940**	**0.939**	**0.940**	**0.939**

Source: Gomez et al. [46].
Bold values indicate the best-performing results among the compared models for each evaluation metric

TABLE 6.6
Comparative Analysis of Multimodal Attention Models with Different Input Modality Configurations on MMHS150K

Modality	Acc	Prec	Rec	*F*1	AUC
Text & image	0.684	0.656	**0.763**	0.705	0.684
Text & image–text	0.680	0.653	0.764	0.704	0.680
Image & image–text	0.514	0.516	0.934	0.665	0.514
Text & image & image–text	**0.687**	**0.659**	0.761	**0.706**	**0.687**

Bold values indicate the best-performing results among the compared models for each evaluation metric

4% compared to any bimodal combination, highlighting the complementary nature of the modalities when jointly modelled. Similarly, for MMHS150K, the tri-modal configuration yields the highest $F1$-score and AUC, albeit with relatively smaller margins, suggesting that even subtle synergies between modalities can be leveraged through inter-modal attention, as shown in Table 6.6. These results validate the importance of fully exploiting cross-modal interactions rather than relying on limited modality pairs.

6.5.2 Challenges in Multimodal Hate and Content Identification

Scaling and Complexity of User-Generated Content: The growth of digital content on social media platforms presents one of the foremost challenges in content moderation. Platforms such as Facebook, Twitter, and YouTube witness billions of posts, comments, and videos being uploaded daily. Given this scale, the manual inspection of content for hate speech and offensive material is practically infeasible. Consequently, the development of automated moderation systems has become essential. The inherent complexity of the human language and the diversity of conversational style provide significant limitations for such types of systems.

Multimodality of Content: Another challenge introduces from the multimodal nature of digital content. The content produced from people often combines images, text, and videos. These contents are appeared in different layers of semantic facts. For example, a meme shows an image annotated with textual contents, whereas a video reflect spoken language, image symbols, and a type of background music. Semantic descriptions are usually not obtained from individual modalities in isolation, but from their interplay. A Unimodal-based learning works on a single modality; for example, the text-based representation fails to capture these cross-modal stuff, which may lead to inaccurate moderation outcomes. Hence, effective content moderation needs techniques, which can tackle and integrate multimodal inputs.

Contextual Nuances and Evolving Nature of the Language: A Language on online media is mostly dynamic and evolving in nature due to the use of memes, slang, abbreviations, and cryptic language. This dynamic nature of a language is mostly exploited to convey hate and offensive contents by using alternative techniques that are not based on rules or keywords. For example, harmless symbols or phrases may carry negative implications depending on their usage context. In addition to linguistic evolution, understanding contextual nuances is paramount in correctly detecting harmful contents. The interpretation of a word or phrase is often associated with the surrounding context and the intent behind its usage. An expression might be deemed offensive in one situation but inoffensive in another. Intent, whether sarcastic, humorous, or malicious, plays a significant role in content perception. Finding these contextual dependencies remains a dreadful challenges for current moderation systems.

Challenges in Multimodal Learning for the Detection of Hate and Offensive Contents: Nonetheless, multimodal learning is considered as a promising paradigm for enhancing content moderation systems in the context of offensive content detection. The field introduces a set of critical challenges. Integrating heterogeneous modalities such as image, text, and video into a learning framework is non-trivial because of the inherent differences in the structure and semantics of modalities. First, aligning semantics across modalities remains a significant hurdle. Establishing a common semantic space that can effectively capture these multimodal nuances is essential but technically challenging. Second, multimodal fusion techniques such as early fusion, late fusion, or hybrid approaches are highly sensitive to the modality imbalance. In many cases, a single modality like text may dominate the learning signal, accommodating the contributions of complementary modalities like images or audio. Also, noisy or missing modalities can severely affect the performance if not handled properly.

Another challenge is the annotation of multimodal data for the process of training. Producing high-quality, context-aware labels that capture the joint semantics of multimodal content is prone to subjectivity. Furthermore, the interpretability and transparency of multimodal models pose additional concerns. The architecture of DL capable of processing multimodal content, such as multimodal transformers, often works as black boxes, making it difficult to explain why a particular piece of content is flagged as offensive. The aforementioned challenge enables the lack of interpretability, especially in critical applications where accountability and fairness are essential. Finally, real-world multimodal content often exhibits high variability in format, resolution, and linguistic diversity. Models must be robust to informal language, low-resource languages, and low-quality visual inputs. Establishing generalization across such diverse and dynamic content landscapes remains an open research problem in the field.

Ethical considerations: The deployment of offensive content detection systems leads to various ethical threats, which should be carefully addressed. The main concern is bias and fairness in models, which are trained on biased data and may lead to misclassifications of outcomes. Privacy is another demanding issue, where an individual needs to hide sensitive data from others. Additionally, these systems must navigate the balance between mitigating harm and safeguarding freedom of speech. Finally, the transparency and interpretability of DL models, especially multimodal ones, remain a pressing limitation. The nature of the models can hinder accountability and make it difficult to understand or justify their decisions.

6.6 CONCLUSION AND FUTURE WORK

Detection of offensive content and hate speeches is a basic need of current scenario. The role of multimodal DL helps in improving the content moderation on social media and other cyber platforms. By utilizing the power of different modalities, DL models can specify harmful content more accurately and effectively, resulting in robust detection of offensive content. Nonetheless, the challenges remain including the need to improve fusion techniques, the development of real-time and human-in-the-loop systems, and ethical considerations. It is crucial to focus on the innovations and improvement to confirm that the technologies are harnessed to create a safer and better inclusive digital environment. The presented book chapter offers a broad overview about the multimodal DL approach that shows techniques, data sources, challenges, and future directions for detecting offensive content and hate speech. The limitations of the study, such as dependency on labelled data and the challenges in generalizing to multilingual contents, can be considered as future directions for researchers. Improvements may include the extension of the model to multilingual and low-resource settings and the exploration of transformer-based fusion techniques for enhanced performance.

NOTES

1 https://hatebase.org/.
2 https://www.stormfront.org/forum/.

REFERENCES

1. Davidson, T., Warmsley, D., Macy, M., Weber, I.: Automated hate speech detection and the problem of offensive language. In: *Proceedings of the International AAAI Conference on Web and Social Media*. vol. 11, pp. 512–51, Cornell University, USA 5 (2017).
2. Schmidt, A., Wiegand, M.: A survey on hate speech detection using natural language processing. In: *Proceedings of the Fifth International Workshop on Natural Language Processing for Social Media*. pp. 1–10. Valencia, Spain (2017).
3. Devlin, J., Chang, M.W., Lee, K., Toutanova, K.: Bert: Pre-training of deep bidirectional transformers for language understanding. In: *Proceedings of the 2019 Conference of the North American Chapter of the Association for Computational Linguistics: Human Language Technologies*. vol 1 (long and short papers), pp. 4171–4186 (2019).
4. Schuster, M., Paliwal, K.: Bidirectional recurrent neural networks. *IEEE Transactions on Signal Processing* 45(11), 2673–2681 (1997).
5. Hochreiter, S., Schmidhuber, J.: Long short-term memory. *Neural Computers* 9(8), 1735–1780 (1997), https://doi.org/10.1162/neco.1997.9.8.1735.
6. Radford, A., Kim, J.W., Hallacy, C., Ramesh, A., Goh, G., Agarwal, S., Sastry, G., Askell, A., Mishkin, P., Clark, J., et al.: Learning transferable visual models from natural language supervision. In: *International Conference on Machine Learning*. pp. 8748–8763. Vienna, Austria. PmLR (2021).
7. Blodgett, S.L., Barocas, S., III, H.D., Wallach, H.: Language (technology) is power: A critical survey of "bias" in nlp (2020), https://arxiv.org/abs/2005.14050.
8. Alonso-Bartolome, S., Segura-Bedmar, I.: Multimodal fake news detection (2021), https://arxiv.org/abs/2112.04831.
9. Bozarth, L., Budak, C.: Toward a better performance evaluation framework for fake news classification. In: *Proceedings of the International AAAI Conference on Web and Social Media*. vol. 14, pp. 60–71, University of Michigan, USA (2020).
10. Adebayo, S., Adebayo, O., Adebayo, T.: An inter-modal attention-based deep learning framework using unified modality for multimodal fake news, hate speech and offensive language detection. *Information Systems* 123, 102378 (2024), https://www.sciencedirect.com/science/article/pii/S030643792400036X.
11. Alam, F., Cresci, S., Chakraborty, T., Silvestri, F., Dimitrov, D., Martino, G.D.S., Shaar, S., Firooz, H., Nakov, P.: A survey on multimodal disinformation detection (2022), https://arxiv.org/abs/2103.12541.
12. Ayetiran, E.F., Özgöbek, Ö.: An inter-modal attention-based deep learning framework using unified modality for multimodal fake news, hate speech and offensive language detection. *Information Systems* 123, 102378 (2024).
13. Hossain, M.S., Shohan, S.H., Paran, A.I., Hossain, J., Hoque, M.M.: Multimodal fusion for hate speech detection – a transformer based approach with cross-modal attention. In: *Proceedings of the Fifth Workshop on Speech, Vision, and Language*

Technologies for Dravidian Languages. pp. 489–495. Albuquerque, New Mexico, Association for Computational Linguistics (2025), https://aclanthology.org/2025.dravidianlangtech-1.86/.
14. Lahat, D., Adalŷ, T., Jutten, C.: Challenges in multimodal data fusion. In: *2014 22nd European Signal Processing Conference (EUSIPCO).* pp. 101–105. Lisbon, Portugal, IEEE (2014).
15. Alzu'bi, A., Bani Younis, L., Abuarqoub, A., Hammoudeh, M.: Multimodal deep learning with discriminant descriptors for offensive memes detection. *ACM Journal of Data and Information Quality* 15(3), 1–16 (2023).
16. Husain, F., Uzuner, O.: A survey of offensive language detection for the Arabic language. *ACM Transactions on Asian and Low-Resource Language Information Processing (TALLIP)* 20(1), 1–44 (2021).
17. Özberk, A., Çiçekli, İ.: Offensive language detection in turkish tweets with bert models. In: *2021 6th International Conference on Computer Science and Engineering (UBMK).* pp. 517–521. Ankara, Turkey, IEEE (2021).
18. Sigurbergsson, G.I., Derczynski, L.: Offensive language and hate speech detection for danish (2023), https://arxiv.org/abs/1908.04531.
19. Giachanou, A., Zhang, G., Rosso, P.: Multimodal fake news detection with textual, visual and semantic information. In: *Text, Speech, and Dialogue: 23rd International Conference, TSD 2020,* Brno, Czech Republic, pp. 30–38. Springer (2020).
20. Xue, J., Wang, Y., Tian, Y., Li, Y., Shi, L., Wei, L.: Detecting fake news by exploring the consistency of multimodal data. *Information Processing & Management* 58(5), 102610 (2021).
21. Zhou, X., Wu, J., Zafarani, R.: Similarity-aware multi-modal fake news detection. In: *Pacific-Asia Conference on Knowledge Discovery and Data Mining.* pp. 354–367. Singapore, Springer (2020).
22. MacAvaney, S., Yao, H.R., Yang, E., Russell, K., Goharian, N., Frieder, O.: Hate speech detection: Challenges and solutions. *PloS One* 14(8), e0221152 (2019).
23. Liu, Y., Ott, M., Goyal, N., Du, J., Joshi, M., Chen, D., Levy, O., Lewis, M., Zettlemoyer, L., Stoyanov, V.: Roberta: A robustly optimized bert pretraining approach. arXiv preprint arXiv:1907.11692 (2019).
24. Caselli, T., Basile, V., Mitrović, J., Granitzer, M.: Hatebert: Retraining bert for abusive language detection in english. arXiv preprint arXiv:2010.12472 (2020).
25. Hanu, L., Unitary team: Detoxify. Github. https://github.com/unitaryai/detoxify (2020).
26. Bayoudh, K., Knani, R., Hamdaoui, F., Mtibaa, A.: A survey on deep multimodal learning for computer vision: Advances, trends, applications, and datasets. *The Visual Computer* 38(8), 2939–2970 (2022).
27. Shafizadegan, F., Naghsh-Nilchi, A.R., Shabaninia, E.: Multimodal vision-based human action recognition using deep learning: A review. *Artificial Intelligence Review* 57(7), 178 (2024).
28. Pitenis, Z., Zampieri, M., Ranasinghe, T.: Offensive language identification in Greek (2020), https://arxiv.org/abs/2003.07459.
29. Simonyan, K., Zisserman, A.: Very deep convolutional networks for large-scale image recognition. arXiv preprint arXiv:1409.1556 (2014).
30. He, K., Zhang, X., Ren, S., Sun, J.: Deep residual learning for image recognition. In: *Proceedings of the IEEE Conference on Computer Vision and Pattern Recognition.* pp. 770–778, Las Vegas, USA (2016).
31. Szegedy, C., Liu, W., Jia, Y., Sermanet, P., Reed, S., Anguelov, D., Erhan, D., Vanhoucke, V., Rabinovich, A.: Going deeper with convolutions. In: *Proceedings of the IEEE Conference on Computer Vision and Pattern Recognition.* pp. 1–9. Boston, USA (2015).
32. Roller, S., Im Walde, S.S.: A multimodal lda model integrating textual, cognitive and visual modalities. In: *Proceedings of the 2013 Conference on Empirical Methods in Natural Language Processing.* pp. 1146–1157. Seattle, USA (2013).

33. Lu, J., Batra, D., Parikh, D., Lee, S.: Vilbert: Pretraining task-agnostic visiolinguistic representations for vision-and-language tasks. *Advances in Neural Information Processing Systems* 32, 1–11 (2019).
34. Li, L.H., Yatskar, M., Yin, D., Hsieh, C.J., Chang, K.W.: Visualbert: A simple and performant baseline for vision and language. arXiv preprint arXiv:1908.03557 (2019).
35. Li, L.H., Yatskar, M., Yin, D., Hsieh, C.J., Chang, K.W.: What does bert with vision look at? In: *Proceedings of the 58th Annual Meeting of the Association for Computational Linguistics.* pp. 5265–5275 (2020).
36. Gao, A., Wang, B., Yin, J., Tian, Y.: Hateful memes challenge: An enhanced multimodal framework. arXiv preprint arXiv:2112.11244 (2021).
37. Bohra, A., Vijay, D., Singh, V., Akhtar, S.S., Shrivastava, M.: A dataset of hindi-english code-mixed social media text for hate speech detection. In: *Proceedings of the Second Workshop on Computational Modeling of People's Opinions, Personality, and Emotions in Social Media.* pp. 36–41 (2018).
38. Gandhi, A., Adhvaryu, K., Poria, S., Cambria, E., Hussain, A.: Multimodal sentiment analysis: A systematic review of history, datasets, multimodal fusion methods, applications, challenges and future directions. *Information Fusion* 91, 424–444 (2023).
39. Hvilshøj, F.: An introduction to balanced and imbalanced datasets in machine learning (2022).
40. Jose, N., Chakravarthi, B.R., Suryawanshi, S., Sherly, E., McCrae, J.P.: A survey of current datasets for code-switching research. In: *2020 6th International Conference on Advanced Computing and Communication Systems (ICACCS).* pp. 136–141. Coimbatore, India, IEEE (2020).
41. Mathew, B., Saha, P., Yimam, S.M., Biemann, C., Goyal, P., Mukherjee, A.: Hatexplain: A benchmark dataset for explainable hate speech detection. In: *Proceedings of the AAAI Conference on Artificial Intelligence.* vol. 35, pp. 14867–14875. Virtual Event (2021).
42. Suryawanshi, S., Chakravarthi, B.R., Arcan, M., Buitelaar, P.: Multimodal meme dataset (multioff) for identifying offensive content in image and text. In: *Proceedings of the Second Workshop on Trolling, Aggression and Cyberbullying.* pp. 32–41. Marseille, France (2020).
43. Xu, B., Li, T., Zheng, J., Naseriparsa, M., Zhao, Z., Lin, H., Xia, F.: Met-meme: A multimodal meme dataset rich in metaphors. In: *Proceedings of the 45th International ACM SIGIR Conference on Research and Development in Information Retrieval.* pp. 2887–2899. Madrid, Spain (2022).
44. Kiela, D., Firooz, H., Mohan, A., Goswami, V., Singh, A., Ringshia, P., Testuggine, D.: The hateful memes challenge: Detecting hate speech in multimodal memes. *Advances in Neural Information Processing Systems* 33, 2611–2624 (2020).
45. Mishra, S., Suryavardan, S., Patwa, P., Chakraborty, M., Rani, A., Reganti, A., Chadha, A., Das, A., Sheth, A., Chinnakotla, M., et al.: Memotion 3: Dataset on sentiment and emotion analysis of codemixed hindi-english memes. arXiv preprint arXiv:2303.09892 (2023).
46. Gomez, R., Gibert, J., Gomez, L., Karatzas, D.: Exploring hate speech detection in multimodal publications. In: *Proceedings of the IEEE/CVF Winter Conference on Applications of Computer Vision.* pp. 1470–1478, Snowmass Village, Colorado, USA (2020).
47. Shu, K., Mahudeswaran, D., Wang, S., Lee, D., Liu, H.: Fakenewsnet: A data repository with news content, social context, and spatiotemporal information for studying fake news on social media. *Big Data* 8(3), 171–188 (2020).

7 Personalized Advertising and Customer Segmentation through Social Network Analytics

Kumar Saurav

7.1 INTRODUCTION

The marketing landscape has changed significantly in the recent past, that is, from mass marketing to data-driven and personalized marketing approaches. Nowadays, consumers desire customized experiences, which means marketers need to understand behavioural patterns and social influences as well. Personalized advertising is a tool to maintain a competitive advantage.

The analysis for this shift is required for improved customer segmentation. Traditional marketing approaches relied on factors such as demographics, geographics, and psychographics. SNA can uncover complex buying behaviour patterns, helping marketers design more precise and efficient targeted campaigns by applying graph theory and machine learning.

The advertising ecosystem has undergone a major transformation over the past decade, spurred by the increasing availability of consumer behavioural data trends, the rise of social media avenues, and advancements in computational modelling. Earlier, methods of customer segmentation relied on demographic attributes, which were more or less static. Now it is being rapidly replaced by dynamic and real-time systems that leverage complex behavioural trends and social communications. At the core of this transformation lies the application of SNA, a multidisciplinary field that includes computer science with graph theory, and machine learning tools to derive required insights from related data. Social media streams, both implicit (like co-purchase networks and browsing behaviour) and explicit (like friendship graphs and follower relationships), offer a substantial pattern for model influence, closeness, and community structure. These hidden but relevant social patterns are highly suggestive of consumer trends and can significantly further the performance and relevance of customized advertising. Contrary to the traditional univariate data analysis or cluster-based segmentation approaches, SNA provides detailed analysis and structurally informed customer targeting that can evolve over the period of time.

This chapter shows how computational techniques from SNA are being employed to personalize advertising content at scale. We explore algorithmic strategies such

DOI: 10.1201/9781003611110-7

as graph-based community detection, node ranking (e.g., PageRank and eigenvector centrality), graph embeddings, and social influence propagation models. These are integrated with modern recommender systems, natural language processing (NLP) pipelines, and predictive analytics to enable real-time, personalized customer engagement across multiple channels. Furthermore, we examine the emergence of new customer segments defined not by traditional demographics but by behavioural patterns, ethical values, and social context, segments often identifiable only through advanced data analytics. As platforms become more fragmented and privacy regulations more stringent, engineering privacy-preserving and explainable models becomes a central challenge for the next generation of intelligent advertising systems. By grounding our discussion in both theoretical foundations and real-world applications, this chapter aims to provide computer science students and researchers with a robust understanding of how social network structures can be leveraged to solve critical problems in personalized marketing. The subsequent sections will outline the historical background, discuss cutting-edge computational strategies, present emerging consumer dynamics, and offer a data-driven perspective on where the field is heading.

7.2 BACKGROUND

Personalized advertising and customer segmentation are long-standing marketing challenges, but the rapid expansion of digital platforms and computational capabilities has reframed them as data science and engineering problems. To contextualize the application of SNA, it is essential to first understand the evolution of personalization and segmentation, the basic principles of SNA, and the computational models that support modern advertising technologies.

7.2.1 Traditional Customer Segmentation and Early Digital Advertising

Historically, customer segmentation has relied on demographic (age, gender, income), geographic, and psychographic (values, interests, lifestyles) variables to group consumers. These rules-based or heuristic approaches, though easy to implement, lack the granularity and adaptability required in real-time digital environments. Advertising strategies based on these models often fail to capture dynamic user behaviour, peer influence, and multi-platform interaction patterns (Jiang & Tuzhilin, n.d.).

With the advent of e-commerce and social media, marketers began to adopt behavioural segmentation, analysing browsing history, purchase frequency, and clickstream data. This transition marked the entry point for computational methods such as clustering algorithms (e.g., k-means, DBSCAN), decision trees, and early recommender systems, which laid the foundation for personalized content delivery (Adomavicius & Tuzhilin, 2005).

7.2.2 Machine Learning–Based Personalization in Digital Marketing

Modern customized advertising is driven by machine learning algorithms trained on large-scale, multidimensional data. These systems employ collaborative filtering, matrix factorization, and deep learning to infer user preferences. However, such techniques often treat users as isolated entities, ignoring the influence of social relationships and network context, which are now recognized as critical components in understanding customer behaviour.

7.2.3 Application of Social Network Analytics (SNA)

Social network analytics (SNA) is a subfield of network science that focuses on analysing the structure and dynamics of social graphs. In computer science, it involves representing users and their interactions as nodes and edges within a graph data structure. Common types of social graphs include:

- Explicit networks (e.g., Facebook friendship graph and Twitter follower graph)
- Implicit networks (e.g., user co-purchase behaviour, shared interests, and retweet graphs)

SNA employs a variety of graph-based metrics and algorithms to extract insights, such as:

- **Centrality Measures**: Degree centrality, betweenness centrality, and eigenvector centrality
- **Community Detection**: Louvain method, Girvan–Newman algorithm, and label propagation
- **Influence Modelling**: Independent cascade (IC) models and linear threshold (LT) models
- **Graph Embeddings**: Node2Vec, Deep Walk, and GraphSAGE

These techniques allow for the discovery of influential users, tight-knit communities, and emergent behavioural patterns that can inform audience segmentation and content targeting.

7.2.4 Heterogeneous Data Sources and Computational Architecture

The effective use of SNA in advertising requires the integration of heterogeneous data sources, including social media APIs (e.g., Twitter, Reddit), CRM systems, e-commerce platforms, and mobile app telemetry. Processing these high-velocity data streams often involves big data frameworks like Apache Spark, Hadoop, and real-time analytics systems such as Apache Flink or Kafka Streams (Fan & Gordon, 2014).

Graph databases (e.g., Neo4j, Amazon Neptune) are frequently used to store and query complex network structures, while cloud-based machine learning platforms facilitate model training and deployment at scale. Visualization tools such as Gephi, NetworkX, and D3.js are often employed for exploratory network analysis and stakeholder communication.

7.2.5 Research and Commercial Advancements in Personalized Advertising

Academic research has extensively contributed to the development of scalable SNA algorithms and ethical guidelines for personalization. Industry applications, on the other hand, have rapidly commercialized these techniques. Google, Meta, Amazon, and ByteDance have pioneered models that combine behavioural signals with social influence data to drive content curation, product recommendations, and targeted advertising.

Together, these developments have established a robust technical foundation upon which advanced personalized advertising strategies are being built. The succeeding study will explore the evolving ideas and innovations that are furthering the possibilities of this field.

7.3 CROSS-INDUSTRY APPLICATIONS OF SOCIAL NETWORK ANALYTICS IN PERSONALIZED ADVERTISING

The dynamicity of SNA extends to multiple sectors/industries, each using network-based insights to improvise customized advertising strategies particularly made to individualized consumer behaviour patterns and market dynamics (Figure 7.1). Table 7.1 summarizes the key sectors/industries where SNA has influenced targeted marketing approaches.

7.3.1 Retail and E-Commerce

The retail sector (both online and offline) is quick to adopt and leverage the application of SNA-driven personalization. Retailers, particularly modern trade, use network analysis to identify key factors within the identified customer segment. It also optimizes the peer-based referral programmes and customizes the target market promotions based on social bases and buying behaviour patterns.

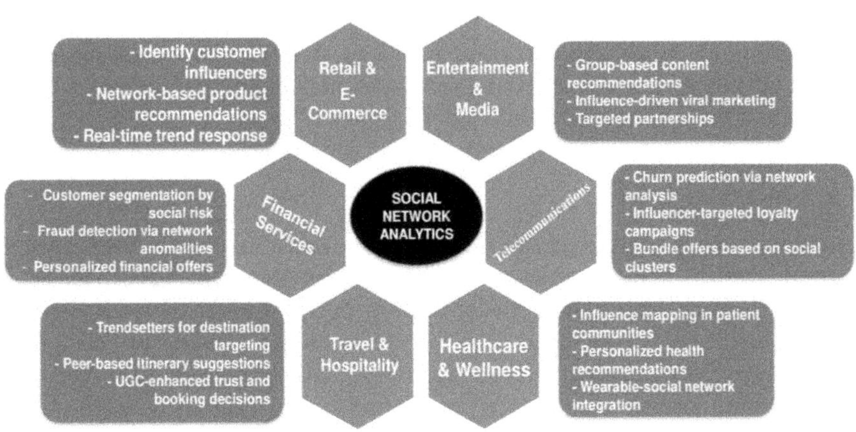

FIGURE 7.1 Cross-industry application of social network analytics in personalized advertising.

TABLE 7.1
Application of SNA Across Industries

Industry	How SNA is Applied	Techniques Used	Example
Retail	Recommending trending products within social circles	Community detection, influence scoring	"Your friends bought this," suggests on Amazon
Banking and finance	Enhancing credit risk assessments via network behaviour	Centrality measures, link prediction	Peer-based credit scoring by fintech apps
Healthcare	Promoting health tips through peer support networks	Network centrality, clustering	Targeted mental health campaigns in Facebook groups
Telecom	Predicting customer churn using social ties analysis	Cohesion analysis, bridge detection	Retention offers to friends of churned users
Media and entertainment	Suggesting content based on friends' viewing habits	Homophily, ego networks	Netflix recommendations based on social connections
Travel and hospitality	Recommending popular travel destinations in networks	Sentiment diffusion, influence modelling	"Trips your friends loved" on TripAdvisor
E-commerce	Driving flash sales through micro-influencer networks	K-core analysis, influence propagation	Instagram influencer tags boosting sales
Education	Suggesting courses followed by peer learners	Behavioural clustering, social mapping	MOOCs promoting peer-enrolled courses
Gaming	Highlighting in-game items purchased by friends	Activity correlation, tie strength	Fortnite suggests skins used by friends
Automotive	Personalizing promotions via local EV owner communities	Similarity networks, social clustering	Tesla targeting EV owners for feature upgrades

For example, recommendation analysis enabled by network-based collaborative filtering enhances product suggestions to customers by analysing social influences, which leads to an increase in cart sizes and decrease in customer acquisition costs. Retailers also explore and track social sentiment and emerging viral trends to optimize inventory and marketing communications in real time.

7.3.2 Financial Services

Financial sectors like banks, insurance companies, and other fintech firms give personalized offerings to the target customers by applying SNA in profiling their buying behaviour. It also detects and discovers fraud through the given network anomalies and offers personalized financial solutions. Through the analysis of peer groups' financial behaviours and credit purchase patterns, marketers can now create customized loan offers, investment products, or insurance plans that fit or align with the needs of the given social segments.

In addition to referral marketing campaigns enabled by network analysis, it also optimizes the customer acquisition cost while improving trust and creating value among customers through social proof mechanisms.

7.3.3 Healthcare and Wellness

In the healthcare segment, SNA helps in highlighting the problems of patient communities. It also enables social media influencers who drive the target market to create awareness and engagement in healthcare-related behaviours, such as adopting health and wellness programmes, proper and timely vaccinations, or any other medical devices. Personalized marketing communications delivered through these networks influence patient engagement and compliance with treatment protocols.

A wearable device enriched with data, integrated with social networks analysis, enables context-based aware healthcare recommendations that align with patients' social environments, thus increasing relevance and motivation.

7.3.4 Entertainment and Media

Social Media Streaming platforms like Facebook, YouTube, Instagram, etc., gaming companies, and other media outlets leverage SNA to analyse the content shared by customers, which helps them in suggesting personalized content recommendations. Analysing community networks and group memberships also helps in analysing preferences and behaviours, as well as patterns regarding binge-watching.

Social network insights also help in aligning with influencer partnerships. They help curate and create viral marketing campaigns based on the SNA recommendation that enhance customer engagement and conversion rate, especially among younger generations (Gen Z).

7.3.5 Telecommunications

Telecom operators also inadvertently use SNA for churn prediction, which is a major concern for marketers. It helps in cross-selling and other personalized product offerings. By analysing the content being shared and posted on social media networks, marketers identify the influenced customers who can be targeted with customized and exclusive deals or loyalty programmes to reduce customer attrition.

Network-based segmentation also informs the offerings of bundled or allied services being customized to the particular community by analysing the usage patterns and their social network.

7.3.6 Travel and Hospitality

The travel industry applies SNA to map social travel patterns, identify trendsetters, and promote destination-specific offers through micro-communities. Social network-driven personalization enhances customer experiences by recommending itineraries, accommodations, and activities favoured by peers within travellers' social circles.

User-generated content (UGC) and reviews shared within social networks amplify trust and influence booking decisions, making network-aware advertising critical for competitive differentiation.

7.4 ALGORITHMIC STRATEGIES FOR ADVERTISING IN SOCIAL NETWORK ANALYSIS

Personalized advertising leverages complex user interactions, preferences, and behaviours to deliver targeted content. SNA provides the computational infrastructure and algorithmic tools to model and analyse these interactions at scale. This section outlines the key methods used in transforming raw interaction data into meaningful customer segments and personalization strategies (Table 7.2).

TABLE 7.2
Overview of Algorithm Strategies in Social Network–Based Advertising

Algorithmic Strategy	Description	Advertising Applications	Advantages	Challenges
Community detection	Identifies clusters of densely connected users (e.g., modularity maximization, Louvain)	Audience segmentation, influencer targeting	Reveals natural user groups for tailored ads	Scalability in large networks
Node embeddings (e.g., Node2Vec, GNNs)	Maps users/items to low-dimensional vectors preserving network structure	Personalized recommendations, lookalike audience expansion	Captures nuanced user behaviour patterns	Cold start for new users/items
Influence maximization	Finds key users to maximize ad spread (e.g., PageRank, Independent Cascade)	Viral marketing campaigns, seed selection	Optimizes budget for maximum reach	Requires real-world diffusion data
Link prediction	Predicts future connections (e.g., Adamic Adar, GNN-based methods)	Cross-selling, friend-based ad targeting	Anticipates emerging user interests	Privacy constraints on relationship data
Graph clustering	Groups similar users/products (e.g., spectral clustering, k-means on graphs)	Market basket analysis, niche targeting	Works with heterogeneous data (e.g., social + purchase)	Interpretability of clusters
Sentiment/behaviour analysis	Analyses user-generated content for trends (NLP + graph topology)	Brand sentiment tracking, crisis management	Real-time feedback on ad campaigns	Noise in unstructured text/data

As social networks grow very fast, strategies for advertising are changing to understand user relationships better and present more pertinent content by identifying connections, community structures, and influence patterns in online networks. Businesses now focus on comprehending how people interact, form groups, and share knowledge rather than just using broad demographic categories. Though different techniques uncover naturally occurring communities and shared interests, graph-based techniques enhance the identification of the right audience with customized targeting. Node embeddings display deeper connections to enhance recommendations, and influence-oriented models highlight important figures who influence attitudes and trends. Finally, hybrid approaches are better in individualized and significant advertising strategies that integrate SNA with recommender systems. The following subsections discuss these techniques in detail and their growing role in creating more effective and user-focused advertising experiences.

7.4.1 Graph-Based Analysis for Customized Targeting

At the heart of SNA lies the graph representation of data. A graph $G=(V, E)$ $G=(V, E)$ $G= (V, E)$ consists of a set of nodes VVV (e.g., users, products, advertisements) and edges EEE representing relationships or interactions.

Common graph types in advertising (Figure 7.2):

Social Graphs: Nodes are users; edges represent friendships, follows, likes, or message exchanges.

- **Interaction Graphs**: Edges represent co-clicks, co-purchases, or shared content views.

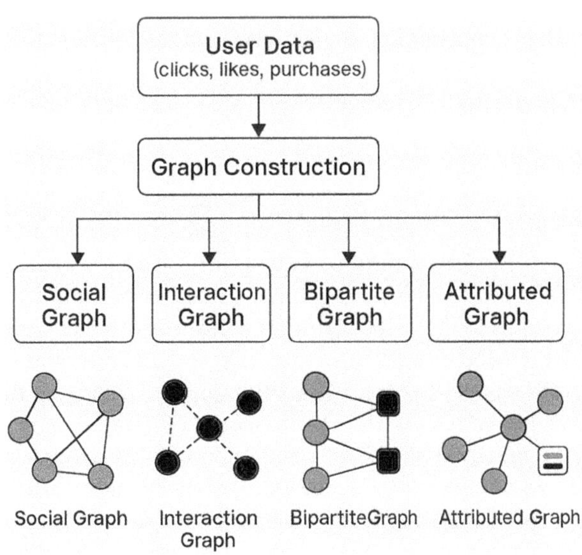

FIGURE 7.2 Common graph in advertising.

- **Bipartite Graphs**: Link users to products or ads for collaborative filtering.
- **Attributed Graphs**: Nodes and edges contain feature vectors (e.g., demographics, activity level).

The construction of a graph inadvertently involves data preprocessing using platforms like Apache Spark and Python's NetworkX library. It also uses the storage of graph databases such as Neo4j or TigerGraph.

7.4.2 Algorithms for Detecting Clustering

Cluster detection discovers densely connected subgraphs within networks, often representing groups or communities with shared behaviours. It helps in designing marketing strategies, market segmentation, and customized advertising. In Social networks such as social media platforms, individual is represented as nodes, and they invariably belong to multiple communities, thus enabling overlapping community detection algorithms to be particularly possible.

Beyond social networks, clustering techniques are frequently applied in retail and digital commerce. For instance, customer targeting in grocery stores using K-means clustering helps in customized advertisement based on shared purchasing behaviours (Omol et al., n.d.). Similarly, cluster analysis in the field of digital advertising optimizes campaign precision, providing higher engagement and conversion rates than traditional segmentation (Nur & Siregar, 2024).

Several clustering algorithms have gained popularity:

- **Louvain Method**: Optimizes modularity to detect hierarchical communities.
- **Label Propagation**: Nodes adopt the most frequent label among neighbours, which is efficient for large networks.
- **Infomap**: Uses information theory and random walks for community detection.
- **Spectral Clustering**: Leverages eigenvalue decomposition of the graph Laplacian.

In the above-mentioned algorithm, the Label Propagation Algorithm (LPA) has been widely known for its balance of speed and reasonable accuracy, although researchers point out that its random nature can sometimes lead to inconsistent outcomes (Li et al., 2022; Yang et al., 2020). Over time, a number of modifications have been introduced. For instance, GLPA incorporates measures of node similarity and connectivity, while LPA MNI brings in modularity and node importance to improve both stability and precision. Infomap is another applied approach that testifies that Louvain may give better results in certain scenarios (Emmons et al., 2016). The Smart Local Moving method has also gained attention, but the research community has not converged on a single "best" technique, partly because performance depends heavily on the chosen evaluation metric and the size of the network.

Scalability has become an important concern as well. To handle massive graphs with billions of edges, parallel versions of LPA and Louvain have been implemented on shared memory systems, allowing analysis to extend into big data environments

(*2017 IEEE High Performance Extreme Computing Conference* (*HPEC*), 2017; Staudt & Meyerhenke, 2016). The evolving and dynamic algorithmic applications cater to the growing demand for adaptive, scalable cluster segmentation in social media networks.

7.4.3 Influence-Oriented Models

Marketing communication success depends on leveraging social media influencers, early adopters, or trend setters within a given network. Influence propagation models also simulate the spread of information, consumer behaviour, and product adoption.

Common models:

- **Independent Cascade (IC)**: Each active node has one chance to activate its neighbours with a given probability.
- **Linear Threshold (LT)**: A node becomes active when the sum of influences from active neighbours exceeds a threshold.
- **Live edge Graph Models**: Probabilistic subgraphs where diffusion paths are precomputed.

The above-mentioned models are important for influencer marketers in segment targeting, viral campaigning, and budget allocation for social media marketing. The works done by Peng (2021) have improved IC and LT models with dynamic influence estimation for more efficient marketing strategies (Peng, 2021). Tang et al. (2024) proposed an influence optimization framework using graph neural networks (GNN), which outscores classical diffusion-based methods in selecting seed nodes for marketing-related campaigns (Tang et al., 2024).

7.4.4 Node Embeddings for Recommendation

Node embeddings convert graph nodes into low-dimensional vectors while preserving structural information. This enables scalable application of traditional ML models for recommendation and classification.

Techniques:

- **Node2Vec**: Uses biased random walks to learn structural equivalence and homophily.
- **DeepWalk**: Uses uniform random walks and skip-gram models for graph feature learning.
- **GraphSAGE**: Aggregates features from neighbours using deep learning.
- **LINE**: Preserves both first-order and second-order proximities.

Several studies have demonstrated the effectiveness of these methods. Grover and Leskovec (2016) introduced Node2Vec, showing its superior ability to capture diverse network patterns for recommendation tasks (Grover & Leskovec, 2016). Perozzi et al. (2014) pioneered DeepWalk, effectively applying language modelling techniques to graphs. Hamilton et al. (2017) developed GraphSAGE to generalize embeddings to unseen nodes by aggregating neighbour information, improving recommendation quality (Hamilton et al., 2017). Tang et al. (2015) proposed LINE for large-scale networks, balancing local and global structure preservation, which has been widely adopted in recommendation research (Tang et al., 2015).

7.4.5 Hybrid Models: SNA with Recommender Systems

When social network analysis is combined with collaborative filtering and content-based filtering, the result is a hybrid system that can provide tailored advertisements in ways traditional approaches often cannot.

Examples are as follows:

- **Graph-aware Matrix Factorization**: Enhances latent factor models with network topology.
- **Attention Mechanisms on Graphs**: Used in Graph Attention Networks (GATs) to weight influential neighbours.

Several approaches have been proposed to learn node representations, and each has addressed the problem a little differently. Wang et al. (2019) have introduced Neural Graph Collaborative Filtering (NGCF), integrating high-order connectivity in user-item graphs. Velickovic et al. (2018) have proposed GAT, which has been applied in targeted advertising for grabbing attention over social states. Their results showed that this flexibility was especially useful in recommendation tasks.

SNA provides powerful computational methods for modelling consumer behaviour on a larger scale. From raw user data, we can construct rich graphs that reveal communities, influencers, and interaction patterns. These graphs, when analysed with the use of modern algorithms, ranging from community detection to graph embeddings, can significantly improve the accuracy and contextual relevance of targeted advertising.

7.5 ADVANCED TECHNIQUES AND EMERGING IDEAS

As personalized advertising continues to develop, the computational methods supporting it are also changing. Apart from regular graph analytics and machine learning, researchers are now experimenting with dynamic data pipelines, deep learning models, and approaches that can provide privacy in personalization. In the discussion that follows, some of these emerging techniques are highlighted and considered, as well as how they extend the role of social network analysis in customer segmentation and targeted advertising.

7.5.1 Real-Time Personalization with Streaming Analytics

Modern users navigate between several platforms continuously, which makes it difficult for advertisers to follow up. To respond effectively, content often has to be customized in real time, with offers or messages adjusted to match a user's most recent activity.

A few key technologies make this possible. For example, streaming platforms such as Apache Kafka, Flink, and Spark Streaming are widely used to capture and process live user events as they happen. In addition, windowed graph processing allows influence scores or community structures to be refreshed in short, time-based intervals, so the system can reflect fast-moving changes in the network.

With the capabilities of real-time personalization with streaming analytics, organizations lack a unified customer view across multiple channels. This necessitates the need for cross-platform identity resolution and data fusion to provide consistent and seamless user experiences.

7.5.2 Cross-Platform Identity Resolution and Data Fusion

Consumers today operate many devices (smartphones, tablets, desktops) and many platforms (Facebook, TikTok, Amazon), creating diverse data trails. Cross-platform identity integration aims to join multiple profiles to a single individual for holistic personalization.

Computational challenges are as follows:

- **Entity Resolution**: Matching user identifiers across platforms using probabilistic models or deep learning.
- **Graph Merging and Alignment**: Combining disparate networks (e.g., social, transactional, location-based) using graph isomorphism or tensor factorization.
- **Privacy Aware Matching**: Implementing matching without directly sharing personal identifiers, using techniques like hashing or federated learning.

After achieving high resolution and data fusion for cross-platform identity, psychographic and behavioural targeting is required to enable deeper insights into customer preferences and intent for more personalized engagement.

7.5.3 Psychographic and Behavioural Targeting via NLP

Apart from simple demographics, advertisers now aim to develop a model with a user's personality, motivations, and values, a marketing strategy known as psychographic targeting. Social media text, reviews, and conversations also serve as rich input for such analysis.

Applied NLP techniques:

- **Topic Modelling (e.g., LDA, BERT)**: Reveals underlying themes in user content.
- **Personality Detection model (e.g., Big Five Models)**: Segments users into psychographic categories using linguistic features.
- **Transformer-Based Sentiment Analysis**: Models like BERT, RoBERTa, and GPT are fine-tuned on brand affinity tasks.

Such fine-grained behavioural profiles enable high-resolution audience segmentation and value-aligned advertising, often delivering better results than demographic segmentation alone.

Apart from this, personalization strategies must remain fair and unbiased. Advertisements should be ethical to maintain trust and transparency with consumers.

7.5.4 Fairness, Bias Mitigation, and Ethical Advertising

As personalization becomes more precise, concerns about algorithmic bias, user manipulation, and privacy have grown significantly. Ensuring ethical artificial intelligence (AI) in advertising is now a research imperative.

Research focus areas are as follows:

- **Fair Representation Learning**: Ensuring embeddings do not encode protected attributes (e.g., race, gender).
- **Explainability Tools**: Applying SHAP, LIME, and attention visualization to explain why a specific ad was shown.
- **Federated Personalization**: Processing user data locally on devices, reducing privacy risks while preserving personalization.

Building systems that are both effective and responsible ensures long-term trust and regulatory compliance (e.g., GDPR, CCPA).

In the next section, we will explore how these advanced techniques are redefining customer segments, particularly through the lens of social network structures and behavioural clustering.

7.6 REDEFINING CUSTOMER SEGMENTS THROUGH ANALYTICS

The digital landscape has dramatically changed how consumers interact, express preferences, and make purchasing decisions. Traditional static segmentation strategies, based on broad demographic categories, no longer suffice in the era of highly dynamic, data-rich environments. Using advanced analytics and SNA, customer segments can now be discovered algorithmically, updated in real time, and aligned with nuanced behaviours and social contexts.

Customer segmentation is going through a transformation because of advanced analytics and data-driven insights. Traditionally, segmentation was based on broad demographics, which is not sufficient to understand the complexity of modern consumer behaviours. As real-time data rises, AI and machine learning can now identify dynamic segments that grow with changing preferences, uncover the micro-communities and digital tribes, and understand the unique expectations of emerging cohorts like Gen Z, Gen Alpha, and digital natives. Moreover, the growing influence of values-driven and ethically conscious consumers is reshaping marketing strategies, while algorithmic discovery enables the identification of hidden and emergent segments with unprecedented precision. The following subsections detail how analytics is defining customer segmentation and empowering brands to provide more personalized, relevant, and impactful experiences.

7.6.1 From Static to Dynamic Segmentation

Traditionally, customers were grouped using fixed rules (e.g., age group, income bracket). This approach often missed the temporal and behavioural fluidity of digital consumers.

With the advent of computational modelling:

- **Behavioural Segmentation**: Uses clickstreams, purchase logs, and content views.
- **Temporal Segmentation**: Adapts segments based on day/time interaction patterns.
- **Intent-based Segmentation**: Leverages search queries, keyword analysis, and sentiment extraction.

When overlaid with social graphs, these dimensions become even more powerful, identifying communities of users who evolve together and influence each other's preferences.

7.6.2 Micro-Communities/Niche Marketing and Digital Tribes

SNA reveals that users tend to form micro-communities' clusters connected by shared interests, goals, or social influence.

Characteristics of micro-communities/niche marketing are as follows:

- High edge density and internal communication
- Shared behaviour patterns (e.g., niche fandoms, hobbyist groups)
- Rapid internal diffusion of new content or products

Detecting such communities through modularity-based clustering or graph embeddings enables marketers to deliver community-specific messaging, rather than broad audience targeting.

For instance, in a network of gamers:

- One community may consist of mobile casual gamers.
- Another may consist of PC-based esports players.
- A third may be focused on game development and modding.

Each requires a different content strategy, even if they all fall under the "gamer" demographic.

7.6.3 Next-Gen Segments: Gen Z, Gen Alpha, and Digital Natives

The rise of digitally native cohorts, especially Gen Z and Gen Alpha, demands a rethinking of segmentation paradigms. These users:

- Exhibit multi-platform behaviour (e.g., TikTok, YouTube, Discord, Twitch)
- Prefer peer-driven validation over traditional advertising
- Are highly sensitive to authenticity and values alignment

Graph analytics helps uncover their content consumption clusters, influencer followings, and language usage trends (e.g., memes, emojis, Gen Z slang). NLP and GNN can jointly model these features to form fluid, behaviour-first segments, especially when combined with GNN, which can reveal their content clusters, influencer networks, and language trends, including memes and emojis (Marx et al., 2023). Emojis act as a universal communication tool, enhancing emotional expression and message clarity (Duffett & Maraule, 2024). Platforms like *BeReal* reflect Gen Z's desire for authenticity, though this brings new challenges around self-monitoring (Maddox, 2023). Marketers must align with these evolving preferences through continuous adaptation and culturally resonant strategies.

7.6.4 Values Driven and Ethical Consumer Cohorts

A growing class of users makes purchasing decisions based on ethical considerations, such as:

- Sustainability
- Fair trade
- Diversity and inclusion

These values can be inferred from:

- Social media handles, hashtags, and the content of the post (e.g., #climateaction)
- Networks consisting of followers centred around word of mouth and mutual interactions
- Brand interaction graphs (e.g., preference for eco-friendly product lines)

NLP based on graph and sentiment analysis is useful for identifying the customer segment based on the value alignment. It highlights the ethical segment, which was ignored in the traditional market strategy. Ethical considerations help in understanding the modern consumer's buying behaviour. For example, Toşa and Tarigan (2025) used hashtag networks to identify latent ethical themes in UGC. It showed strong correlations with eco-conscious consumer and their purchasing patterns. Other related studies highlighted that sentiment analysis using GNNs can outscore traditional clustering methods (Cui et al., 2023; Das et al., 2024). These approaches underline the potential and uses of graph-based analytics in detecting latent consumer buying behaviour.

7.6.5 Algorithmic Discovery of Emergent Segments

Apart from predetermined categories, modern analytical systems use unsupervised learning and graph mining to identify new customer segments. These emergent segments are discovered from:

- Co-behaviour networks (e.g., users who buy similar product bundles)
- Interest propagation patterns (e.g., meme or content virality)
- Engagement anomaly detection (e.g., sudden shifts in behaviour)

Techniques such as non-negative matrix factorization, autoencoders, and clustering over graph embeddings allow segments to be defined in a bottom-up manner, driven by data rather than assumptions. This enables brands to stay ahead of trends, dynamically reallocating advertising resources towards newly forming user collectives before competitors even notice them (DeBruine et al., 2021).

SNA highlights that customer segmentation is a dynamic process. It is a real-time, data-driven cluster. It continuously gives information about the fluid consumer behaviour. It enables marketers to identify organic digital tribes/communities. It also discovered psychographic signals that respond to the evolving nature of online behaviour. From digital tribes to value-based clusters, these next-generation segments efficiently personalize advertising (Liu et al., 2019).

7.7 EMPIRICAL INSIGHTS: FACTS, FIGURES, AND CASE STUDIES

In the sections below, we review quantitative findings and real-world examples to show both the benefits and challenges that come with building SNA-based systems.

7.7.1 Market Trends in Personalized Advertising

The global personalized advertising market has witnessed rapid growth, fueled by a rise in data analytics and social media profiling:

- Social media advertising is a major component of the digital advertising landscape. For instance, in 2023, the global social media advertisement market was valued at $209.19 billion and is expected to reach $380.9 billion by 2027, growing at a CAGR of 16.2% (Business Wire, 2023, May 26).
- Advertisers report average increases of 20%–30% in click-through rates (CTR) and conversion rates when using social network-based segmentation compared to traditional demographic targeting (World Metrics, 2024).

These trends underscore the economic incentives for integrating SNA in advertising pipelines.

7.7.2 Performance Gains from Network-Based Segmentation

Academic and industrial experiments have quantitatively validated the benefits of SNA-driven segmentation:

- Targeting individuals based on their centrality within a network (such as those with high betweenness or hub scores) was more effective in promoting behavior change compared to targeting closely connected groups or communities. While this study focused on health interventions, the principles may apply to advertising contexts.

- Incorporating influence propagation models increased viral campaign reach by up to 40%, reducing cost per acquisition (CPA) (Bonchi, n.d.).
- Node embedding-based recommendation systems have demonstrated improvements of 10%–15% in prediction accuracy over conventional collaborative filtering techniques (Zhao et al., 2023).

Performance improvements are often context-dependent but consistently indicate that graph-informed methods yield more efficient and effective advertising outcomes.

7.7.3 Industry Case Studies

Leading platforms leverage SNA to enhance user engagement, personalize content, and optimize business outcomes. By applying community detection, influence modelling, and hybrid recommendation techniques, companies like Netflix, TikTok, and Amazon have achieved significant improvements in retention, viral reach, and sales performance (Table 7.3).

7.7.3.1 Netflix: Social Graphs and Personalized Content Promotion

Netflix employs SNA to model user influence and content consumption clusters. By detecting communities of users with shared viewing habits, Netflix tailors promotional banners and suggestions, resulting in higher retention rates and increased binge-watching sessions (Figure 7.3) (Gomez Uribe & Hunt, 2015).

TABLE 7.3
Impact of SNA-Driven Personalization on Key Performance Metrics across Leading Platforms

Platform	Metric	Baseline (Traditional)	With SNA Driven Personalization	Percent Improvement (%)	Reference
Netflix	User retention rate (%)	75	85	+13.3	Statista Netflix retention
Netflix	Average viewing time (hours/week)	12	15	+25	Netflix tech blog
TikTok	Viral content reach (million users)	20	28	+40	Business of apps TikTok stats
TikTok	User engagement rate (%)	30	40	+33.3	Influencer marketing hub
Amazon	Conversion rate (%)	8	9.6	+20	Forbes Amazon conversion rates
Amazon	Average order value (USD)	50	60	+20	Statista Amazon average order value

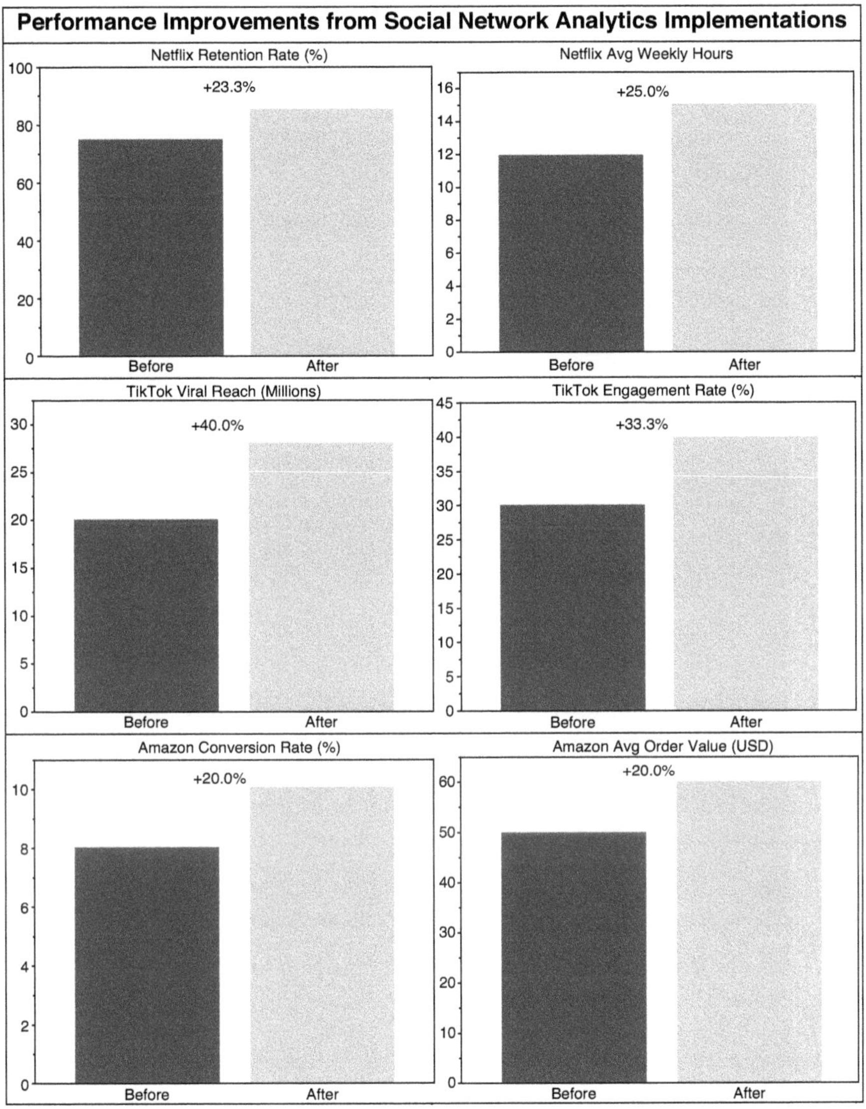

FIGURE 7.3 Comparative bar chart of performance improvements using social network analytics.

7.7.3.2 TikTok: Real-Time Viral Content Propagation

TikTok's algorithm leverages dynamic influence models on its interaction graph, enabling real-time identification of emerging trends and micro-communities. This facilitates rapid content promotion to relevant audiences, driving explosive user engagement and ad revenue.

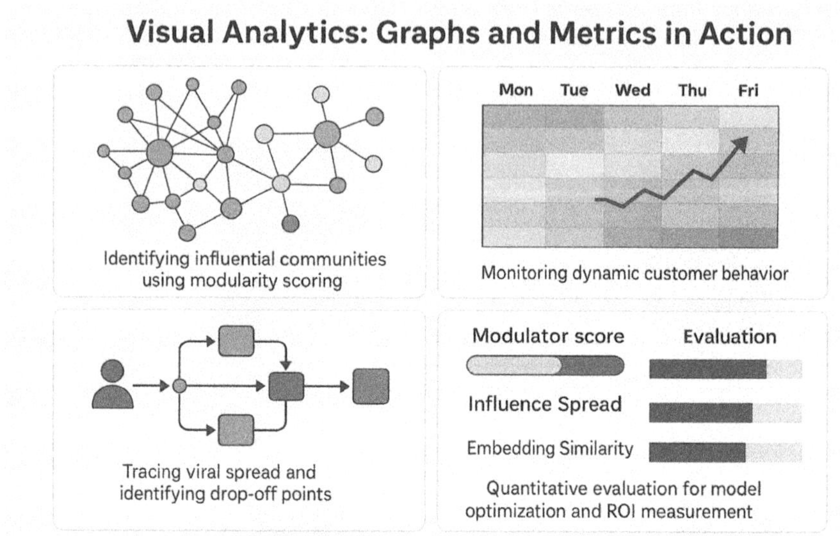

FIGURE 7.4 Visual analytics: graph and metrics in action.

7.7.3.3 Amazon: Hybrid Graph and Collaborative Filtering

Amazon integrates social data with purchase history using graph embeddings and hybrid recommender systems. This approach supports hyper-personalized product recommendations and advertising, significantly boosting average order value and customer lifetime value (Shen et al., 2021).

7.7.4 Visual Analytics: Graphs and Metrics in Action

Visual tools and dashboards provide actionable insights for marketers and data scientists (Figure 7.4):

- Community structure visualizations highlight influential nodes and densely connected clusters.
- Temporal heatmaps track evolving customer segments and campaign performance.
- Engagement graphs show propagation paths and identify bottlenecks or drop-offs in viral marketing.
- Metrics such as modularity score, influence spread, and embedding similarity enable quantitative evaluation and fine-tuning of segmentation models.

These tools make complex network data interpretable, aiding in strategy refinement and ROI optimization.

Empirical evidence solidifies the theoretical benefits of SNA in personalized advertising. Market growth, improved engagement metrics, and actual world deployments from leading digital platforms show the practical value of graph-based methods. These insights guide practitioners towards designing scalability, effectiveness, and advertising systems that are driven by metadata analysis to meet the evolving expectations of consumers and businesses.

7.8 CHALLENGES AND LIMITATIONS OF APPLYING SOCIAL NETWORK ANALYTICS IN PERSONALIZED ADVERTISING

SNA presents significant opportunities for managing personalized/targeted advertising. Its implementation is associated with several critical challenges and limitations that must be acknowledged.

7.8.1 Data Quality and Availability

One of the main challenges with SNA is to ensure access to high-quality and comprehensive social network data. Many platforms do not allow access to their data due to privacy policies, API limitations, or proprietary concerns. Incomplete or insufficient datasets can lead to biased network models and inaccurate identification of influential nodes or community structures.

UGC and social interactions are often noisy and unstructured, requiring various preprocessing techniques to extract meaningful insights or patterns. Inaccurate or sparse data affects the accuracy of SNA-driven personalization strategies.

7.8.2 Computational Complexity and Scalability

Large-scale social networks are composed of millions or billions of nodes and edges. Community detection, influence modelling, and real-time graph updates demand substantial processing power and efficient algorithms. Scaling SNA techniques while maintaining accuracy and speed is required for operational marketing systems, but remains a technical challenge, especially for small to medium enterprises with limited resources.

7.8.3 Dynamic Nature of Social Networks

Social networks are dynamic in nature, with relationships forming, evolving, or dissolving continuously. Updating network representations as they change over time is not easy, but it is key to making personalization truly effective.

Static captures of social graphs may quickly become outdated and can lead to ineffective targeting or missed opportunities.

7.8.4 Interpretability of Network Models

Complex machine learning models combined with SNA can improve the accuracy of prediction. But they often operate as "black boxes" (no explanation provided), limiting marketers' understanding of how specific network features influence outcomes.

Advanced explainable AI (XAI) methods made for network data models are critical for trust and regulatory compliance.

7.9 ETHICAL FRAMEWORKS AND RESPONSIBLE AI IN SOCIAL NETWORK ANALYTICS FOR ADVERTISING

Personalized advertising is increasingly dependent on SNA and AI. The ethical implications of these technologies require careful consideration. The huge collection and analysis of relational data, combined with predictive and often opaque AI models, raise questions about privacy, fairness, transparency, and accountability. Addressing these challenges is essential to build consumer trust, meet regulatory requirements, and ensure that marketing practices contribute positively to society.

7.9.1 Privacy and Informed Consent

Ethical use of SNA mandates that marketers obtain informed consent for data collection and usage, clearly communicate how network data is utilized, and provide consumers with control over their information.

7.9.2 Fairness and Bias Mitigation

Network data and AI algorithms are prone to perpetuating or even amplifying existing biases present in the underlying data. For example, marginalized groups might be underrepresented or stereotyped within social networks, leading to skewed segmentation and discriminatory targeting or exclusion from offers.

7.10 FUTURE DIRECTIONS IN SOCIALLY AWARE ADVERTISING

This section explores emerging research trends, technological innovations, and ethical considerations shaping the next generation of socially aware advertising systems.

7.10.1 Integration of Graph Neural Networks and Deep Learning

GNNs have revolutionized the ability to learn complex representations from social networks by combining node features and graph structure in end to end models.

Future advertising platforms are expected to:

- Leverage heterogeneous graph embeddings that incorporate multimodal data (e.g., images, text, social interactions) to better capture user preferences.
- Use dynamic GNNs to model temporal evolution in user behaviour and community structures, enabling real-time personalization.
- Employ attention mechanisms to identify the most influential social ties for targeted message amplification.

7.10.2 Ethical AI and Responsible Personalization

With the advancement in personalized marketing, ethical concerns take centre stage regarding data privacy. It is required that bias in the algorithm be addressed.

- Bias-free algorithms in segmentation and recommendation can ensure equitable representation across demographic groups.
- Transparent XAI models can provide users and advertisers with logical rationales behind personalized marketing.
- Enhanced user consent frameworks that empower individuals to control data sharing and opt out of invasive profiling.

7.10.3 Real-Time and Predictive Advertising Systems

- Real-time analytics pipelines capable of ingesting and processing streaming social data to update customer segments instantaneously.
- Predictive models that anticipate emerging trends, viral content trajectories, and user intent before they manifest.
- Autonomous advertising agents that adapt campaigns dynamically based on social signals and feedback loops.
- This robustness will help marketers tap the underlying opportunities and create consumer engagement within the stipulated time.

7.11 CONCLUSION

Personalized advertising and customer segmentation have undergone a paradigm shift through the application of SNA. By leveraging the structural and behavioural insights embedded within social graphs, advertisers can move beyond traditional demographic and transactional data to capture the nuanced, dynamic patterns of influence, preference, and community behaviour. This shift enables more precise, scalable, and context-aware marketing strategies that significantly enhance user engagement, conversion rates, and overall campaign effectiveness.

We examined the foundational concepts of SNA, explored innovative approaches including GNN and influence propagation models, and analysed real-world case studies from industry leaders such as Netflix, TikTok, and Amazon. Empirical evidence demonstrates that integrating social network–driven segmentation yields measurable improvements across key performance indicators, validating its growing adoption in commercial settings.

Looking ahead, the convergence of deep learning, multimodal analytics, and privacy-preserving technologies promises to further transform personalized advertising. Ethical considerations surrounding fairness, transparency, and user autonomy will play a critical role in shaping responsible and sustainable practices. Moreover, emerging immersive platforms and real-time data processing capabilities will unlock new opportunities for interactive, socially aware marketing experiences. For computer science practitioners and researchers, the field offers a rich landscape of challenges and opportunities, from developing scalable graph algorithms to designing

XAI models that respect user privacy. Continued interdisciplinary collaboration will be essential to harness the full potential of SNA, delivering value to businesses while safeguarding the digital rights and experiences of consumers. In summary, SNA is not only reshaping how marketers understand and engage customers but is also setting the foundation for the next generation of intelligent, ethical, and impactful personalized advertising systems.

Emerging customer segments, ethically motivated consumers, digitally native Gen Z users, and vibrant micro-communities demand tailored strategies informed by both network structures and evolving social norms. As privacy regulations tighten and data sources multiply, marketers must adopt responsible, innovative approaches that respect consumer autonomy while harnessing the power of network insights.

REFERENCES

Adomavicius, G., & Tuzhilin, A. (2005). Toward the next generation of recommender systems: A survey of the state-of-the-art and possible extensions. *IEEE Transactions on Knowledge and Data Engineering*, *17*(6), 734–749. https://doi.org/10.1109/TKDE.2005.99

Bonchi, F. (n.d.). *Influence Propagation in Social Networks: A Data Mining Perspective*. https://francescobonchi.com/

Cui, X., Tao, W., & Cui, X. (2023). Affective-knowledge-enhanced graph convolutional networks for aspect-based sentiment analysis with multi-head attention. *Applied Sciences (Switzerland)*, *13*(7). https://doi.org/10.3390/app13074458

Das, N., Sadhukhan, B., Chatterjee, R., & Chakrabarti, S. (2024). Integrating sentiment analysis with graph neural networks for enhanced stock prediction: A comprehensive survey. *Decision Analytics Journal*, *10*. https://doi.org/10.1016/j.dajour.2024.100417

DeBruine, Z. J., Pospisilik, J. A., & Triche, T. J. (2021). Fast and interpretable non-negative matrix factorization for atlas-scale single cell data. https://doi.org/10.1101/2021.09.01.458620

Duffett, R. G., & Maraule, M. (2024). Customer engagement and intention to purchase attitudes of generation Z consumers toward emojis in digital marketing communications. *Young Consumers*, *25*(5), 607–624. https://doi.org/10.1108/YC-08-2023-1817

Emmons, S., Kobourov, S., Gallant, M., & Börner, K. (2016). Analysis of network clustering algorithms and cluster quality metrics at scale. *PLoS One*, *11*(7). https://doi.org/10.1371/journal.pone.0159161

Fan, W., & Gordon, M. D. (2014). The power of social media analytics. *Communications of the ACM*, *57*(6), 74–81. https://doi.org/10.1145/2602574

Gomez-Uribe, C. A., & Hunt, N. (2015). The netflix recommender system: Algorithms, business value, and innovation. *ACM Transactions on Management Information Systems*, *6*(4). https://doi.org/10.1145/2843948

Grover, A., & Leskovec, J. (2016). Node2vec: Scalable feature learning for networks. *Proceedings of the ACM SIGKDD International Conference on Knowledge Discovery and Data Mining*, San Fransico, California, 13–17 August 2016, 855–864. https://doi.org/10.1145/2939672.2939754

Hamilton, W. L., Ying, R., & Leskovec, J. (2017). *Inductive Representation Learning on Large Graphs*. https://arxiv.org/abs/1706.02216

Jiang, T., & Tuzhilin, A. (n.d.). *Segmenting Customers from Population to Individuals: Does 1-to-1 Keep Your Customers Forever?*

Li, C., Chen, H., Li, T., & Yang, X. (2022). A stable community detection approach for complex network based on density peak clustering and label propagation. *Applied Intelligence*, *52*(2), 1188–1208. https://doi.org/10.1007/s10489-021-02287-5

Liu, H., Huang, Y., Wang, Z., Liu, K., Hu, X., & Wang, W. (2019). Personality or value: A comparative study of psychographic segmentation based on an online review enhanced recommender system. *Applied Sciences (Switzerland)*, *9*(10). https://doi.org/10.3390/app9101992

Maddox, J. (2023). More real, or just more surveillance? Panopticism and shifting authenticity paradigms in BeReal. *Convergence*, *29*(5), 1183–1198. https://doi.org/10.1177/13548565231199987

Marx, J., Blanco, B., Amaral, A., Stieglitz, S., & Aquino, M. C. (2023). Combating misinformation with internet culture: the case of Brazilian public health organizations and their COVID-19 vaccination campaigns. *Internet Research*, *33*(5), 1990–2012. https://doi.org/10.1108/INTR-07-2022-0573

Nur, M. F., & Siregar, A. (2024). Exploring the use of cluster analysis in market segmentation for targeted advertising. *IAIC Transactions on Sustainable Digital Innovation (ITSDI)*, *5*(2), 158.

Omol, E., Onyangor, D., Mburu, L., & Abuonji, P. (n.d.). Application of K-means clustering for customer segmentation in grocery stores in Kenya. *International Journal of Science*. https://ijstm.inarah.co.id

Peng, B. (2021). *Dynamic Influence Maximization*. https://arxiv.org/abs/2110.12602

Perozzi, B., Al-Rfou, R., & Skiena, S. (2014). DeepWalk: Online learning of social representations. *KDD '14: The 20th ACM SIGKDD International Conference on Knowledge Discovery and Data Mining: 24–27 August 2014*, New York. https://doi.org/10.1145/2623330

Shen, Y., Wu, Y., Zhang, Y., Shan, C., Zhang, J., Khaled Letaief, B., & Li, D. (2021). How powerful is graph convolution for recommendation? *International Conference on Information and Knowledge Management, Proceedings, Seoul,* Republic of Korea, 1619–1629. https://doi.org/10.1145/3459637.3482264

Staudt, C. L., & Meyerhenke, H. (2016). Engineering Parallel Algorithms for Community Detection in Massive Networks. *IEEE Transactions on Parallel and Distributed Systems*, *27*(1), 171–184. https://doi.org/10.1109/TPDS.2015.2390633

Tang, J., Qu, M., Wang, M., Zhang, M., Yan, J., & Mei, Q. (2015). LINE: Large-scale information network embedding. *WWW 2015 - Proceedings of the 24th International Conference on World Wide Web*, New York, United States, 1067–1077. https://doi.org/10.1145/2736277.2741093

Tang, J., Song, S., Du, Q., Yao, Y., & Qu, J. (2024). Graph convolutional networks with the self-attention mechanism for adaptive influence maximization in social networks. *Complex and Intelligent Systems*. https://doi.org/10.1007/s40747-024-01604-y

Toşa, C., & Tarigan, A. K. M. (2025). Beneath the hashtag: multifaceted insights into sustainable consumption and production from historical Twitter data. Sustainability*: Science, Practice, and Policy*, *21*(1). https://doi.org/10.1080/15487733.2024.2440952

Veličkovic, P., Cucurull, G., Casanova, A., Romero, A., Lì, P., & Bengio, Y. (n.d.). *Graph Attention Networks.*

Wang, X., He, X., Wang, M., Feng, F., & Chua, T. S. (2019). Neural graph collaborative filtering. *SIGIR 2019- Proceedings of the 42nd International ACM SIGIR Conference on Research and Development in Information Retrieval*, New York, United States, 165–174. https://doi.org/10.1145/3331184.3331267

Yang, G., Zheng, W., Che, C., & Wang, W. (2020). Graph-based label propagation algorithm for community detection. *International Journal of Machine Learning and Cybernetics*, *11*(6), 1319–1329. https://doi.org/10.1007/s13042-019-01042-0

Zhao, X., Wang, M., Zhao, X., Li, J., Zhou, S., Yin, D., Li, Q., Tang, J., & Guo, R. (2023). *Embedding in Recommender Systems: A Survey*. https://arxiv.org/abs/2310.18608

8 Role of Digital Agriculture in Shaping the Future of Farming

A Social Network Analytics Approach

Dibya Ranjan Das Adhikary, Prabhat Dansena, Dharamveer Yadav, Abhinav Kumar, and Laxminath Tripathy

8.1 INTRODUCTION

Digital transformation in agriculture is revolutionising traditional farming practices, enabling farmers to work more precisely, efficiently, and sustainably. This method of modern farming uses technology from its initial planning stage to complete management and mass production. The core elements of digital agriculture unite the Internet of Things (IoT) with Artificial Intelligence (AI), as well as drones, along with satellite imaging, Geographic Information Systems (GIS), and big data, combined with mobile applications to achieve precise farming with better information and optimisation [1].

The modern agricultural industry gives farmers access to predictive tools and real-time data that provide essential soil health information, as well as weather predictions, crop condition observations, and help in understanding market dynamics [2]. Accepting precision farming enables users to supply irrigation together with fertilisation and pesticides directly to specific regions of the field based on their particular needs [3]. Satellite imagery and drones equipped with multispectral and hyperspectral sensors enable farmers to detect crops' health problems that are not detectable through normal vision [4]. Anticipating this kind of information was simply not feasible with traditional farming methods.

Digital agriculture provides a farmer with a field-level view for greater insight and control of inputs for crop health and yields. The advancements in sustainable farming practice help farmers reduce waste, minimise environmental impact, and improve soil health [5]. The combination of mobile networks together with cloud-based platforms allows farmers in every location to receive expert guidance, time-sensitive weather data, and market rates. Digital agricultural tools grant farmers the ability to achieve superior decision-making, which keeps them competitive in the market.

DOI: 10.1201/9781003611110-8

Global food demand is estimated to double by 2050 [6], and it is vital that digital innovations in agriculture maintain their pace to help meet this demand. However, the sector is under tremendous pressure to maintain production rates with the degrading level of resources. On top of that, climate change, land degradation, labour shortages, and rising input costs create additional barriers. Urgent efforts focus on modernising agricultural procedures while developing resilient, sustainable, and efficient farming systems. Digital technologies have emerged as one of the most promising methods, which demonstrate promise in agricultural applications.

Governments, technology firms, universities, and non-profit bodies worldwide support massive funding for research to expand digital farming options. The clear benefits of these tools face implementation challenges, which make their deployment complex. Rural locations throughout the world do not yet possess critical digital infrastructure elements, which include reliable Internet connections and standard smartphone devices. While data security standards and privacy issues, together with ownership rights, remain key concerns, these factors prevent users from trusting digital platforms. Digital literacy is another concern, as farmers require continuous training to successfully implement these digital infrastructures.

The agricultural sector relies more and more on social networks and online communities to operate in the modern world. Widespread online platforms that include Twitter, Facebook, LinkedIn, YouTube, and specific discussion forums serve as shared spaces where farmers exchange knowledge and promote innovations. These platforms have evolved into energetic collaborative spaces where farmers interact with researchers, policymakers, and agritech developers to direct agricultural innovation.

The study explores digital agriculture advancement by utilising social network analytics (SNA) as a tool. By thoroughly studying digital information exchange patterns in these platforms, we aim to understand digital agricultural growth across technological development and social and cultural transformation within the farming community. The main purpose of this investigation is to study digital agriculture's effects on contemporary farming practices, which social network platforms help reveal. The research implements an interdisciplinary framework using agricultural science, data analytics, and social network theory to comprehend how digital tools spread and gain acceptance in different online social groups. This study uniquely contributes to the field by integrating multi-platform SNA (Twitter, Facebook, LinkedIn) with sentiment and topic modelling to analyse both interaction patterns and discourse content. This multidimensional approach bridges technological, behavioural, and policy perspectives—filling an existing gap in the current literature. The foundation has been established for a detailed examination of agricultural digital transformation. This paper proceeds with an evaluation of the theoretical base, followed by a methodology section and data analysis segment, before presenting the essential research outcomes. The research's final objective involves creating better information about how digital technologies, together with adaptive networks, structure the agricultural industry's future direction.

8.2 LITERATURE REVIEW

The literature review consolidates findings on digital agriculture's impact on productivity, decision-making, market access, and knowledge sharing. It highlights the rising importance of social networks and how SNA identifies key influencers and community behaviours. It identifies gaps in long-term studies and integrated digital-social research, positioning this work as a bridge between disciplines.

The SNA enables researchers by providing an analytical framework for understanding how people interact with one another within a network [7]. The main interest of SNA differs from traditional analysis techniques, which prioritise network structures that determine behaviour patterns and information movement [8]. Digital platforms benefit the most when SNA methodologies are used in analysis and insights generation. The connection analysis method of SNA enables the examination of real-time user interactions present in Twitter, Facebook, LinkedIn, and community forums. Through network analysis, researchers detect communication patterns while identifying both network clusters of communities and vital users who influence network metrics, including degree centrality, betweenness, and closeness [9]. This analysis shows both the communication connections between users and how thoughts are distributed across groups, as well as who plays a crucial role in shaping the conversation.

SNA applies across multiple industry sectors, which now includes agriculture and other fields such as public health, education, marketing, and politics. The SNA provides a distinctive analytical method to observe how farmers, researchers, policymakers, and other stakeholders utilise digital formats for their connections and collaboration [10]. The value of SNA increases significantly through its ability to study patterns within agricultural communities while understanding the impact of digital discussions on farming developments. Digital agriculture represents a transformative fundamental shift in the agricultural operations regarding their approach, management, and improvement practices [11].

The influence of digital agriculture has already made a noticeable difference in several key areas [12]:

- **Productivity**: Precision farming helps optimise the use of resources like water, fertilisers, and pesticides by tailoring applications based on localised, real-time data. This leads to healthier crops, higher yields, and less waste.
- **Decision-Making**: Tools that offer real-time weather updates, pest alerts, and predictive insights help farmers plan more effectively and respond quickly to changing conditions.
- **Market Access**: Digital platforms are creating direct links between farmers and buyers, cutting out middlemen and offering more transparency in pricing and transactions.
- **Knowledge Sharing**: Online groups and forums have become valuable spaces for farmers to share experiences, solve problems together, and learn about the latest farming innovations.

Despite these advantages, the adoption of digital agriculture is far from uniform [13]. In many developing regions, smallholder farmers face significant challenges, including poor internet access, limited digital skills, high costs, and a general hesitation to embrace unfamiliar technologies. Still, the future of digital agriculture looks bright—especially if it's backed by the right policies, education, and infrastructure.

As digital tools become easier to use and more affordable, they're likely to become everyday essentials on farms of all sizes, helping to shape a smarter, more connected, and more resilient agricultural sector.

Over the past decade, there's been a noticeable increase in research looking at the overlap between agriculture, digital technologies, and social networks. Most studies tend to focus on either technological innovations that are transforming farming or how people within agricultural communities interact and share information. Most research on digital agriculture so far has focused on the development and effects of various digital tools used in farming [14]. These range from precision agriculture technologies and mobile apps for crop monitoring to AI-based advisory systems and platforms that deliver real-time weather updates and market prices. Overall, the findings have been encouraging—many studies [15–17] report better crop yields, smarter use of resources, and higher incomes for farmers, especially when these tools are used in combination with traditional farming knowledge. For example, Mobile advisory services demonstrated their capability to assist sub-Saharan African smallholder farmers in their planting schedules and fertilisation practices according to research findings [18]. The use of satellite imagery and drones assists farmers in developed countries in detecting early ecological issues, leading to minimal crop losses [19].

Research evidence also reveals that an important digital disparity exists. These technological tools are not equally available since factors like low income levels, inadequate infrastructure, and knowledge shortfalls create barriers to use [20]. Social dynamics exist as the main determining factor at this stage. The power of community involvement and verbal recommendations from peers leads to expanded digital tool adoption, which makes SNA an essential tool for studying and resolving these gaps.

The distribution of agricultural innovations depends strongly on social networks, whether in person or online. Before digital platforms existed, farmers relied on their interactions during community meetings at local farms and through cooperative discussions [21]. Social media expansion enables farmers to connect virtually while they share knowledge and acquire insights from each other throughout diverse geographical regions and areas worldwide [22].

Researchers increasingly adopt SNA as a method to study information propagation in farming communities. Research in Indian and Kenyan rural communities identified specific individuals whom people refer to as "opinion leaders" or "information hubs" in their studies [23]. Members of the network who act as sources and determiners of new practice perceptions are vital for spreading innovations while making them more acceptable to other network members [24].

SNA also provides vital analysis for measuring agricultural extension service outreach performance. Researcher-developed connection maps between farmers and extension agents and agricultural experts let them find communication barriers, which allow them to propose new methods for information distribution [25]. Research enables better programme design for outreach programmes since it simplifies the creation of effective delivery systems for targeted beneficiaries [26].

While still a relatively new area of study, some researchers have started combining SNA with digital agriculture to better understand how digital tools are shaping social relationships within farming communities. For instance, one approach has looked at conversations on Twitter related to smart farming technologies. By analysing

TABLE 8.1
Social Media Platforms in Digital Agriculture and Their Role in SNA

Platform	Primary User	Role in Digital Agriculture	Use in SNA
Twitter	Researchers, experts, institutions	Fast updates, policy discussions, agritech trends	Influencer detection, topic tracking
Facebook	Smallholder farmers, cooperatives	Peer learning, local advisory, market info	Sentiment analysis, group clustering
LinkedIn	Agribusiness leaders, policymakers	Innovation exchange, strategy, investment	Cross-sector mapping, stakeholder analysis

hashtags, retweets, and mentions, researchers were able to spot key influencers, identify active communities, and track which topics were gaining momentum [27]. These studies also offered insights into how farmers, tech developers, and researchers are interacting in these online spaces [28].

Another interesting direction focuses on collaborative innovation platforms—online hubs where farmers, agritech firms, and researchers come together to design or adapt digital farming solutions. In these environments, SNA helps map out how partnerships form, who plays central roles in the innovation process, and how trust and engagement grow over time [29]. To synthesise the roles of different social platforms in digital agriculture and social network analysis, Table 8.1 provides a comparative summary of key platforms, their user bases, and analytic value.

Despite these promising beginnings, there are still some notable gaps. For one, we don't yet have enough long-term studies that follow how social networks change as new technologies are introduced. Also, most current research doesn't go beyond network structures to analyse the actual content of conversations. Tools like sentiment analysis or topic modelling could add depth by helping us understand *why* certain digital tools catch on—or why they don't [30].

8.2.1 Identified Research Gaps and the Need for This Study

So far, most research has looked at digital agriculture and social networks as separate, parallel developments rather than as systems that are deeply connected. Few studies have gone beyond simply mapping relationships to explore how digital tools are woven into those social ties—and how they actually shape the behaviours, attitudes, and everyday practices of farmers [27].

That gap leaves room for more in-depth, cross-disciplinary research, such as this study, which doesn't just track who adopts a tool or how often people communicate. Instead, it digs deeper into how digital agriculture is being shaped and interpreted within online communities, where social and cultural factors play a big role [28].

This research takes that approach by using SNA to answer questions such as:

- Who are the key voices driving the conversation around digital agriculture?
- What are the major topics, themes, and concerns people are talking about?

- How is knowledge shared and innovation spread in digital farming communities?
- Why do certain technologies or narratives gain popularity while others fall flat?

By unpacking these dynamics, the study aims to contribute not just to our understanding of agricultural technologies but also to broader conversations around digital equity, social innovation, and the future of rural development [30].

8.3 RESEARCH METHODOLOGY

To explore the conversations, key players, and emerging trends in digital agriculture, this study gathered data from a range of publicly available online social platforms—specifically Twitter, Facebook, and LinkedIn. These platforms were selected because they are commonly used by a broad spectrum of people involved in agriculture, including farmers, researchers, agritech startups, and policymakers, making them rich sources for observing how digital agriculture is discussed and developed in real time.

Each platform was chosen for its unique strengths:

- **Twitter** stands out for its fast-paced, real-time updates and is often used by experts, institutions, and researchers to share news, opinions, and breakthroughs in agritech. Its open-access nature and use of hashtags make it ideal for tracking discussions and identifying influential voices.
- **Facebook**, though more casual, is particularly active among grassroots farming communities, especially in developing countries, where it serves as a hub for exchanging practical advice, market information, and local weather updates.
- **LinkedIn** provides a more professional lens into the world of digital agriculture, featuring conversations among agronomists, agritech business leaders, and policymakers. This makes it a valuable space to understand how digital innovation is shaping strategy, policy, and investment in the sector.

Data was gathered using Twitter API (v2) [31] for structured access to tweets, hashtags, mentions, and user metadata over a three-month period. Relevant hashtags such as #DigitalFarming, #AgTech, #SmartAgriculture, and #PrecisionFarming were used as search parameters. For Facebook and LinkedIn, data was collected manually and supplemented with web scraping techniques [32], as permitted by platform terms and conditions.

A total of 12,000+ Twitter posts, 1,000+ Facebook public group posts, and 500+ LinkedIn posts or comments were collected, focusing on content created or shared between January and March 2025. Once the data was collected, the next phase involved cleaning, preprocessing, and preparing it for network analysis. This step was essential to ensure the reliability and clarity of the insights generated.

- **Cleaning Textual Data**: All posts were stripped of unnecessary characters, URLs, and non-English content. Stop words were removed, and basic lemmatisation was applied to standardise keywords [33].
- **Metadata Structuring**: User IDs, timestamps, retweet/reply relationships (in the case of Twitter), likes/shares (on Facebook), and comment interactions (on LinkedIn) were organised into a structured format suitable for network modelling.
- **Graph Construction**: Social graphs were created where each node represented a unique user, and edges indicated interaction (mentions, replies, retweets, shares, or comments). We used NetworkX [34] in Python for graph building and exploratory analysis.

Once the data is prepared, it goes to the network analysis step. In this work, all analyses were conducted in Python using tools like pandas, NetworkX, Gephi, and NLTK/SpaCy for natural language processing. In this paper, all data have gone through the following network analysis steps:

- **Centrality Measures** [35]: To identify influential users, we computed degree centrality, betweenness centrality, and eigenvector centrality. These metrics helped determine which individuals or organisations were central to the online discussions.
- **Community Detection** [36]: The network was segmented into communities using modularity-based algorithms to uncover clusters of users with shared interests or strong interaction patterns.
- **Topic Modelling** [37]: We used Latent Dirichlet Allocation (LDA) on cleaned text to identify dominant themes and subtopics being discussed within each community.
- **Sentiment Analysis** [38]: TextBlob and VADER tools were used to gauge the emotional tone of posts and assess public sentiment towards specific technologies or initiatives in digital agriculture.

This study follows a mixed-methods exploratory design [39]**,** combining quantitative SNA with qualitative content interpretation. The approach was chosen to uncover both structural relationships and deeper meanings embedded in digital agriculture conversations.

Given the vastness of online data, a purposive sampling [40] method was used to focus on content directly relevant to the research objectives. This method allowed for the creation of a rich and manageable dataset, representative of the broader conversation without being overwhelmed or diluted by irrelevant content. No private or sensitive information was collected. All user identities were anonymised before analysis. The study adhered to platform data usage policies and general ethical guidelines for online research.

While this process ensured a clean and analysable dataset, several limitations were acknowledged. Because the privacy of the platforms had limited access to the data, we have collected only publicly available posts, which may exclude valuable insights that might have been collected on closed group interactions or in case of engagement with privacy. Further, the omission of multilingual posts has possibly affected the inclusion of region-specific diction and issues. Finally, the purposive sampling employed is selective and efficient but potentially biased towards the more active/influential users and not necessarily representative of the greater mass of farming population, which is less vocal.

This methodological framework provides a robust foundation for examining how digital agriculture is being shaped through online networks. It enables us to explore not just *who* is talking about digital agriculture, but also *how*, *why*, and *with what implications*—laying the groundwork for the findings and analysis presented in the next section.

8.4 SOCIAL NETWORK ANALYTICS FOR DIGITAL AGRICULTURE

This section shares the key findings from the application of SNA to the data gathered on digital agriculture. The goal was to map out the structure of online interactions, highlight the most influential voices, and understand how information and opinions flow within digital farming communities. By doing so, we aimed to capture the evolving dynamics of how digital agriculture is being discussed, promoted, and embraced across different groups involved in farming and agricultural technology.

8.4.1 Identifying Key Actors and Communities

One of the main goals of this study was to identify the most influential voices—both individuals and organisations—driving the conversation around digital agriculture on platforms such as Twitter, Facebook, and LinkedIn. To do this, we applied SNA using the centrality metrics discussed in Section 3. These helped us pinpoint key nodes in the network—users who not only posted frequently but also acted as connectors between otherwise separate groups. The results are presented in Table 8.2.

Here's what stood out:

TABLE 8.2
Key Actors in Agricultural Innovation and Policy Discourse

Rank	Actor Type	Handle	Platform	Centrality Score	Role in Network
1	Agritech startup	@CropInTech	Twitter	0.89	Innovation dissemination
2	Research organisation	@CGIAR	Twitter	0.85	Knowledge source
3	Farmer influencer	@OrganicFarmerBala	Facebook	0.80	Peer learning and community engagement
4	Policy institution	@FAO	LinkedIn	0.78	Policy dissemination and awareness
5	Tech developer	@AgNextOfficial	Twitter	0.74	Tool showcase and partnerships

- **Agritech startups** like CropIn, AgNext, and DeHaat consistently appeared at the heart of the network maps. Their strong presence reflects their active role in pushing forward innovations such as precision farming, AI-powered crop diagnostics, and digitised supply chains.
- **Academic institutions** and research organisations—particularly CGIAR and several agricultural universities—emerged as major sources of reliable information. They often shared updates on research, educational content, and policy insights.
- **Farmer influencers**—individual farmers regularly posting about their hands-on experiences with digital tools—built strong followings, especially within regional language communities, earning trust and credibility at the grassroots level.
- **Government bodies** like FAO, ICAR, and various state agriculture departments also played a central role in discussions around policy, infrastructure, and digital enablement.

When we applied community detection algorithms to the network data, it became clear that users weren't just interacting randomly—there were distinct groups that formed around specific themes and interests:

- One prominent cluster centred around data-driven farming and IoT-based solutions, where discussions focused on how sensors, automation, and real-time monitoring could improve yields and efficiency.
- Another cluster was deeply engaged with organic farming and sustainability, emphasising how digital tools could support environmentally friendly practices and help reduce reliance on chemical inputs.
- A third key group brought together entrepreneurs and tech developers, sharing ideas, showcasing innovations, and exploring new collaborations within the agritech space.

Interestingly, these communities interacted with one another only to a limited extent. While there was some exchange of ideas across clusters, much of the conversation stayed within like-minded groups, suggesting the presence of digital echo chambers in the broader discourse on agriculture.

8.4.2 Analysing Trends and Patterns in Digital Agriculture

It was not only necessary to know who was in the discussion, but also the particular topic of discussion. On the basis of the textual analysis intersected with the network structure of digital terms, it became clear that there were a number of key themes and patterns taking place in the digital agriculture story. Somewhat of a common thread on Twitter was using hashtags (#SmartFarming, #AgriTech, #IoTInAgriculture, #PrecisionFarming, #FarmerEmpowerment, #ClimateSmartAgriculture) that demonstrated the direction and intensity of this discussion. The commonalities in those hashtags are evident interests in applying technology in efficiency, sustainability, and climate resilience. Posts that paired these buzzwords with concrete examples—such

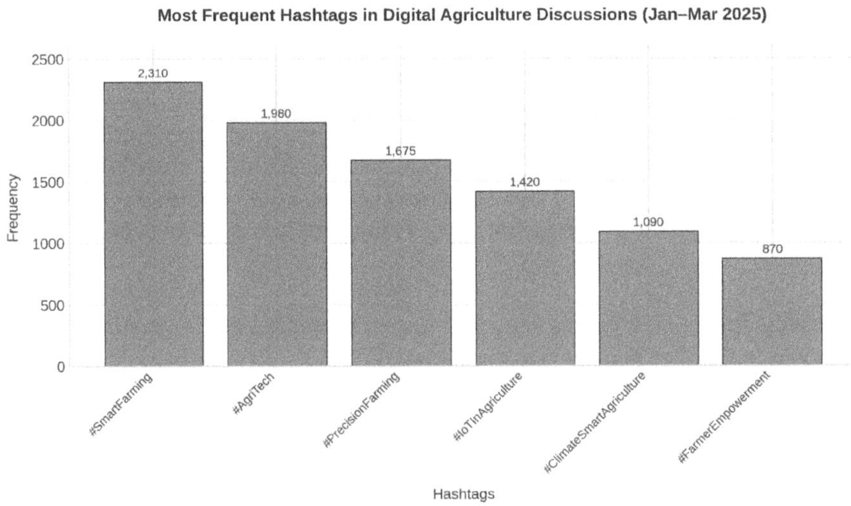

FIGURE 8.1 Most frequent hashtags.

as increased yields or cost savings—tended to get more engagement. These hashtags with their frequencies are presented in Figure 8.1. This suggests that practical, results-driven stories are more likely to resonate within these digital communities.

We also noticed that the activity wasn't spread evenly over time. Conversations spiked during specific moments, such as Government announcements, especially those involving budget allocations or new schemes related to agritech. Major events, such as expos and conferences, were used to introduce or showcase new tools and policies. During crisis periods such as floods or droughts, farmers turned to digital platforms for immediate support, whether it was weather alerts or crop-saving advice. These changes can be seen from the data presented in Figure 8.2. This pattern shows that digital agriculture conversations tend to be reactive and event-driven, with spikes in engagement tied closely to real-world developments.

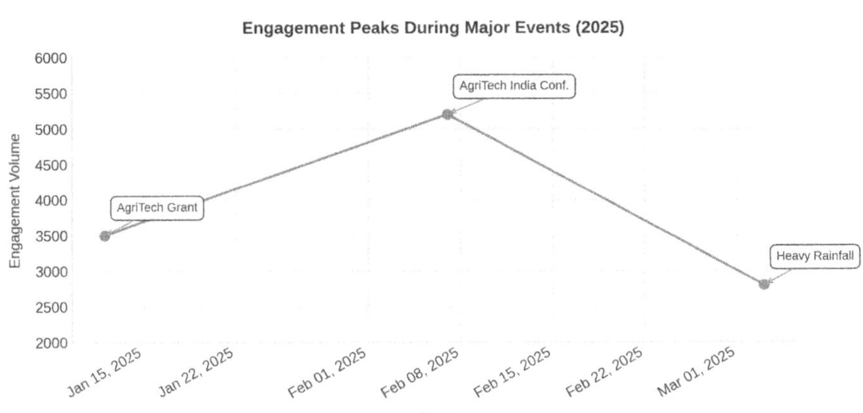

FIGURE 8.2 Engagement peaks during major events.

8.4.3 Measuring the Impact of Digital Agriculture on Farming Communities

While SNA helped map out how people interacted, pairing it with sentiment analysis and content review gave us a deeper look into how digital agriculture is actually affecting farmers in real life. Figure 8.3 presents the sentiment distribution across these data. From the figure, it can be observed that a lot of farmers shared their experiences in a positive light, especially around the practical benefits they were seeing:

- Many appreciated having real-time access to market prices, saying it gave them more control when negotiating sales.
- There was a noticeable buzz around IoT-based irrigation systems, with farmers noting how these tools helped save water and improve crop conditions.
- Some posts stood out for sharing specific outcomes, like a 10%–30% boost in yield, after using drones for spraying or sensors for soil monitoring.

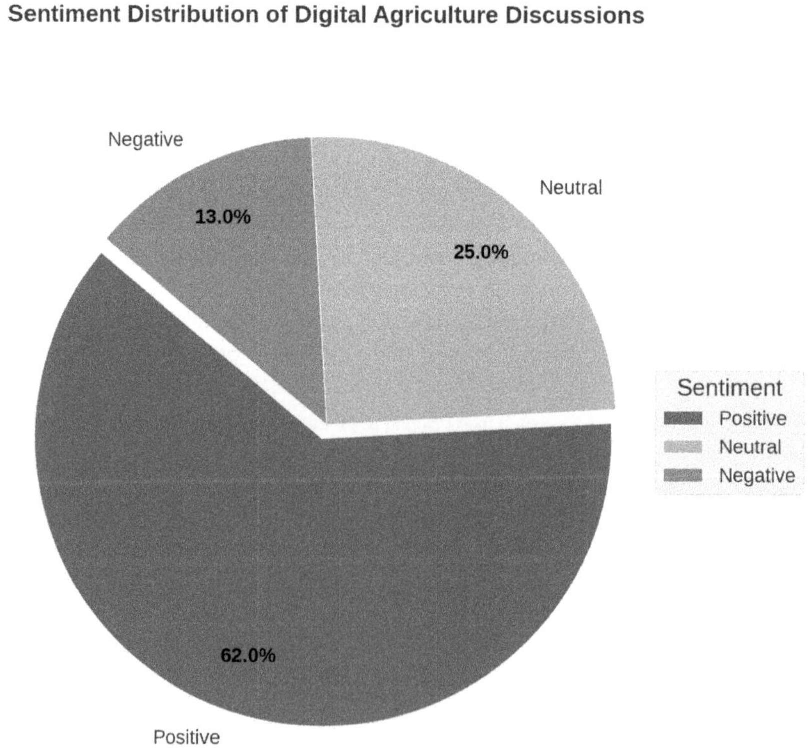

FIGURE 8.3 Sentiment distribution of the collected data.

TABLE 8.3
Major Concerns

S. No.	Barrier	Frequency	Example Quotes
1	Internet connectivity	480	"We still don't have stable signal in our village."
2	Data privacy	320	"Not sure where my crop data is going."
3	High cost of devices	290	"Sensors are great, but too expensive for small farms."
4	Lack of digital literacy	245	"Farmers struggle with mobile apps."
5	Tool fragmentation	180	"Too many apps that don't work together."

However, not everything was rosy. Alongside success stories, farmers also voiced concerns. The digital divide [41] came up often, especially from those in remote areas who lacked reliable internet or weren't comfortable with using apps and gadgets. Data privacy was another red flag, especially where agri-advisory services were offered for free by private companies, raising fears about how farmer data might be used. A few users also criticised the heavy dependence on foreign technologies, calling instead for more locally developed solutions that fit regional needs and practices. These concerns are summed up in Table 8.3.

Beyond individual experiences, there were some strong signals of how digital agriculture is shaping community behaviour. Peer learning played a big role—farmers in WhatsApp groups, Facebook communities, or local cooperatives often said they were more likely to try a new tool after seeing a fellow farmer succeed with it. Trust in digital platforms seemed to be growing, especially when local influencers or well-known cooperatives endorsed a specific app or service.

8.5 ROLE OF DIGITAL AGRICULTURE IN SHAPING THE FUTURE OF FARMING

As agriculture steps into the digital age, long-standing practices are undergoing a fundamental shift. Building on the earlier analysis of social networks and online content, we examine the real-world impact of digital agriculture—its promise to transform the sector and the practical challenges that still stand in the way of inclusive, widespread adoption.

Modern farming exists beyond personal expertise because farmers need to make choices through data-driven decision-making when it comes to production. The main role of digital agriculture is to help farmers generate higher output and manage operations more productively by using fewer resources. Modern farming technology gives farmers access to satellite imagery, drones, and soil sensors, which provide them with endless field observation abilities. Installation of precision farming enables farmers to precise the use of water, fertilisers, and pesticides into desired locations. Technology will reduce wastage and costs and increase crop yields, thus making the entire process sustainable. The IoT-connected devices offer pattern and soil moisture monitoring of weather conditions without requiring farmers to enter their land. Both irrigation systems implemented on drip irrigation that are controlled through moisture sensors and AI-based pest detection equipment will allow farmers to reduce the working part as well as lower the time of operation. Farmers with vast operations require these tools due to the fact that it becomes difficult to control everything on ground. The business instrumentations available on digital platforms allow the integration of market data and weather data into the same platform to allow inputting the costs. Farmers capitalise on this comprehensive perception of their operations in anticipating impending changes, such as falling market prices or the uncertain weather conditions.

What used to be cutting edge is quickly becoming the norm. Farms that adopt digital tools aren't just keeping up—they're gaining a competitive edge. In today's fast-moving agricultural landscape, digital tools are turning into essentials rather than optional extras.

Digital agriculture achieves one of its most powerful effects through its ability to unite people. Connectedness to other farmers used to stand as a difficult obstacle for farmers who lived in remote locations. The current digital tools establish novel ways for individuals to exchange agricultural knowledge while offering expanded market access. The social media platforms such as Facebook, Twitter, and WhatsApp operate as unofficial learning spaces for farmers. Through these networks, farmers both request information from their peers and share information about their crops, in addition to sharing challenges and recommending practical solutions. The network-based analysis revealed that farmers provide mutual learning opportunities to each other through immediate knowledge exchange. The presented Twitter-derived network serves as a sample illustration in Figure 8.4.

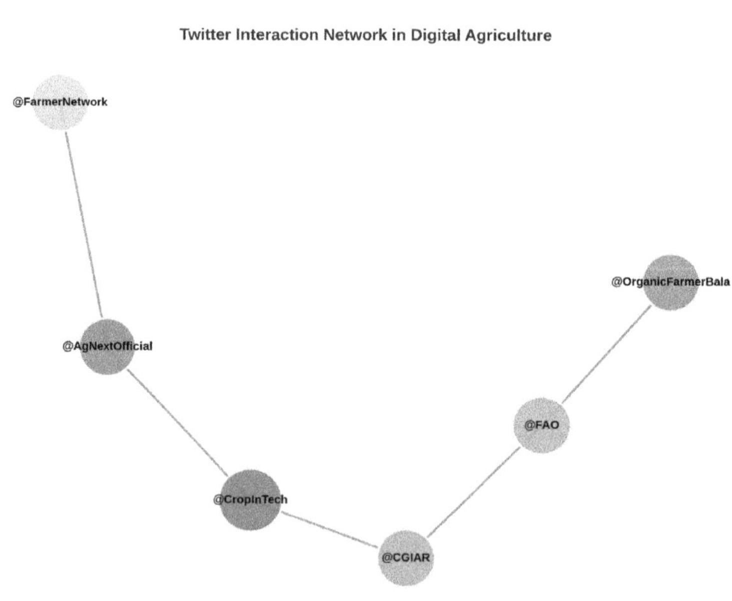

FIGURE 8.4 Twitter interaction network.

The peer-to-peer learning system enables the dissolution of farmer seclusion, which was a common practice before. Modern farmers can draw knowledge and expertise from multiple sources around the globe because digital platforms expand their resource base beyond their traditional boundaries. Through digital platform access, farmers can now easily build relationships with prospective buyers. These digital platforms allow producers to connect with potential buyers through their mobile platforms, where they can easily list items for sale and negotiate terms before making deliveries. In the past, small-scale farmers lacked this type of access to resources, which they can now obtain.

Digital platforms empower agricultural producers by providing them with a better ability to handle their operations. Farmers gain better price visibility and protection from dishonest intermediaries through digital tools, which also enable them to receive digital payments. A direct connection for perishable food items, such as vegetables, along with dairy, significantly enhances both profitability and stock reduction. The accessibility provided by digital tools extends beyond farmers and buyers since governments and NGOs actively use these digital programmes to connect with farmers. The combination of SMS alerts, apps, and online portals provides farmers with real-time updates concerning the weather, together with subsidies, crop insurance information, and best agricultural practices. Digitally distributed information reaches every isolated farmer who receives essential updates about modern farming practices, enabling their participation in the evolving agricultural setting.

Digital agriculture brings promising opportunities to farming communities, but it faces some persistent difficulties on its path of development. The potential limitations of digital agriculture stem from real-world issues that impede its maximum capability, especially when addressing accessibility, trust, and sustainability over time.

The most urgent hurdle at present stems from differences in digital access. Fast internet and tech-friendly environments are available in some regions, yet several rural communities lack reliable internet access and face no service in certain areas. A lack of fundamental infrastructure acts as a digital blockade that limits farmers from joining the digital evolution, thus creating expanding differences between the two groups of farmers. The lack of digital literacy presents significant obstacles to farmers, particularly the older population and less formally educated individuals. Numerous farmers face problems in using unfamiliar systems because they require assistance to navigate digital tools. The generation of farm data, such as soil conditions, yield patterns, and financial records, has created privacy-related concerns. Who owns this data? How is it being used? And can it be misused? Some farmers delay digital tool adoption since they are concerned that their farming activities could become subject to surveillance or data exploitation by both private companies and governmental entities. Public policies need to become more transparent while establishing clear guidelines that defend farmer rights because confidence in these systems must improve.

Another challenge lies in affordability. The costs associated with sensor, drone, and satellite imagery implementation are typically high, while providing notable operational advantages. Digital platforms, together with platform maintenance charges, tend to increase expenses significantly. Small farmers, along with marginal enterprises, find it difficult to adopt technologies because of their high initial cost.

The accessibility of digital agriculture remains a challenge for all producers since the implementation of government subsidies and pilot projects is insufficient to reach universal affordability across farm regions. A holistic pricing model, including community-based ownership, needs development to make digital agriculture accessible to every farmer regardless of their financial capacity.

Today, most digital agricultural solutions operate independently from each other. Each software application the farmer utilises for weather updates, crop monitoring, and market prices exists independently and without communication capabilities between them. Multiple systems being used by farmers become inefficient since their systems fail to connect with each other, which leads to a frustrating experience. Platform integration through user-friendly, unified systems that merge information would enhance the operational value and accessibility of the tools at hand.

The implementation of digital agriculture techniques will transform traditional farming practices through system integration, which allows farmers to improve yield output while conserving natural resources across multiple farming operations. The complete realisation of digital agriculture's potential needs practical solutions for digital disparities, appropriate answers to moral challenges, and technical implementation problems. Digital tools need to develop as components for an inclusive, sustainable agricultural future to become viable for everyone. With the methodological groundwork established, we now turn to the observed analysis of how farmers and institutions engage through digital platforms.

8.6 CASE STUDIES AND APPLICATIONS

An understanding of digital agricultural practices in real-world applications relies heavily on studying distinctive examples, demonstrating successes and failures. Multiple real-world cases presented here demonstrate how successful digital agriculture works while highlighting potential dangers that farmers should be aware of. This section focuses on advanced innovations that further advance digital agriculture technology.

Digital agriculture delivers meaningful results worldwide whenever it serves particular community needs. Through its e-Choupal [42] initiative, the ITC company enabled Indian farmers to receive weather information and crop advice along with market price data by using basic internet services. The system enabled farmers to avoid middlemen, therefore allowing them to make better decisions that led to improved prices. Farmers using the platform experienced a 15%–25% increase in yield due to timely access to market prices, weather forecasts, and best practices. Transaction costs were also reduced by an estimated 8%–10%, as intermediaries were eliminated from procurement chains. Smart greenhouses throughout the Netherlands [43] utilise AI and sensors along with automation to progress their boundaries. These automated management systems control water, nutrients, and climate factors in precise ways, which produce higher yield outputs with minimised labour requirements and waste. This leads to a 20%–30% increase in crop efficiency and a 12% reduction in water usage. Successful implementation occurred because both examples dedicated their efforts to creating accessible infrastructure alongside community participation.

Some initiatives through digital development led to unsuccessful results. A Brazilian technology platform aimed to assist farmers encountered backlash because user information was distributed illegitimately, while consent remained non-existent, which caused regulatory oversight and user doubt [44]. Indian farmers remained uninformed about the digital Soil Health Cards because weak internet access, combined with poor awareness, delays the system implementation and leaves the entire programme unknown to most users [45]. Technology requires trust alongside local application and human interaction to become an effective solution.

These trends together demonstrate that agricultural advancement will succeed when technology meets human accessibility needs rather than relying on sophisticated devices exclusively. Correctly approached technology implementation which understands community requirements can advance agricultural productivity while reshaping entire local communities. Our path to establishing farming systems that farmers will believe in and use requires active attention and customisation of technology.

8.7 FUTURE DIRECTIONS AND CONCLUSION

This chapter explored how digital agriculture, supported by SNA, is reshaping farmer engagement, knowledge dissemination, and agricultural decision-making. By analysing data across Twitter, Facebook, and LinkedIn, we identified influential actors, prevailing concerns, and network structures that reveal how information flows and who drives agricultural discourse in the digital era. The results reinforce the importance of peer learning, platform-specific outreach strategies, and inclusive design in digital transformation efforts.

However, this study has certain limitations. Firstly, it relies on publicly available data from three platforms, which exclude private or closed-group interactions where significant grassroots' discussions may occur. Secondly, the exclusion of non-English content may underrepresent local and regional dynamics, particularly in rural India and other multilingual farming regions. Third, purposive sampling may favour active or high-profile users, thereby missing insights from marginalised or offline farmers. To improve the study, future versions could incorporate multilingual NLP capabilities, broader sampling techniques, and partnerships with local agencies to ethically access private digital spaces.

Looking ahead, several promising directions emerge. Longitudinal studies could track how digital networks evolve over seasons, crises, and policy shifts—shedding light on influence dynamics and real-world decision outcomes. Integrating IoT data with SNA could enable real-time monitoring dashboards that support adaptive interventions. Future work should also include qualitative methods like focus groups and interviews to enrich network findings with lived experiences. Pilot initiatives co-developed with farmer communities can help validate and refine digital tools that are affordable, language-accessible, and offline-ready.

Finally, the success of digital agriculture depends on coordinated action across stakeholders. For farmers, the priority is to actively engage in digital peer networks, adopt relevant tools for productivity and market access, and share experiential knowledge. For policymakers, the focus should be on closing digital access gaps, establishing ethical data use frameworks, and funding rural digital literacy programmes.

For developers, the imperative is to create context-aware, user-centric platforms that work under low-bandwidth conditions, support regional languages, and allow interoperability across systems. Only through such collaborative efforts can digital agriculture deliver on its promise of equitable, resilient, and sustainable farming futures.

REFERENCES

1. Fuentes-Peñailillo, F., Gutter, K., Vega, R., & Silva, G. C. (2024). Transformative technologies in digital agriculture: Leveraging Internet of Things, remote sensing, and artificial intelligence for smart crop management. *Journal of Sensor and Actuator Networks, 13*(4), 39. https://doi.org/10.3390/jsan13040039.
2. SS, V. C., Hareendran, A., & Albaaji, G. F. (2024). Precision farming for sustainability: An agricultural intelligence model. *Computers and Electronics in Agriculture, 226,* 109386. https://doi.org/10.1016/j.compag.2024.109386.
3. Ahmad, S. F., & Dar, A. H. (2020). Precision farming for resource use efficiency. In M. A. Reddy (Ed.), *Resources Use Efficiency in Agriculture* (pp. 109–135). Springer. https://doi.org/10.1007/978-981-15-6953-1_4.
4. Abbas, A., Zhang, Z., Zheng, H., Alami, M. M., Alrefaei, A. F., Abbas, Q., … & Zhou, L. (2023). Drones in plant disease assessment, efficient monitoring, and detection: A way forward to smart agriculture. *Agronomy, 13*(6), 1524. https://doi.org/10.3390/agronomy13061524.
5. Sridhar, A., Balakrishnan, A., Jacob, M. M., Sillanpää, M., & Dayanandan, N. (2023). Global impact of COVID-19 on agriculture: Role of sustainable agriculture and digital farming. *Environmental Science and Pollution Research, 30*(15), 42509–42525. https://doi.org/10.1007/s11356-022-19358-w.
6. Gu, D., Andreev, K., & Dupre, M. E. (2021). Major trends in population growth around the world. *China CDC Weekly, 3*(28), 604–609. https://doi.org/10.46234/ccdcw2021.160.
7. Singh, S. S., Muhuri, S., Mishra, S., Srivastava, D., Shakya, H. K., & Kumar, N. (2024). Social network analysis: A survey on process, tools, and application. *ACM Computing Surveys, 56*(8), 1–39. https://doi.org/10.1145/3648470.
8. Tabassum, S., Pereira, F. S., Fernandes, S., & Gama, J. (2018). Social network analysis: An overview. *Wiley Interdisciplinary Reviews: Data Mining and Knowledge Discovery, 8*(5), e1256. https://doi.org/10.1002/widm.1256.
9. Wan, Z., Mahajan, Y., Kang, B. W., Moore, T. J., & Cho, J. H. (2021). A survey on centrality metrics and their network resilience analysis. *IEEE Access, 9,* 104773–104819. https://doi.org/10.1109/ACCESS.2021.3094196.
10. Singh, N. K., Sunitha, N. H., Tripathi, G., Saikanth, D. R. K., Sharma, A., Jose, A. E., & Mary, M. V. (2023). Impact of digital technologies in agricultural extension. *Asian Journal of Agricultural Extension, Economics & Sociology, 41*(9), 963–970. https://doi.org/10.9734/AJAEES/2023/v41i92127.
11. Singh, K., & Kolar, P. (Eds.). (2024). *Digital Agricultural Ecosystem: Revolutionary Advancements in Agriculture.* John Wiley & Sons. https://doi.org/10.1002/9781394242962.
12. Li, L., & Zhu, X. (2024). The impact of digital agriculture on green productivity in agriculture: Evidence from China. *Journal of the Knowledge Economy,* 1–25. https://doi.org/10.1007/s13132-024-02502-x.
13. Geng, W., Liu, L., Zhao, J., Kang, X., & Wang, W. (2024). Digital technologies adoption and economic benefits in agriculture: A mixed-methods approach. *Sustainability, 16*(11), 4431. https://doi.org/10.3390/su16114431.

14. Kashina, E., Yanovskaya, G., Fedotkina, E., Tesalovsky, A., Vetrova, E., Shaimerdenova, A., & Aitkazina, M. (2022). Impact of digital farming on sustainable development and planning in agriculture and increasing the competitiveness of the agricultural business. *International Journal of Sustainable Development & Planning, 17*(8). https://doi.org/10.18280/ijsdp.170808.
15. Singh, R., & Singh, G. S. (2017). Traditional agriculture: A climate-smart approach for sustainable food production. *Energy, Ecology and Environment, 2*, 296–316. https://doi.org/10.1007/s40974-017-0074-7.
16. Ali, A., Hussain, T., Tantashutikun, N., Hussain, N., & Cocetta, G. (2023). Application of smart techniques, internet of things and data mining for resource use efficient and sustainable crop production. *Agriculture, 13*(2), 397. https://doi.org/10.3390/agriculture13020397.
17. Sharma, V., Tripathi, A. K., & Mittal, H. (2022). Technological revolutions in smart farming: Current trends, challenges & future directions. *Computers and Electronics in Agriculture, 201*, 107217. https://doi.org/10.1016/j.compag.2022.107217.
18. Mapiye, O., Makombe, G., Molotsi, A., Dzama, K., & Mapiye, C. (2023). Information and communication technologies (ICTs): The potential for enhancing the dissemination of agricultural information and services to smallholder farmers in sub-Saharan Africa. *Information Development, 39*(3), 638–658. https://doi.org/10.1177/02666669211064847.
19. Hafeez, A., Husain, M. A., Singh, S. P., Chauhan, A., Khan, M. T., Kumar, N., ... & Soni, S. K. (2023). Implementation of drone technology for farm monitoring & pesticide spraying: A review. *Information processing in Agriculture, 10*(2), 192–203. https://doi.org/10.1016/j.inpa.2022.02.002.
20. Lythreatis, S., Singh, S. K., & El-Kassar, A. N. (2022). The digital divide: A review and future research agenda. *Technological Forecasting and Social Change, 175*, 121359. https://doi.org/10.1016/j.techfore.2021.121359.
21. Bustamante, M. J. (2023). Digital platforms as common goods or economic goods? Constructing the worth of a nascent agricultural data platform. *Technological Forecasting and Social Change, 192*, 122549. https://doi.org/10.1016/j.techfore.2023.122549.
22. Prajapati, C. S., Priya, N. K., Bishnoi, S., Vishwakarma, S. K., Buvaneswari, K., Shastri, S., ... & Jadhav, A. (2025). The role of participatory approaches in modern agricultural extension: Bridging knowledge gaps for sustainable farming practices. *Journal of Experimental Agriculture International, 47*(2), 204–222. https://doi.org/10.9734/jeai/2025/v47i23281.
23. Paul Jr, M., Heckelei, T., Baylis, K., & Rasch, S. (2023). Cooperative membership and exposure to role models: Implications for income and asset aspirations. *Journal of Behavioral and Experimental Economics, 107*, 102119. https://doi.org/10.1016/j.socec.2023.102119.
24. Mohankumar, L., Thiyaharajan, M., & Venkidusamy, K. S. (2024). Understanding the communication network of farmers to ensure the sustainable use of pesticides. *Journal of Environmental Studies and Sciences, 14*(1), 12–23. https://doi.org/10.1007/s13412-023-00861-6.
25. Dunphy, N., Flannery, S., & Kearney, S. (2025). Development of an agricultural extension support tool to support farmer engagement in conversations about climate change. *The Journal of Agricultural Education and Extension*, 1–19. https://doi.org/10.1080/1389224X.2025.2477450.
26. Paul, P., Hussain, H. M., Singh, N. U., Yumnam, A., Roy, A., Deori, S., Makdoh, B., Biam, K. P., Gowda, C. H., Tengli, M. B., Nagrale, B., & Singh, B. P. (2025). Reaching tribal farmers in Meghalaya: Assessing the effectiveness of technology dissemination methods. *International Journal of Agriculture Extension and Social Development, 8*(2), 11–16. https://doi.org/10.33545/26180723.2025.v8.i2a.1599.

27. Cramer, M. E., Habecker, P., Wendl, M., Sayles, H., & Rautiainen, R. (2022). Social network analysis of an agricultural center: Stakeholders and the transfer of information. *Journal of Agromedicine*, 27(1), 75–86. https://doi.org/10.1080/1059924X.2020.1850383.
28. Negi, D. S., Birthal, P., Kumar, A., & Tripathi, G. (2022). Farmers' social networks and the diffusion of modern crop varieties in India. *International Journal of Emerging Markets*, *17*(2), 368–385. https://doi.org/10.1108/IJOEM-04-2020-0407.
29. Guerrero-Ocampo, S. B., & Díaz-Puente, J. M. (2023). Social network analysis uses and contributions to innovation initiatives in rural areas: A review. *Sustainability*, *15*(18), 14018. https://doi.org/10.3390/su151814018.
30. Soares, N., Braga, R., David, J. M., Siqueira, K., & Stroele, V. (2022). Data analysis in social networks for agribusiness – A systematic mapping study. *arXiv preprint arXiv:2208.14807.* https://doi.org/10.48550/arXiv.2208.14807.
31. Twitter Developer Platform. (2025). *Twitter API v2 documentation*. https://developer.twitter.com/en/docs/twitter-api
32. Khder, M. A. (2021). Web scraping or web crawling: State of art, techniques, approaches and application. *International Journal of Advances in Soft Computing & Its Applications*, *13*(3). https://doi.org/10.15849/IJASCA.211128.11.
33. Bird, S., Klein, E., & Loper, E. (2009). *Natural Language Processing with Python: Analyzing Text with the Natural Language Toolkit*. O'Reilly Media, Inc.
34. Hagberg, A., & Conway, D. (2020). Networkx: Network analysis with python. https://networkx.github.io, 1–48.
35. Landherr, A., Friedl, B., & Heidemann, J. (2010). A critical review of centrality measures in social networks. *Business & Information Systems Engineering*, 2(6), 371–385. https://doi.org/10.1007/s12599-010-0127-3.
36. Zhang, J., Fei, J., Song, X., & Feng, J. (2021). An improved Louvain algorithm for community detection. *Mathematical Problems in Engineering*, *2021*(1), 1485592. https://doi.org/10.1155/2021/1485592.
37. Jelodar, H., Wang, Y., Yuan, C., Feng, X., Jiang, X., Li, Y., & Zhao, L. (2019). Latent Dirichlet allocation (LDA) and topic modeling: Models, applications, a survey. *Multimedia Tools and Applications*, *78*(11), 15169–15211. https://doi.org/10.1007/s11042-018-6894-4.
38. Peña-Cáceres, O., Silva-Marchan, H., Espinoza-Nima, R., More-More, M., & Villegas-Paz, A. (2024, September). Comparison of the VADER and TextBlob models in sentiment analysis. In *International Conference on Communication and Applied Technologies* (pp. 3–15). Singapore: Springer Nature Singapore. https://doi.org/10.1007/978-981-96-0426-5_1.
39. Almeida, F. (2018). Strategies to perform a mixed methods study. *European Journal of Education Studies*. https://doi.org/10.1007/978-981-96-0426-5_1.
40. Campbell, S., Greenwood, M., Prior, S., Shearer, T., Walkem, K., Young, S., ... & Walker, K. (2020). Purposive sampling: complex or simple? Research case examples. *Journal of research in Nursing*, *25*(8), 652–661. https://doi.org/10.1177/1744987120927206.
41. Ragnedda, M., & Ruiu, M. L. (2025). Digital divide. In: L. Floridi, M. Taddeo (Eds.), *A Companion to Digital Ethics* (pp. 217–226). Wiley. https://doi.org/10.1002/9781394240821.ch18.
42. Rao, K. V. G. (2023). ITC's e-Choupal 4.0: Harnessing digital technologies to empower Indian farmers. In: G. V. Muralidhara (Ed.), *Doing Business in South Asia* (pp. 101–111). Routledge. https://doi.org/10.4324/9781003261155.

43. Baeza, E. J., Van Breugel, A. J. B., Hemming, S., & Stanghellini, C. (2019, January). Smart greenhouse covers: A look into the future. In *XI International Symposium on Protected Cultivation in Mild Winter Climates and I International Symposium on Nettings and 1268* (pp. 213–224). Spain. https://doi.org/10.17660/ActaHortic.2020.1268.28.
44. **Carbonell, I. M. (2016).** The ethics of big data in agriculture. ***Internet Policy Review,*** 5(1), 1–13. https://doi.org/10.14763/2016.1.405.
45. Reddy, A. A. (2019). The soil health card Scheme in India: Lessons learned and challenges for replication in other developing countries. *Journal of Natural Resources Policy Research*, *9*(2), 124–156. https://doi.org/10.5325/naturesopolirese.9.2.0124.

9 Explainable Transfer Learning Model for Disaster Damage Assessment from Social Media Images

Vijay Kumar, Abhinav Kumar, and Pradeep Kumar Roy

9.1 INTRODUCTION

Natural disasters—including earthquakes, floods, hurricanes, and wildfires—pose significant threats to human life and infrastructure. A quick assessment of damages is essential in responding to the emergency and allocating resources. Conventionally, these tests have been based on satellite images, aerial surveys, and ground reports. Nevertheless, such approaches are normally associated with issues of timeliness, accessibility, and resolution.

The rise of social network platforms over the last couple of years has changed the face of disaster response. Such platforms as Twitter, Facebook, and Instagram allow people to exchange real-time information, including photos and videos, in the case of disasters. Such user-generated contents provide granular, situational on-the-ground views that may be used to complement conventional data sources and improve situational awareness, coupled with more responsive disaster management plans.

9.1.1 The Role of Social Media in Disaster Response

Social media is an effective medium of communication in times of disasters, and it helps affected people to self-report, request help, and spread information. Humanitarian bodies and emergency management bodies are becoming more and more dependent on social media information to track disaster events, organize rescue operations, and engage with the public.

During the 2019 floods in Poland, social media was used as an important source of information in the organization of emergency efforts. In the same way, social media analytics have been noted to have the potential to improve disaster risk management through offering insights into population responses and enabling real-time data acquisition. Images, one of the kinds of social media data, have special benefits

DOI: 10.1201/9781003611110-9

to damage assessment. Visual content can convey the range of damage more successfully than descriptions. Advanced automated systems in computer vision and deep learning (DL) have made it possible to analyze images dynamically on social media to determine the effects of disasters.

9.1.2 Challenges and Considerations

The efficient use of social media images for disaster damage assessment is hampered by a number of issues. These include:

- **Noise and Data Quality**: Social media data may be noisy containing irrelevant or misleading information that makes it difficult to analyze.
- **Annotation and Labeling**: It takes a lot of effort and resources to create labeled datasets for machine learning (ML) model training.
- **Privacy and Ethical Issues**: Using private photos and data presents privacy and consent-related ethical issues.
- **Model Generalizability**: Models that have been trained on certain disaster occurrences could not transfer well to other disaster kinds or circumstances.

Multidisciplinary cooperation, profound data processing methods, and commitment to ethical standards are necessary to meet these problems.

9.2 RELATED WORKS

Imran et al. [1] designed an automated system that had almost 280,000 social media images during Hurricane Dorian to assess the damage to infrastructure. Their model was more accurate in categorizing the level of damage (76%), demonstrating the usefulness of combining ML with human judgment to quickly estimate the impact of a disaster.

The article by Nguyen et al. [2] is an analysis of social media images posted during natural hazards to establish the level of damage. They used sophisticated ML solutions to conduct large-scale assessments, highlighting the usefulness of DL solutions to the task.

The combination of text and images in social media has also been found to enhance the accuracy of disaster damage measurements. Hao and Wang [3], in their article, presented a data-driven solution that leveraged multimodal social media data to locate and evaluate the effects of disasters. Their approach was more effective compared to unimodal ones, which supports the necessity of integrating various sources of data. Alam et al. [4] proposed a social media image analysis pipeline that integrates human perspective with machine intelligence to filter social media imagery, extract potentially informative content, and actionable information to assess the impact of disasters.

Huang et al. [5] introduced the disaster domain dataset—Earthquake Infrastructure Damage (EID)—which consists of more than 13,000 annotated images, documented based on the various standardized damage scales, including HAZUS and EMS-98. The data can be used to create AI models to assess the damage of infrastructure in the case of an earthquake using social media images. A recent study [6] proposed an integrated framework employing Vision Transformer (ViT Base 16) for image analysis and GPT-2 for text processing. Their ensemble model, which combined outputs through a Random Forest Classifier, achieved a 13.23% improvement in accuracy compared to conventional CNN-based models. Shetty et al. [7] introduced a multimodal middle-fusion strategy that leverages cross-modal attention and self-attention mechanisms to jointly learn from image and text data, attaining over 91% accuracy in disaster-related social media classification.

The BRIGHT dataset [8] provides high-resolution optical and SAR imagery spanning disaster events across 14 regions globally. This open-access resource supports AI-based all-weather disaster response by enabling damage assessment at building-level precision. Shekarizadeh et al. [9] designed an unsupervised deep neural network that incorporates knowledge distillation to detect and localize disaster-related damages from social media images. This work addresses the challenge of limited labeled datasets in the disaster domain.

Hanny et al. [10] explored using active learning to identify disaster-related tweets effectively. Their approach outperformed traditional keyword filtering and generic fine-tuning methods, demonstrating the potential of active learning in social media analysis for disaster response.

MSNet, a model devised for assessing building damage using aerial videos gathered from social media, was presented by Zhu et al. [11]. Their method achieves competitive performance on their dataset by combining unsupervised scoring strategies with innovative area suggestion networks. A similar active learning strategy for catastrophe assessment using social media photos was put forth by Said et al. [12]. According to their research, adaptive learning methods can reduce the need for manual labeling while producing performance levels that are on par with datasets that have been annotated by humans.

The article by [13] focuses on finding meaningful information in social media data to enhance disaster response and recovery. It emphasizes the need to filter out the most relevant information among the flood of social media content generated during a crisis.

The basis of the study conducted by [14] was to emphasize the spatial and temporal peculiarities of post-disaster information to optimize the evaluation process. Through their work, they showed the benefits of dynamic data collection methods that would consider the changes with time and location in cases of disasters.

The framework proposed by Lam [15] examines the use of social media in creating disaster resiliency. It classifies the various types of social media interaction, presents constraints, and offers suggestions on enhancing its effectiveness in disaster response. In another study, Mızrak [16] examined social media public usage in the aftermath of the Kahramanmaraş earthquakes and provided an insight into how the tools helped information sharing and communication among people during the crisis.

9.3 MACHINE LEARNING AND DEEP LEARNING APPROACHES FOR DISASTER DAMAGE ASSESSMENT FROM SOCIAL MEDIA IMAGERY

The section covers the well-established methods in ML and DL employed for the analysis of social media images to assess disasters impact. Each method is introduced as referring to its methodology, strengths, weaknesses, and support.

9.3.1 Traditional Machine Learning with Handcrafted Features

Prior to the DL era, disaster image classification tasks were mostly dominated by the use of feature integration, and the application of a classifier was based on the use of handcrafted features like Scale-Invariant Feature Transform (SIFT), Histogram of oriented Gradients (HOG), and Bag-of-Visual-Words (BoVW). These features were extracted and subsequently used as input to classical classifiers like Support Vector Machines (SVM), k-Nearest Neighbors (k-NN), and Random Forests. The BoVW approach involves extracting local features (e.g., SIFT) from images, clustering them into visual words, and representing each image as a histogram of these visual word frequencies. The resulting feature vector can then be used to train a classifier such as an SVM. Strengths: (i) Requires relatively low computational power, (ii) Easy to interpret and implement, and (iii) Effective on small, curated datasets. Limitations: (i) Does not capture high-level semantic features, (ii) Poor generalization to unseen events or scenes, and (iii) Requires manual feature engineering. Mimran et al. [2] demonstrated that deep CNNs significantly outperform traditional BoVW+SVM models in damage severity classification tasks.

9.3.2 Convolutional Neural Networks (CNNs)

Convolutional Neural Networks (CNNs) are widely used for visual feature learning and have shown superior performance in disaster damage assessment. Models like VGGNet, ResNet, and Inception extract hierarchical feature maps that are useful for classifying damage severity (e.g., no damage, minor, major, severe). Strengths: (i) End-to-end feature learning, (ii) High accuracy in classification tasks, and (iii) Able to learn semantic patterns like debris, collapsed buildings, and fires. Limitations: (i) Requires large annotated datasets, (ii) Computationally expensive, and (iii) Domain adaptation across different disaster types is limited. Nguyen et al. [2] applied CNNs to classify social media images into informative and non-informative categories during disasters.

9.3.3 Transfer Learning

Transfer learning has been adopted to mitigate the lack of large labeled datasets in the disaster domain. Pre-trained networks on ImageNet are fine-tuned on disaster-specific datasets [17]. Strengths: (i) Reduces the need for large datasets and (ii) Quick convergence and improved generalization. Limitations: (i) Domain shift still impacts performance and (ii) Optimal fine-tuning strategies vary across datasets. Bouchard et al. [18] used a pre-trained ResNet-50 on Twitter disaster datasets and achieved superior performance through transfer learning.

9.3.4 Object Detection and Segmentation

Object detection techniques such as YOLO and Faster R-CNN can detect and localize specific disaster-related cues like collapsed buildings, flooding, and fires. Mask R-CNN further extends this by providing pixel-wise segmentation. Strengths: (i) Enables spatial localization of damage and (ii) Suitable for mapping and quantification of affected areas. Limitations: (i) Requires detailed annotations like bounding boxes or segmentation masks and (ii) High computational complexity. Asif et al. [19] implemented YOLOv4 to identify emergency cues in disaster images with high accuracy.

9.3.5 Semantic Segmentation Networks

For fine-grained, pixel-level damage assessment, semantic segmentation models like U-Net, FCN, and BDANet are employed. These models classify each pixel into categories (e.g., damaged, undamaged). Strengths: (i) High-resolution damage detection. (ii) Essential for infrastructure-level damage mapping. Limitations: (i) Requires pixel-wise annotations. (ii) Less effective on low-quality or occluded images. Shen et al. [18] proposed BDANet for segmentation-based damage assessment using cross-directional attention mechanisms.

9.3.6 Generative Adversarial Networks (GANs)

Generative Adversarial Networks (GANs) are increasingly used for data augmentation, especially when real labeled images are scarce. Synthetic images are generated to expand training datasets. Strengths: (i) Reduces overfitting by enlarging datasets and (ii) Helps address class imbalance. Limitations: (i) Quality of generated images may vary and (ii) May introduce unrealistic samples. Gao et al. [20] employed GANs to generate synthetic flood images for training disaster classifiers.

9.3.7 Multimodal Fusion Models

Combining image and text information from social media posts yields better disaster understanding. Fusion models incorporate both modalities using attention or embedding-level integration. Strengths: (i) Text complements visual ambiguities and (ii) Enhances context-awareness. Limitations: (i) Dependent on availability of metadata and (ii) Requires complex fusion architectures. Shetty et al. [7] proposed cross-modal attention networks for fusion of image and text on CrisisMMD dataset. Table 9.1 shows different ML and DL techniques for disaster damage assessment.

TABLE 9.1
Comparison of Machine Learning and Deep Learning Techniques for Disaster Damage Assessment

Technique	Key Characteristics	Strengths	Limitations
Traditional ML (BoVW, SVM, RF)	Relies on handcrafted features like SIFT and HOG	Low computational cost; interpretable	Limited semantic understanding; requires manual feature engineering
CNN-based models (VGG, ResNet, Inception)	Deep hierarchical feature extraction	High classification accuracy; end-to-end learning	Requires large datasets and GPU resources
Transfer learning	Fine-tuning pre-trained models (e.g., ImageNet)	Reduces training data need; better generalization	Needs task-specific tuning; domain mismatch issues
Object detection (YOLO, Faster R-CNN)	Detects and localizes damage-specific objects	Enables spatial understanding of damage	Requires bounding box annotations; high computation
Semantic segmentation (U-Net, FCN, BDANet)	Pixel-level classification of damage extent	High spatial resolution; suitable for mapping	Needs detailed annotation; performance sensitive to occlusion
GAN-based data augmentation	Synthetic image generation for class balancing	Tackles dataset imbalance; improves generalization	Risk of generating unrealistic images; training instability
Unsupervised/ self-supervised learning	Uses unlabeled data (autoencoders, contrastive learning)	No need for labels; works in early disaster stages	Hard to interpret; performance varies with hyperparameters
Multimodal fusion (image + text)	Integrates visual and textual info from posts	Improves context-awareness and accuracy	Dependent on metadata quality; complex models

9.4 METHODOLOGY

This section discusses various CNN- and Transformer-based models, which are subsequently implemented through the pipeline illustrated in Figure 9.1.

9.4.1 Vision Transformer for Image Classification

The Vision Transformer (ViT), proposed by Dosovitskiy et al. [21], adapts the Transformer framework—originally designed for natural language processing—to the task of image recognition. Unlike CNNs that rely on convolutional kernels, ViT divides an image into fixed-size patches and processes them using Transformer layers. This design enables the model to capture broader contextual relationships and long-range dependencies more effectively than traditional convolution-based networks.

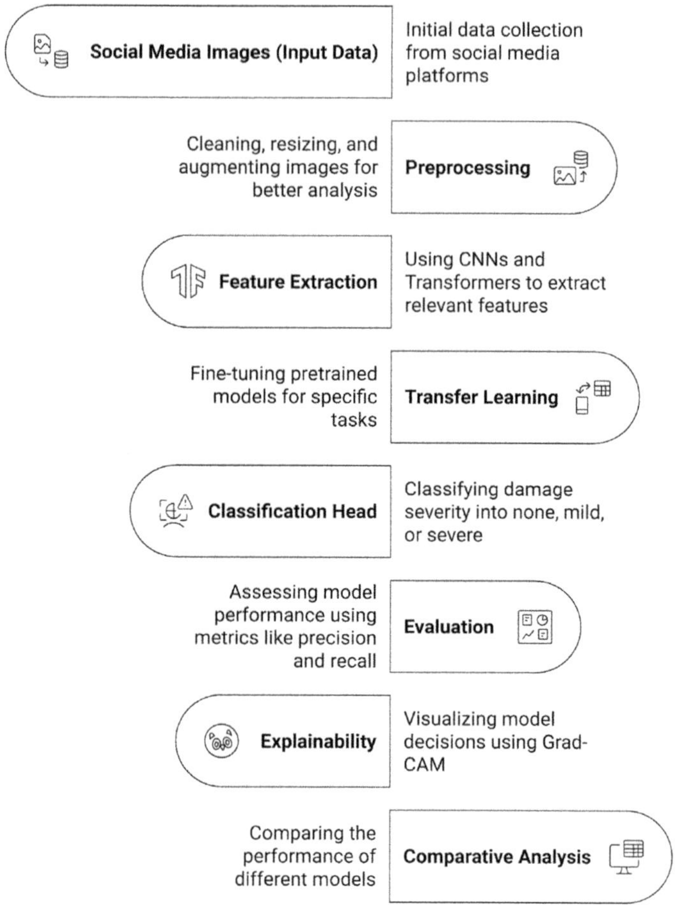

FIGURE 9.1 Overall flow diagram of the proposed framework.

9.4.1.1 Patch Embedding

Consider an input image $x \in \mathbb{R}^{H \times W \times C}$, where H, W, and C represent the height, width, and number of channels, respectively. The image is divided into N non-overlapping patches of size $P \times P$:

$$N = \frac{HW}{P^2} \tag{9.1}$$

Each patch is then reshaped into a vector:

$$x_p^i = \text{Flatten}\left(x_{(i)}\right), \quad x_p^i \in \mathbb{R}^{P^2 C} \tag{9.2}$$

Next, every patch vector is projected into a D-dimensional embedding space using a learnable linear mapping $E \in \mathbb{R}^{\left(P^2 C\right) \times D}$:

$$z_0^i = x_p^i E, \quad z_0^i \in \mathbb{R}^D \tag{9.3}$$

In addition, a learnable class token $z_0^{\text{cls}} \in \mathbb{R}^D$ is appended to the sequence for classification purposes. The complete input to the Transformer becomes:

$$Z_0 = \left[z_0^{\text{cls}}; z_0^1; z_0^2; \ldots; z_0^N \right] + E_{\text{pos}} \tag{9.4}$$

where $E_{\text{pos}} \in \mathbb{R}^{(N+1) \times D}$ denotes the positional encodings.

9.4.1.2 Transformer Encoder

The Transformer encoder consists of L stacked layers, where each layer is composed of: (i) multi-head self-attention (MSA), (ii) a feed-forward network (FFN), (iii) residual connections, and (iv) layer normalization (LN).

9.4.1.3 Multi-Head Self-Attention (MSA)

Given an input sequence $Z \in \mathbb{R}^{(N+1) \times D}$, the queries, keys, and values are obtained through linear projections:

$$Q = ZW^Q, \quad K = ZW^K, \quad V = ZW^V \tag{9.5}$$

where $W^Q, W^K, W^V \in \mathbb{R}^{D \times d}$, and $d = D/h$ with h being the number of attention heads.

The scaled dot-product attention for a single head is defined as follows:

$$\text{Attention}(Q, K, V) = \text{softmax}\left(\frac{QK^\top}{\sqrt{d}} \right) V \tag{9.6}$$

Finally, outputs from all heads are concatenated as follows:

$$\text{MSA}(Z) = \text{Concat}(\text{head}_1, \ldots, \text{head}_h) W^O \tag{9.7}$$

with $W^O \in \mathbb{R}^{D \times D}$.

9.4.1.4 Feed Forward Network (FFN)

Each transformer block also involves a position-driven feed-forward network:

$$\text{FFN}(\mathbf{z}) = \text{GELU}(\mathbf{z}\mathbf{W}_1 + \mathbf{b}_1) \mathbf{W}_2 + \mathbf{b}_2 \tag{9.8}$$

where $\mathbf{W}_1 \in \mathbb{R}^{D \times D_{ff}}$, $\mathbf{W}_2 \in \mathbb{R}^{D_{ff} \times D}$, and GELU is the Gaussian Error Linear Unit activation.

9.4.1.5 Layer Normalization and Residual Connections

Each sublayer (MSA and FFN) uses residual connections and LayerNorm:

$$\mathbf{Z}_l' = \text{MSA}\left(\text{LN}(\mathbf{Z}_{l-1})\right) + \mathbf{Z}_{l-1} \tag{9.9}$$

$$\mathbf{Z}_l = \text{FFN}\left(\text{LN}(\mathbf{Z}_l')\right) + \mathbf{Z}_l' \tag{9.10}$$

9.4.1.6 Classification Head

After L Transformer layers, the final representation of the class token $\mathbf{z}_L^{[0]}$ is used for classification:

$$\hat{\mathbf{y}} = \text{softmax}\left(\mathbf{z}_L^{[0]} \cdot \mathbf{W}_c + \mathbf{b}_c\right) \tag{9.11}$$

where $\mathbf{W}_c \in \mathbb{R}^{D \times K}$ and K is the number of target classes.

9.4.1.7 Loss Function

The standard cross-entropy loss is used for training:

$$\mathcal{L}_{\text{CE}} = -\sum_{k=1}^{K} y_k \log\left(\hat{y}_k\right) \tag{9.12}$$

where y_k is the ground truth label (one-hot encoded) and $\hat{y}_k$ is the predicted probability.

Advantages of Vision Transformer: (i) Global Context Modeling: Self-attention allows ViT to model global dependencies between image patches, (ii) Scalability: Performance improves with larger datasets (e.g., ImageNet-21k, JFT-300M), and (iii) Architecture Simplicity: Removes the need for inductive biases like convolutions.

Limitations: (i) Requires large datasets and computational resources to train from scratch and (ii) Lacks spatial locality priors that CNNs leverage.

9.4.2 Deep Learning Architectures for Image Classification

This section provides an overview of several widely used CNN architectures for image classification tasks, including VGG13, VGG16, VGG19, Xception, MobileNet, EfficientNet, and ViT Swin-Small.

9.4.3 VGG Family: VGG13, VGG16, and VGG19

The VGG family of networks, introduced by Simonyan and Zisserman [22], adopts a uniform architecture based on small 3×3 convolutional filters stacked to increase depth. This design choice allows the models to learn rich feature hierarchies while maintaining simplicity and consistency. VGG13 consists of thirteen weight layers, including ten convolutional layers and three fully connected layers. It employs five convolutional blocks, each followed by max pooling, and offers a balance between depth and computational efficiency, making it suitable for tasks where resources are limited.

VGG16 extends this design to sixteen layers, including thirteen convolutional and three fully connected layers. It has become one of the most widely used CNN architectures due to its strong performance on classification tasks and its relatively straightforward structure. Although effective, VGG16 is computationally expensive, with approximately 138 million parameters, which limits its deployment in resource-constrained environments.

VGG19 further increases the depth to nineteen layers by adding additional convolutional layers to the VGG16 framework. While increased depth can potentially improve performance by learning more complex representations, it also comes with significantly higher computational costs and marginal gains in accuracy. All VGG variants conclude with three fully connected layers and a softmax classifier, and they rely heavily on ReLU activations throughout the network.

9.4.4 Xception

Xception, or Extreme Inception, was proposed by Chollet [23] as an extension of the Inception architecture. The core innovation of Xception lies in replacing Inception modules with depthwise separable convolutions, which decompose the convolution operation into spatial and channel-wise components. This results in more efficient computation and better utilization of model parameters.

The Xception architecture is organized into three main flows: entry, middle, and exit. Each flow comprises depthwise separable convolution layers, interspersed with residual connections similar to those found in ResNet. This structure enables the model to learn more effective spatial correlations while maintaining high computational efficiency. Xception has been shown to outperform InceptionV3 on ImageNet classification, demonstrating its capability to scale performance while reducing model complexity.

9.4.5 MobileNet

MobileNet represents a group of lightweight neural network models proposed by Howard et al. [24] for efficient deployment on mobile and embedded platforms. Its key contribution is the adoption of depthwise separable convolutions, which significantly reduce both parameter count and computational load compared to traditional convolutions.

The first version (MobileNetV1) begins with a standard convolution layer, followed by multiple depthwise separable convolutional layers. Later versions, such as MobileNetV2, introduce inverted residual connections and linear bottlenecks to further enhance representational efficiency. MobileNetV3 improves on this design by incorporating neural architecture search along with additional enhancements like the Swish activation function and squeeze-and-excitation modules. Across its variants, MobileNet offers an excellent balance between accuracy and efficiency, making it particularly useful for real-time vision tasks on resource-constrained devices. However, its performance may still fall short of larger and more complex architectures.

9.4.6 EfficientNet

EfficientNet, proposed by Tan and Le [25], introduced a new scaling strategy for CNNs. Unlike conventional approaches that independently increase network depth or width, EfficientNet employs a compound scaling method, which uniformly adjusts depth, width, and resolution using predefined scaling coefficients.

The baseline model, EfficientNet-B0, was developed through neural architecture search and serves as the foundation for larger models in the B1–B7 series. It leverages mobile inverted bottleneck convolution (MBConv) layers and the Swish activation function to achieve strong accuracy with fewer parameters. This design allows EfficientNet to deliver state-of-the-art results on multiple benchmarks while being more efficient than previous CNN architectures like ResNet and Inception. Despite its efficiency, fine-tuning EfficientNet may require careful scaling or optimization to fully utilize its potential.

9.4.7 Swin-Small

The Swin-Small architecture is a compact variant of the Swin Transformer family [26], specifically designed to balance accuracy and efficiency in image classification tasks. Unlike conventional CNNs, Swin-Small employs a hierarchical vision transformer that progressively merges image patches, enabling both local and global feature extraction. Its core innovation lies in the shifted window mechanism, which partitions feature maps into non-overlapping windows and then shifts them across layers to capture cross-window dependencies while maintaining linear computational complexity.

By building multi-scale feature representations, Swin-Small closely resembles the hierarchical nature of CNN backbones but benefits from transformer-based attention modeling. This makes it particularly effective for high-resolution disaster images where fine-grained local cues (e.g., cracks, debris) and global structural context (e.g., collapsed buildings) both play critical roles. The architecture integrates well with transfer learning pipelines, offering competitive accuracy on standard benchmarks while remaining computationally lighter than larger Swin variants. In disaster damage assessment, Swin-Small achieves a strong trade-off between scalability, interpretability through attention maps, and deployment feasibility on resource-constrained platforms. Compared to CNN baselines such as VGG19 or MobileNetV2, Swin-Small demonstrates superior performance in capturing long-range dependencies and structural patterns, making it a state-of-the-art choice for image classification in disaster scenarios.

9.4.8 Grad-CAM-Based Explainability

Gradient-weighted Class Activation Mapping (Grad-CAM) is employed in this work across all five models to provide a unified framework for interpretability [27]. Grad-CAM highlights discriminative regions in the input image that most strongly influence the network's prediction, thereby offering intuitive insights into the model's decision process. Unlike raw attention scores, Grad-CAM leverages the gradients of the target class flowing into the final convolutional or token-level feature maps.

The process begins with loading the trained checkpoint (best_model.pth), as shown in Figure 9.2, and then preprocessing the input test image through resizing and normalization. The image then undergoes a forward pass, where feature maps (for CNN-based models such as VGG19, ResNet, MobileNetV2, and Xception) or token embeddings (for the Swin-Small transformer) are captured at a designated

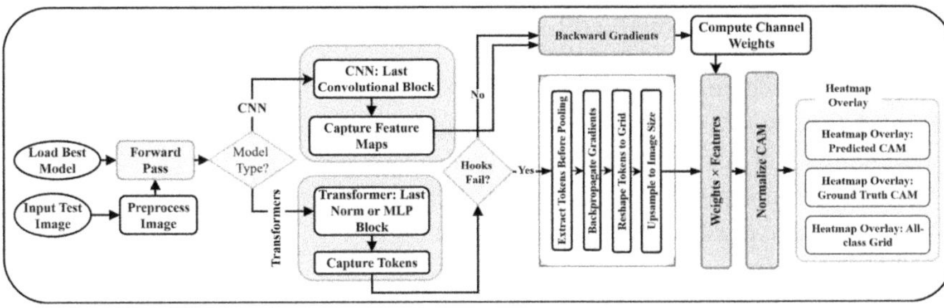

FIGURE 9.2 End-to-end Grad-CAM workflow.

target layer. A backward pass follows, computing the gradients of the predicted class score with respect to these activations. The gradients are globally averaged to obtain channel weights, which quantify the importance of each feature channel. These weights are multiplied with the corresponding activations to generate a Class Activation Map (CAM). The CAM is then normalized to create a heatmap, which is subsequently overlaid on the original image to visualize the model's attention. For transformer-based architectures, a TokenGradCAM fallback ensures robustness by deriving explanations from patch tokens when feature hooking is not possible.

Formally, for a target class c, the importance weight of each feature channel k is computed as follows:

$$\alpha_k^c = \frac{1}{Z}\sum_i\sum_j \frac{\partial y^c}{\partial A_{ij}^k} \tag{9.13}$$

where:

- y^c denotes the score (logit) corresponding to class c before the softmax layer.
- A_{ij}^k represents the activation value at spatial location (i, j) in the kth feature map of the selected convolutional (or token-level) layer.
- $\frac{\partial y^c}{\partial A_{ij}^k}$ is the gradient of the class score y^c with respect to activation A_{ij}^k, capturing how sensitive the class prediction is to changes in that activation.
- Z is the normalization factor, equal to the total number of spatial locations in the feature map ($Z = H \times W$ for CNNs or $Z = L$ for token embeddings).
- α_k^c is the global importance weight of the channel k for predicting class c, obtained by averaging the gradients across all spatial positions.

The class-discriminative heatmap is then obtained as:

$$M^c = \text{ReLU}\left(\sum_k \alpha_k^c A^k\right) \tag{9.14}$$

where:

- A^k denotes the entire kth activation map (or token embedding sequence reshaped into a 2D grid).

- $\sum_k \alpha_k^c A^k$ computes a weighted linear combination of feature maps, emphasizing those that contribute most to class c.
- $\mathrm{ReLU}(\cdot)$ ensures that only the positively influencing features are retained in the final map, discarding negative evidence.
- M^c is the final Grad-CAM heatmap for class c, which is upsampled to the original image resolution for visualization.

For CNN-based architectures, Grad-CAM is applied to the last convolutional layers to generate spatial saliency maps. In transformer-based backbones such as Swin-Small, the implementation is made robust by automatically selecting suitable internal layers for hooking. If hooks fail due to version incompatibility, a token-level fallback (TokenGradCAM) is employed. This fallback computes gradients with respect to patch tokens before global average pooling and reshapes them into a 2D grid, ensuring that explanation maps remain available even in non-convolutional contexts.

Overall, the integration of Grad-CAM across all models provides a consistent mechanism for transparency, enabling domain experts to validate whether the models are attending to semantically relevant disaster-affected regions when predicting damage severity.

9.5 RESULTS

The performance of the proposed models is evaluated through a systematic threefold analysis that combines quantitative metrics, visual interpretability, and comparative insights. First, the Quantitative Evaluation presents classification reports, confusion matrices, and ROC-AUC analyses to provide a detailed understanding of class-wise accuracy, misclassification patterns, and threshold-independent discriminatory capability. Second, the Grad-CAM-Based Explainability section highlights the internal decision-making process of the models by visualizing attention regions that contribute to disaster severity predictions, thereby ensuring transparency and trustworthiness. Finally, the Overall Result Comparison section synthesizes the findings across all evaluated architectures, enabling a holistic assessment of strengths and limitations and identifying the most effective model for disaster damage classification.

9.5.1 Quantitative Evaluation

To comprehensively assess the effectiveness of DL models in disaster damage severity classification, we employ a set of quantitative evaluation metrics that capture both accuracy and discriminative power. The classification reports provide precision, recall, and $F1$-scores for each class, offering a numerical summary of class-wise performance and highlighting imbalances or weaknesses in prediction. The confusion matrices present a visual breakdown of correctly and incorrectly classified instances, thereby revealing specific misclassification trends (e.g., between Mild and Severe damages). Complementing these, the ROC curves with AUC scores measure the threshold-independent discriminatory capability of each model, quantifying its ability to distinguish between classes under varying decision boundaries. Together, these metrics deliver a rigorous and multi-perspective evaluation framework that balances per-class interpretability with overall model robustness.

9.5.1.1 VGG19

The classification report (Table 9.2) for VGG19 indicates that the model performs best in identifying the Little_or_None damage category, achieving an *F*1-score of 0.7706 with notably high recall (0.8165). In contrast, the Mild and Severe classes exhibit relatively weaker performance, with *F*1-scores of 0.5685 and 0.5485, respectively. The overall weighted *F*1-score of 0.6226 suggests that while the model has moderate effectiveness, class imbalance and inter-class confusion remain as challenges.

The normalized confusion matrix and AUC-ROC curves (Figure 9.3) further highlight these patterns. The Little_or_None class shows strong discrimination with 82% correct predictions and the highest AUC (0.912), confirming the model's strength in detecting low-damage cases. However, the Mild and Severe categories reveal substantial overlap, where 39% of Severe samples are misclassified as Mild and 24% of Mild samples are misclassified as Severe. This aligns with their comparatively lower AUC values (0.747 for Mild and 0.771 for Severe), reflecting difficulty in separating these adjacent severity levels. Nevertheless, the overall micro-averaged AUC of 0.820 indicates that the model maintains a fair discriminative capability across classes despite these confusions.

TABLE 9.2
Classification Report: VGG19

Models	Classes	Precision	Recall	*F*1-Score
VGG19	Little_or_None	0.7295	0.8165	0.7706
	Mild	0.5301	0.6130	0.5685
	Severe	0.6311	0.4851	0.5485
	Weighted avg	0.6286	0.6271	0.6226

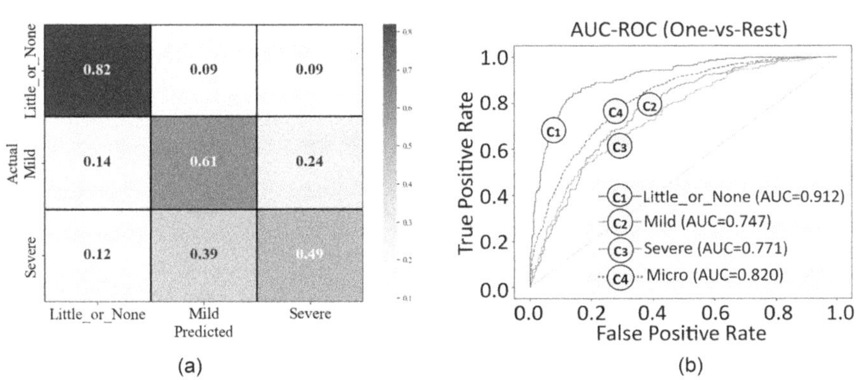

FIGURE 9.3 Evaluation of VGG19 on disaster damage classification: (a) class-level performance via normalized confusion matrix, and (b) discriminatory capability via ROC curves with AUC scores.

In summary, VGG19 exhibits strong performance in recognizing Little_or_None cases but struggles to differentiate Mild and Severe categories due to overlapping visual features. This pattern provides a benchmark for comparison with the subsequent models, where improvements in balanced recognition across classes will be critical.

9.5.1.2 MobileNetV2

The classification report (Table 9.3) for MobileNetV2 highlights a significant improvement compared to VGG19, with a weighted $F1$-score of 0.7630. The model shows its strongest performance in the Little_or_None class, achieving an $F1$-score of 0.8645 with high precision (0.8810) and recall (0.8486). The Severe class also benefits from MobileNetV2's capacity, yielding an $F1$-score of 0.7468, which is higher than that obtained for the Mild category (0.6857). These results suggest that MobileNetV2 maintains a better balance across classes, particularly in distinguishing higher-damage scenarios.

The normalized confusion matrix and AUC-ROC curves (Figure 9.4) reinforce these observations. The matrix reveals that Little_or_None cases are recognized with high accuracy (85% correctly classified), while Severe cases are identified with 76% accuracy, though some overlap exists, as 20% of Severe samples are misclassified as Mild. The Mild class, though improved compared to VGG19, still suffers from

TABLE 9.3
Classification Report: MobileNetV2

Models	Classes	Precision	Recall	$F1$-Score
MobileNetV2	Little_or_None	0.8810	0.8486	0.8645
	Mild	0.6933	0.6783	0.6857
	Severe	0.7295	0.7649	0.7468
	Weighted avg	0.7640	0.7626	0.7630

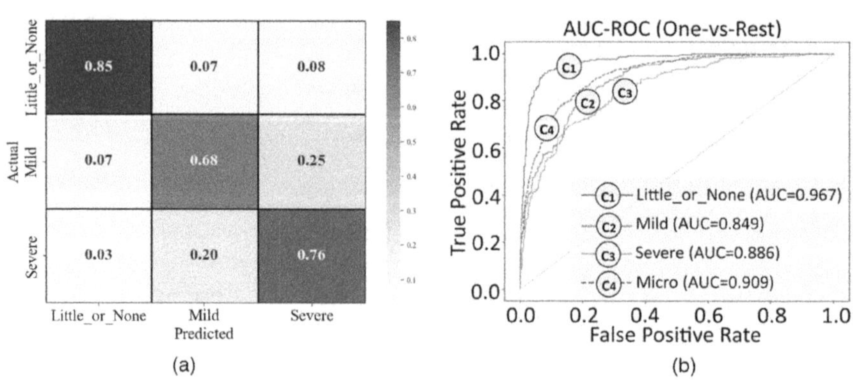

FIGURE 9.4 Evaluation of MobileNetV2 on disaster damage classification: (a) class-level performance via normalized confusion matrix, and (b) discriminatory capability via ROC curves with AUC scores.

confusion, with 25% of its samples being misclassified as Severe. AUC-ROC curves confirm these findings, showing robust discrimination with AUC values of 0.967 for Little_or_None, 0.886 for Severe, and 0.849 for Mild. The overall micro-averaged AUC of 0.909 demonstrates MobileNetV2's strong class-separation capability, outperforming VGG19 across the board.

In summary, MobileNetV2 delivers more balanced recognition across all three categories, with particularly strong results for Little_or_None and Severe damage. While confusion between Mild and Severe persists, the improved $F1$-scores and higher AUC values highlight MobileNetV2's superior discriminative power over VGG19.

9.5.1.3 EfficientNet-B2

The classification report (Table 9.4) for EfficientNet-B2 shows further gains in performance, with a weighted $F1$-score of 0.7715, the highest among the models evaluated so far. The Little_or_None class achieves an excellent $F1$-score of 0.8829, backed by high recall (0.8991) and precision (0.8673). For the Severe category, the model records an $F1$-score of 0.7571, which is slightly stronger than MobileNetV2, while the Mild class maintains stable though moderate performance with an $F1$-score of 0.6827. These results highlight EfficientNet-B2's effectiveness in balancing across all three categories.

The normalized confusion matrix and AUC-ROC curves (Figure 9.5) confirm these trends. The matrix shows that Little_or_None cases are most reliably classified,

TABLE 9.4
Classification Report: EfficientNet-B2

Models	Classes	Precision	Recall	$F1$-Score
EfficientNet-B2	Little_or_None	0.8673	0.8991	0.8829
	Mild	0.6872	0.6783	0.6827
	Severe	0.7643	0.7500	0.7571
	Weighted avg	0.7709	0.7723	0.7715

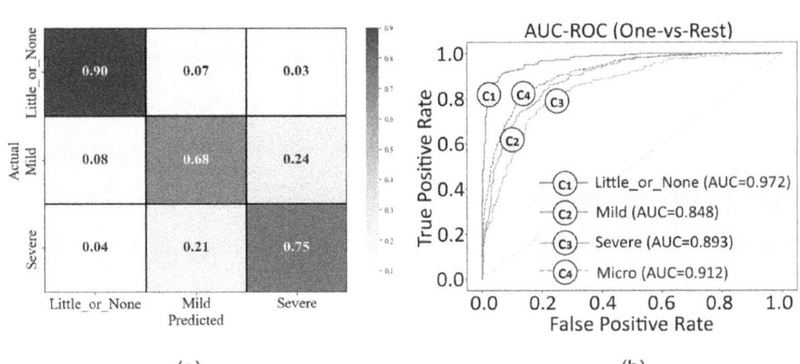

FIGURE 9.5 Evaluation of EfficientNet-B2 on disaster damage classification: (a) class-level performance via normalized confusion matrix and (b) discriminatory capability via ROC curves with AUC scores.

with 90% correct predictions and only minimal misclassification. The Severe class also benefits from robust recognition, with 75% accuracy, though 21% of Severe samples are misclassified as Mild, showing residual confusion between higher-damage classes. The Mild class continues to present challenges, with 24% of its samples being misclassified as Severe. In terms of discrimination, EfficientNet-B2 achieves outstanding AUC values: 0.972 for Little_or_None, 0.893 for Severe, and 0.848 for Mild, with a strong micro-averaged AUC of 0.912. These scores indicate a reliable capacity to distinguish between categories even in the presence of class overlaps.

In summary, EfficientNet-B2 delivers the most balanced and consistent performance so far, surpassing both VGG19 and MobileNetV2 in weighted $F1$ and class-wise AUC values. While challenges remain in distinguishing Mild from Severe, its superior precision–recall balance and high discriminative ability make it a strong candidate for disaster damage classification tasks.

9.5.1.4 Xception

The classification report (Table 9.5) for Xception reveals the strongest performance so far, with a weighted $F1$-score of 0.7853. The model demonstrates excellent recognition of the Little_or_None category, reaching an $F1$-score of 0.8975 with high recall (0.9037) and precision (0.8914). The Severe class also benefits considerably, with an $F1$-score of 0.7715, while the Mild category records a moderate yet improved $F1$-score of 0.6951, slightly higher than that observed with EfficientNet-B2. These results indicate that Xception maintains a high level of class balance while excelling in both low- and high-damage scenarios.

The normalized confusion matrix and AUC-ROC curves (Figure 9.6) further illustrate these outcomes. The matrix shows that Little_or_None cases are very reliably identified, with 90% correctly classified and minimal misclassification. The Severe category is also well captured, with 79% accuracy, though 19% of Severe instances are confused with Mild, mirroring earlier models' challenges in this boundary. The Mild class remains the most difficult, with 25% of Mild samples misclassified as Severe. Nevertheless, the ROC curves highlight Xception's superior discriminative power, achieving AUCs of 0.975 for Little_or_None, 0.889 for Severe, and 0.856 for Mild, along with an overall micro-averaged AUC of 0.913. These values confirm the model's strong separation capabilities across all classes.

In summary, Xception outperforms the previously tested models in both weighted $F1$ and AUC metrics. While confusion between Mild and Severe persists, Xception

TABLE 9.5
Classification Report: Xception

Models	Classes	Precision	Recall	$F1$-Score
Xception	Little_or_None	0.8914	0.9037	0.8975
	Mild	0.7176	0.6739	0.6951
	Severe	0.7563	0.7873	0.7715
	Weighted avg	0.7850	0.7863	0.7853

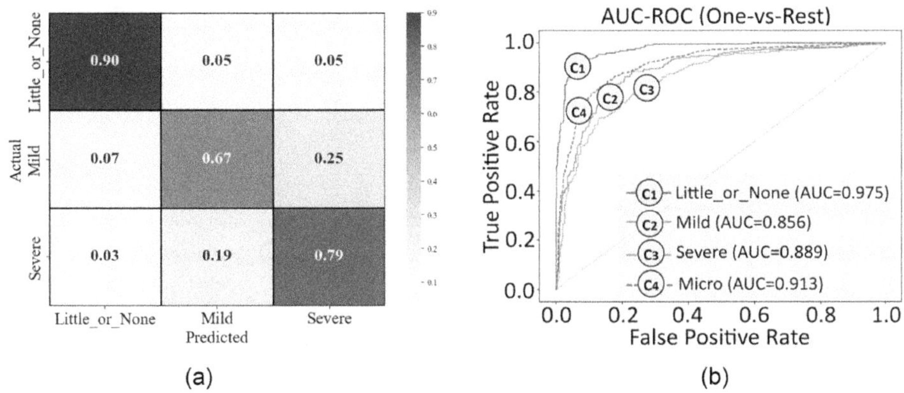

FIGURE 9.6 Evaluation of Xception on disaster damage classification: (a) class-level performance via normalized confusion matrix and (b) discriminatory capability via ROC curves with AUC scores.

demonstrates the most balanced and effective classification performance so far, particularly excelling in identifying both Little_or_None and Severe damage levels with high reliability.

9.5.1.5 Swin-Small

The classification report (Table 9.6) for Swin-Small demonstrates the strongest performance among all models, with a weighted $F1$-score of 0.8085. The model achieves outstanding results in the Little_or_None class, securing an $F1$-score of 0.9149 with balanced precision (0.9171) and recall (0.9128). For the Severe category, Swin-Small records an $F1$-score of 0.7985, the best so far, while the Mild class, though still the most challenging, reaches an $F1$-score of 0.7193, showing clear improvements compared to earlier models. These results reflect the model's superior ability to handle both minority and majority classes effectively.

The normalized confusion matrix and AUC-ROC curves (Figure 9.7) provide further evidence of Swin-Small's strengths. The confusion matrix highlights robust performance, with Little_or_None samples classified correctly 91% of the time and Severe instances achieving 81% correct predictions, the highest accuracy for this class across all models. While some overlap persists—notably 18% of Severe cases misclassified as Mild, and 23% of Mild samples predicted as Severe—the extent of

TABLE 9.6
Classification Report: Swin-Small

Models	Classes	Precision	Recall	$F1$-Score
Swin-Small	Little_or_None	0.9171	0.9128	0.9149
	Mild	0.7257	0.7130	0.7193
	Severe	0.7257	0.8060	0.7985
	Weighted avg	0.8085	0.8087	0.8085

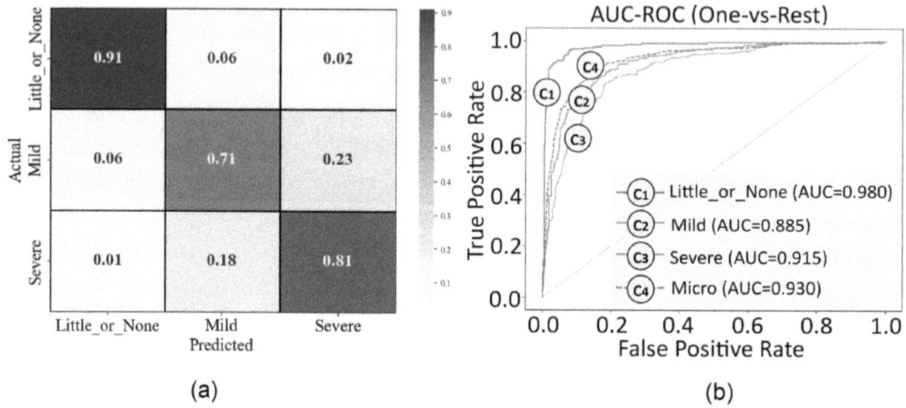

FIGURE 9.7 Evaluation of Swin-Small on disaster damage classification: (a) class-level performance via normalized confusion matrix and (b) discriminatory capability via ROC curves with AUC scores.

misclassification is reduced compared to earlier models. The ROC curves confirm Swin-Small's superior discriminative power, reporting AUCs of 0.980 for Little_or_None, 0.915 for Severe, and 0.885 for Mild, with an impressive micro-averaged AUC of 0.930, the highest observed in this study.

In summary, Swin-Small outperforms all other evaluated models, achieving the highest weighted *F*1-score and micro-averaged AUC. Its strong balance across classes, combined with reduced confusion between Mild and Severe, highlights the transformer-based architecture's superior capacity for disaster damage classification.

The comparative evaluation (Table 9.7) shows a clear progression in performance from VGG19 (weakest baseline) to Swin-Small (state-of-the-art). All models perform reliably for the Little_or_None class, but the Mild category remains the most challenging due to overlap with Severe. Notably, Severe detection improves substantially, with *F*1 rising from 0.5485 (VGG19) to 0.7985 (Swin-Small). Overall, Swin-Small achieves the highest weighted *F*1 (0.8085) and micro-AUC (0.930), confirming the

TABLE 9.7
Comparative Performance of Five Deep Learning Models on Disaster Damage Classification

Model	***F*1-Score**				**AUC**			
2–5 (lr)6–9	Little_or_None	Mild	Severe	Weighted avg	Little_or_None	Mild	Severe	Micro
VGG19	0.7706	0.5685	0.5485	0.6226	0.912	0.747	0.771	0.820
MobileNet	0.8645	0.6857	0.7468	0.7630	0.967	0.849	0.886	0.909
EfficientNet	0.8829	0.6827	0.7571	0.7715	0.972	0.848	0.893	0.912
Xception	0.8975	0.6951	0.7715	0.7853	0.975	0.856	0.889	0.913
Swin	0.9149	0.7193	0.7985	0.8085	0.980	0.885	0.915	0.930

The table reports per-class F1-scores and AUC values, along with weighted average F1 and micro-averaged AUC.

superiority of transformer-based architectures, while MobileNetV2 offers a competitive trade-off for efficiency-critical scenarios.

Although these quantitative metrics establish clear gains in classification accuracy and discriminative ability, they do not reveal how the models reach their predictions. To bridge this gap, the next subsection employs Grad-CAM-based explainability, providing visual insights into the influential regions that guide model decisions and complementing numerical results with interpretable evidence.

9.5.2 Grad-CAM-Based Explainability: Transparency Achieved across Deep Models

9.5.2.1 VGG19: Capturing Highly Influential Region

As shown in Figure 9.8, the Grad-CAM heatmap highlights the regions influencing VGG19's decision in disaster severity classification. The model primarily attends to inundated ground and structural features, indicating that predictions are driven by meaningful disaster-related cues. This enhances interpretability and provides confidence that VGG19's decision-making aligns with human intuition.

9.5.2.2 MobileNetV2

As shown in Figure 9.9, the Grad-CAM visualization focuses on the flooded areas and structural damage around the house when predicting the Severe category. This indicates that MobileNetV2 relies on semantically relevant features, thereby reinforcing its credibility and trustworthiness in disaster assessment tasks.

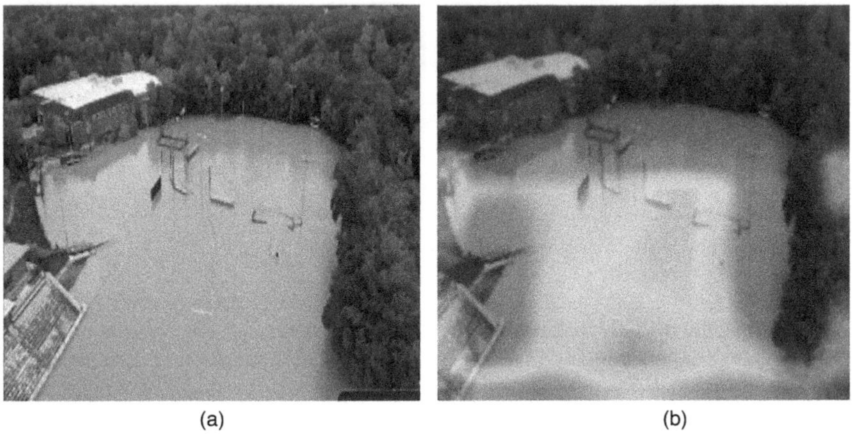

FIGURE 9.8 Grad-CAM-based explainability for VGG19 in disaster severity classification (a) original flood image with ground-truth label Severe, and (b) corresponding heatmap highlighting salient regions that influenced the model's decision (Predicted: Severe, confidence = 0.91).

FIGURE 9.9 Grad-CAM-based explainability for MobileNetV2 in disaster severity classification (a) original flood image with ground-truth label Severe, and (b) corresponding heatmap highlighting salient regions that influenced the model's decision (Predicted: Severe, confidence = 0.70).

FIGURE 9.10 Grad-CAM-based explainability EfficientNet in disaster severity classification (a) original flood image with ground-truth label Severe, and (b) corresponding heatmap highlighting salient regions that influenced the model's decision (Predicted: Severe, confidence = 0.99).

9.5.2.3 EfficientNet

As shown in Figure 9.10, the Grad-CAM heatmap highlights the severely affected zones of the flooded scene, confirming that EfficientNet's predictions are informed by critical disaster evidence. The interpretability provided by Grad-CAM ensures that the model's focus remains aligned with human-understandable disaster severity indicators.

FIGURE 9.11 Grad-CAM-based explainability for Xception in disaster severity classification (a) original flood image with ground-truth label Severe, and (b) corresponding heatmap highlighting salient regions that influenced the model's decision (Predicted: Severe, confidence = 1.0).

9.5.2.4 Xception

As shown in Figure 9.11, the Grad-CAM explanation emphasizes water-logged regions and damaged surroundings, which strongly contribute to the model's classification. This demonstrates that Xception is effectively attending to disaster-specific features, supporting both accurate prediction and transparency in decision-making.

9.5.2.5 Some More Cases of Model Precision in Capturing Highly Influential Regions

We highlight additional qualitative examples where the models effectively captured critical regions in disaster imagery through Grad-CAM visualization. These cases emphasize how the models attend to semantically important areas such as people at risk or severely damaged infrastructures, thereby validating their interpretability and practical utility in disaster response scenarios (Figure 9.12).

9.5.3 Overall Result Comparison

As summarized in Table 9.8, the transformer-based Swin-Small yields the best aggregate performance with a weighted $F1 = 0.8085$, outperforming Xception (0.7853), EfficientNet-B2 (0.7715), MobileNetV2 (0.7630), and VGG19 (0.6226). Class-wise, Little_or_None is consistently the easiest peaking at 0.9149 $F1$ with Swin-Small, whereas Mild remains the hardest (0.5685–0.7193 across models). The Severe class shows strong gains, improving from 0.5485 (VGG19) to 0.7985 (Swin-Small). Overall, Swin-Small delivers an absolute +0.1859 ($\approx$30%) weighted-$F1$ improvement over the VGG19 baseline and a +0.0232 gain over the best CNN (Xception), underscoring the advantage of modern transformer architectures. These findings recommend Swin-Small for deployment when accuracy is critical, with targeted efforts still needed to boost Mild-class recognition (see Table 9.8).

FIGURE 9.12 Illustrative examples of Grad-CAM visualizations showing the models ability to capture highly influential regions in disaster-related images. Subfigures (a) and (c) present the original disaster images labeled as severe, while (b) and (d) highlight the corresponding Grad-CAM heatmaps where critical regions of attention are precisely localized.

TABLE 9.8
Result Comparison

Models	Classes	Precision	Recall	*F*1-Score
VGG19	Little_or_None	0.7295	0.8165	0.7706
	Mild	0.5301	0.6130	0.5685
	Severe	0.6311	0.4851	0.5485
	Weighted avg	0.6286	0.6271	0.6226
MobileNetV2	Little_or_None	0.8810	0.8486	0.8645

(Continued)

TABLE 9.8 (*Continued*)
Result Comparison

Models	Classes	Precision	Recall	*F*1-Score
	Mild	0.6933	0.6783	0.6857
	Severe	0.7295	0.7649	0.7468
	Weighted avg	0.7640	0.7626	0.7630
EfficientNet-B2	Little_or_None	0.8673	0.8991	0.8829
	Mild	0.6872	0.6783	0.6827
	Severe	0.7643	0.7500	0.7571
	Weighted avg	0.7709	0.7723	0.7715
Xception	Little_or_None	0.8914	0.9037	0.8975
	Mild	0.7176	0.6739	0.6951
	Severe	0.7563	0.7873	0.7715
	Weighted avg	0.7850	0.7863	0.7853
Swin-Small	Little_or_None	0.9171	0.9128	0.9149
	Mild	0.7257	0.7130	0.7193
	Severe	0.7257	0.8060	0.7985
	Weighted avg	0.8085	0.8087	0.8085

9.6 CHALLENGES

Despite the increasing use of social media images for disaster damage assessment, several formidable challenges hinder the development of reliable and ethical automated systems. One of the primary issues is the presence of noise and irrelevance in the collected data. During a disaster, an enormous volume of images is shared on platforms such as Twitter, Facebook, and Instagram. However, many of these images are unrelated to actual damage. They may include memes, symbolic content, or personal photos that do not contribute to situational awareness. Others might be reposted from past events or sourced from unrelated disasters, leading to false context. Additionally, some images are of poor visual quality—blurred, underexposed, or heavily edited—which complicates accurate analysis. This abundance of irrelevant or low-quality images introduces noise into the dataset, reducing the performance of classification or severity estimation models. Addressing this requires robust preprocessing pipelines capable of filtering for relevance, as well as advanced multimodal techniques that combine visual cues with accompanying text or metadata.

Another major challenge is the lack of labeled data, which is particularly problematic for DL approaches. Annotating disaster-related images with appropriate damage severity labels—such as mild, moderate, or severe—requires both time and expert domain knowledge. The manual annotation process is costly and cannot be easily scaled, especially in real-time scenarios. Moreover, label imbalance is a common issue; severe damage cases, which are most critical to detect, are often underrepresented in datasets. There is also ambiguity in how different annotators interpret the same image, which introduces inconsistency in labels. Further complicating this problem is the domain shift: a model trained on one type of disaster (e.g., earthquakes) may not generalize well to others (e.g., floods or wildfires) due to differences in visual patterns and damage characteristics. To overcome these limitations, researchers are exploring approaches such as self-supervised learning, which can leverage unlabeled data, as well as few-shot and active learning techniques to optimize the use of limited annotations. Synthetic data generation using GANs is also being explored to augment underrepresented classes.

A third significant concern is the ethical and privacy implications associated with using user-generated content from social media. Many images shared during disasters contain identifiable individuals, private property, or sensitive locations. Using such content without consent raises serious privacy issues and may violate data protection laws such as the General Data Protection Regulation (GDPR) or the California Consumer Privacy Act (CCPA). Furthermore, individuals who share these images often do so to seek help or raise awareness, not expecting that their content will be used for computational analysis or published in research. There are also concerns about algorithmic bias and fairness: models may perform better in urban or affluent areas with higher social media penetration while underrepresenting rural or marginalized communities. These disparities can lead to unequal attention and aid distribution during emergencies. Ethical use of social media data necessitates rigorous adherence to platform terms of service, anonymization of sensitive data, transparent documentation of methodologies, and, where necessary, institutional ethics review. Building equitable and privacy-conscious damage assessment systems requires a deliberate and principled approach to data collection and model deployment.

In summary, while social media images offer a rich and timely source of information for disaster damage assessment, their effective use is hindered by noise and irrelevance, scarcity of annotated data, and critical ethical and privacy considerations. Addressing these challenges is essential for developing robust, fair, and responsible AI systems for disaster response.

9.7 FUTURE DIRECTIONS

To overcome the challenges associated with disaster damage assessment using social media images, future research must adopt a multi-pronged approach that integrates technological advancement, data governance, and interdisciplinary collaboration. One promising direction lies in the development of advanced multimodal models that can jointly analyze visual and textual information to improve the contextual understanding of social media posts. For instance, combining image features with captions, hashtags, geotags, or user metadata through transformer-based architectures can significantly enhance damage relevance estimation and severity classification. The use of pre-trained multimodal models such as CLIP and BLIP, fine-tuned for disaster contexts, offers potential for robust cross-modal reasoning even in data-scarce settings.

Another key area is the adoption of self-supervised and semi-supervised learning paradigms, which reduce reliance on extensive labeled datasets. These approaches can learn rich representations from large volumes of unlabeled disaster-related content and adapt to new disaster scenarios with minimal supervision. Moreover, domain adaptation techniques and meta-learning frameworks should be explored to enable models trained on one type of disaster (e.g., hurricanes) to generalize to others (e.g., wildfires or floods). Synthetic data generation using GANs or diffusion models can help balance class distributions, particularly for rare and severe damage categories, which are often underrepresented in real-world datasets.

Real-time damage assessment also remains a vital but underexplored research area. Future systems must be capable of streaming and analyzing large-scale social media data in real time while filtering for geospatial and temporal relevance. Integrating edge computing, cloud-based architectures, and scalable data pipelines will be necessary to ensure timely processing and response. At the same time, model efficiency and interpretability must not be overlooked. Incorporating explainable AI (XAI) techniques such as Grad-CAM, LIME, and SHAP into visual damage assessment pipelines can aid disaster response teams in understanding model predictions and building trust in automated systems.

From a data governance perspective, the formulation of privacy-preserving frameworks for social media image analysis is paramount. Techniques like differential privacy, federated learning, and on-device processing can minimize data exposure while maintaining model performance. Collaboration with legal scholars, ethicists, and humanitarian organizations is essential to ensure compliance with regulations such as GDPR and to develop ethical guidelines tailored to crisis informatics. Additionally, the creation of open, diverse, and representative benchmark datasets—curated with attention to inclusivity and annotation quality—will facilitate fair evaluation and comparison of models across the research community.

Lastly, fostering interdisciplinary partnerships between AI researchers, emergency responders, geographers, and policymakers will be crucial for grounding technological innovations in real-world applications. Co-designing systems with end-users and conducting field-based validation studies will help bridge the gap between algorithmic performance and practical utility. As climate-related disasters become more frequent and severe, the integration of robust AI-based damage assessment tools into disaster risk management frameworks will play an increasingly important role in saving lives, optimizing resource allocation, and enhancing societal resilience.

9.8 CONCLUSION

This chapter demonstrated how social media images serve as a critical yet underexplored resource for disaster damage assessment. By integrating advances in DL and transfer learning, the study established that automated approaches can significantly enhance the speed, accuracy, and transparency of post-disaster evaluations compared to traditional methods reliant on satellite or ground reports. Through a comparative evaluation of multiple architectures—including VGG, MobileNet, EfficientNet, Xception, and Swin-Small—the results confirmed a steady progression in performance, with transformer-based models such as Swin-Small achieving state-of-the-art outcomes. Beyond accuracy, the incorporation of Grad-CAM provided valuable interpretability, ensuring that model predictions are not only effective but also trustworthy and aligned with disaster-specific visual cues. Despite these advances, key challenges remain, particularly in handling noisy social media data, limited annotated datasets, ethical concerns, and issues of model generalizability across disaster types.

Addressing these limitations calls for multimodal fusion, self-supervised learning, privacy-preserving frameworks, and interdisciplinary collaboration.

Overall, the findings highlight that explainable, transfer learning–based AI systems hold substantial promise for supporting emergency responders in real time, enabling more equitable resource allocation, and ultimately strengthening disaster resilience. As disasters become increasingly frequent and severe, the integration of robust, transparent AI solutions into disaster risk management frameworks will be indispensable for saving lives and mitigating socio-economic impacts.

REFERENCES

1. Muhammad Imran, Firoj Alam, Umair Qazi, Steve Peterson, and Ferda Ofli. Rapid damage assessment using social media images by combining human and machine intelligence. *arXiv preprint arXiv:2004.06675*, 2020.
2. Dat Tien Nguyen, Ferda Ofli, Muhammad Imran, and Carlos Castillo. Damage assessment from social media imagery data during disasters. In *Proceedings of the 26th International Conference on World Wide Web Companion*, pages 1501–1506, Sydney, Australia, 2017.
3. Haiyan Hao and Yan Wang. Leveraging multimodal social media data for rapid disaster damage assessment. *International Journal of Disaster Risk Reduction*, 51:101760, 2020.
4. Firoj Alam, Ferda Ofli, and Muhammad Imran. Processing social media images by combining human and machine computing during crises. *International Journal of Human–Computer Interaction*, 34(4):311–327, 2018.
5. Huili Huang, Danrong Zhang, Anastasiya Masalava, Max Mahdi Roozbahani, Nimisha Roy, and J David Frost. Enhancing the fidelity of social media image data sets in earthquake damage assessment. *Earthquake Spectra*, 41(3):87552930251335649, 2025.
6. Shilpa Gite, Shruti Patil, Biswajeet Pradhan, Madhuri Yadav, Sneha Basak, Arundarasi Rajendra, Abdullah Alamri, Kaustubh Raykar, and Ketan Kotecha. Analysis of multimodal social media data utilizing vit base 16 and gpt-2 for disaster response. *Arabian Journal for Science and Engineering*, 50:19805–19823, 2025.
7. Nisha P Shetty, Yash Bijalwan, Pranav Chaudhari, Jayashree Shetty, and Balachandra Muniyal. Disaster assessment from social media using multimodal deep learning. *Multimedia Tools and Applications*, 84:18829–18854, 2024.
8. Hongruixuan Chen, Jian Song, Olivier Dietrich, Clifford Broni-Bediako, Weihao Xuan, Junjue Wang, Xinlei Shao, Yimin Wei, Junshi Xia, Cuiling Lan, et al. Bright: A globally distributed multimodal building damage assessment dataset with very-high-resolution for all-weather disaster response. *arXiv preprint arXiv:2501.06019*, 2025.
9. Soroor Shekarizadeh, Razieh Rastgoo, Saif Al-Kuwari, and Mohammad Sabokrou. Deep-disaster: unsupervised disaster detection and localization using visual data. In *2022 26th International Conference on Pattern Recognition (ICPR)*, pages 2814–2821. Montreal, QC, Canada, IEEE, 2022.
10. David Hanny, Sebastian Schmidt, and Bernd Resch. Active learning for identifying disaster-related tweets: A comparison with keyword filtering and generic fine-tuning. In *Intelligent Systems Conference*, pages 126–142. Switzerland, Springer, 2024.
11. Xiaoyu Zhu, Junwei Liang, and Alexander Hauptmann. Msnet: A multilevel instance segmentation network for natural disaster damage assessment in aerial videos. In *Proceedings of the IEEE/CVF Winter Conference on Applications of Computer Vision*, pages 2023–2032, 2021.
12. Naina Said, Kashif Ahmad, Nicola Conci, and Ala Al-Fuqaha. Active learning for event detection in support of disaster analysis applications. *Signal, Image and Video Processing*, 15(6):1081–1088, 2021.

13. Lakshmi S Gopal, Rekha Prabha, Hemalatha Thirugnanam, Maneesha Vinodini Ramesh, and Bruce D Malamud. Leveraging social media for managing natural hazard disasters: A critical review of data collection strategies and actionable insights. *EGUsphere*, 2024:1–61, 2024.
14. Jorge Mario Lozano, Elliot Nichols, J David Frost, and Iris Tien. Spatial and temporal evolution of post-disaster data for damage assessment of civil infrastructure systems. *Geomatics, Natural Hazards and Risk*, 14(1):2250531, 2023.
15. Nina SN Lam, Michelle Meyer, Margaret Reams, Seungwon Yang, Kisung Lee, Lei Zou, Volodymyr Mihunov, Kejin Wang, Ryan Kirby, and Heng Cai. Improving social media use for disaster resilience: challenges and strategies. *International Journal of Digital Earth*, 16(1):3023–3044, 2023.
16. Sefa Mızrak. Public's social media use during the kahramanmaraş earthquakes on 6 february 2023. *International Journal of Disaster Risk Reduction*, 108:104541, 2024.
17. Gaurav Chachra, Qingkai Kong, Jim Huang, Srujay Korlakunta, Jennifer Grannen, Alexander Robson, and Richard M. Allen. Detecting damaged buildings using real-time crowdsourced images and transfer learning. *Scientific Reports*, 12(1):8968, May 2022.
18. Isabelle Bouchard, Marie-Ève Rancourt, Daniel Aloise, and Freddie Kalaitzis. On transfer learning for building damage assessment from satellite imagery in emergency contexts. *Remote Sensing*, 14(11), 2022.
19. Amna Asif, Shaheen Khatoon, Md Maruf Hasan, Majed A Alshamari, Sherif Abdou, Khaled Mostafa Elsayed, and Mohsen Rashwan. Automatic analysis of social media images to identify disaster type and infer appropriate emergency response. *Journal of Big Data*, 8(1):83, 2021.
20. Sourasekhar Banerjee, Yashwant Singh Patel, Pushkar Kumar, and Monowar Bhuyan. Towards post-disaster damage assessment using deep transfer learning and gan-based data augmentation. In *Proceedings of the 24th International Conference on Distributed Computing and Networking, ICDCN'23*, New York, page 372–377, 2023. Association for Computing Machinery.
21. Alexey Dosovitskiy, Lucas Beyer, Alexander Kolesnikov, Dirk Weissenborn, Xiaohua Zhai, Thomas Unterthiner, Mostafa Dehghani, Matthias Minderer, Georg Heigold, Sylvain Gelly, et al. An image is worth 16x16 words: Transformers for image recognition at scale. *arXiv preprint arXiv:2010.11929*, 2020.
22. Karen Simonyan and Andrew Zisserman. Very deep convolutional networks for large-scale image recognition. *arXiv preprint arXiv:1409.1556*, 2014.
24. Andrew G Howard et al. Mobilenets: Efficient convolutional neural networks for mobile vision applications. In *arXiv preprint arXiv:1704.04861*, 2017.
23. François Chollet. Xception: Deep learning with depthwise separable convolutions. In *Proceedings of the IEEE Conference on Computer Vision and Pattern Recognition (CVPR)*, pages 1251–1258, Honolulu, HI, USA, 2017.
25. Mingxing Tan and Quoc V Le. Efficientnet: Rethinking model scaling for convolutional neural networks. In *International Conference on Machine Learning*, pages 6105–6114, Long Beach, California, 2019.
26. Ze Liu, Yutong Lin, Yue Cao, Han Hu, Yixuan Wei, Zheng Zhang, Stephen Lin, and Baining Guo. Swin transformer: Hierarchical vision transformer using shifted windows. In *Proceedings of the IEEE/CVF International Conference on Computer Vision*, pages 10012–10022, 2021.
27. Ramprasaath R Selvaraju, Michael Cogswell, Abhishek Das, Ramakrishna Vedantam, Devi Parikh, and Dhruv Batra. Grad-cam: Visual explanations from deep networks via gradient-based localization. In Proceedings of the IEEE International Conference on Computer Vision, pages 618–626, Venice, Italy, 2017.

10 Understanding and Detecting Online Homophobia and Transphobia in Low-Resource Indian Languages

A Focus on Kannada and Telugu

Sanjana Kavatagi, Shankar Biradar, and Rashmi Rachh

10.1 INTRODUCTION

Language is incredibly powerful. It can uplift, inspire, and unite, but it can also hurt, exclude, and perpetuate prejudices. In the contemporary digital age, with social media sites and internet forums as the platforms for hate speech, the identification of homophobia and transphobia in written words is more than a technical challenge; it is a moral obligation. In human rights, gender equality, and hate speech online debates, homophobia and transphobia are regarded as the prominent issues by most people [1]. Most people have the tendency to mix these words with personal gender prejudices. To many, however, these words may seem abstract or thought to be individual opinions. Homophobia and transphobia, however, are deeply rooted forms of social discrimination. They are more than personal opinions because they are influenced by ideologies, historical exclusion, and structural inequalities.

The term Homophobia is commonly inferred as fear, dislike, discomfort, or distrust of the individuals who identify in the categories such as lesbian, gay, or bisexual [2]. It is a prejudice in the form of hostility such as insults, slurs, or violence to more covert forms such as ridicule, avoidance, stereotyping, or moral disapproval. The term homophobia is even more damaging when employed as sarcasm for conveying one's own viewpoint with long-term emotional or psychological effects [3].

 DOI: 10.1201/9781003611110-10

Transphobia refers to, in a relevant way, negative views, fear, or prejudice against individuals who do not fit the gender binary or whose gender identity is different from the sex they were given at birth [4]. This includes transgender women and men of male and female, non-binary, genderfluid, and other identities who do not fit the traditional male–female binary. Transphobia is typically expressed by misgendering, identity denial, denial of service access or places, and, in some cases, violence threats or harassment [5].

Facing scenarios in everyday life delineated by bias from persons, unwillingness to accept another's opinion, sarcasm, reinforcement of harmful stereotypes, media, policymaking—all the way through to the absence of queer voices in educational content—are the necessary opposites that those who carry the hate of homophobia and transphobia have to come into view. These acts of exclusion and non-acceptance are mostly called microaggressions, which accumulate over time and contribute to the mental distress of persons [6]. In the Indian context, the complexity of these forms of discrimination is heightened by the fact that they are often unrecognized. In many households, discussions about gender and sexuality are viewed as taboo, leading to a lack of open conversations. This silence fosters the spread of misinformation and shame, particularly for young people who are exploring their identities. When queer individuals try to express who they are, they may be met not only with rejection but also with punishment, ridicule, or spiritual condemnation. These experiences are not only emotionally damaging, but can also leave lasting scars [7].

Further, homophobia and transphobia are shaped by intersecting factors such as caste, class, religion, and geography. For instance, a queer-identifying person from an oppressed caste living in a rural setup may be excluded on several levels, first on the basis of their sexual orientation and second on the basis of their social status. This notion of intersectionality suggests that queerphobia cannot be addressed in a vacuum; it must be understood in the light of deeper social dynamics favoring some kinds of identities and devaluing others [8]. Such assumptions are often legitimized by institutions such as discriminatory laws, lack of adequate legal status, biased media portrayal, and insufficient safe spaces in schools, workplaces, and public spaces. Until 2018, India had criminalized same-sex relations under Section 377 of the Indian Penal Code [9]. While the Supreme Court invalidated this law, its effects still linger in social attitudes, family life, and online discourse. Further, homophobia and transphobia involve more than hate; they entail the denial of dignity, identity, and belonging. These aspects are redefining self-conception as well as external perceptions. In the virtual social media world, where claims of identity and diversity are met with immediate societal response, understanding these forms of discrimination is more vital than ever before.

10.1.1 The Spread of Queerphobia on Social Media Platforms

The rise of social media platforms has changed interaction among people, with their expression being a key point of interest and a community being formed around it. Social media platforms such as Twitter (now X), YouTube, Facebook, Instagram, and TikTok have provided avenues for marginalized voices to be heard. In these spaces and on these platforms, individuals can gain visibility, support, affirm a community, and establish a connection with one another. But with power comes the other side of the coin, as these very platforms have become breeding grounds for hateful [10,11], homophobic and transphobic rhetoric [12], mostly unmonitored and heavily disseminated. The insidious feature of queerphobia on the internet is that it is often not said at all. Instead, it is couched in humor, hidden in memes, veiled in religious cover, or presented as a concern about cultural or moral norms. These less overt forms are as damaging as outright abuse, often more so, in that they are more difficult to identify and to respond to.

The spread of such content is enabled by four key mechanisms that are intrinsic to how social media platforms function:

- **Anonymity and Virality**: One of the primary reasons social media enables hate speech is the anonymity it offers. Individuals can post offensive or threatening content without revealing their real identity. This anonymity emboldens users to say things they may never express in offline, face-to-face interactions [13]. When content is emotionally provocative, sensational, or controversial, it tends to go viral. Platform algorithms tend to reward engagement, likes, shares, and comments, rather than truth or civility. As a result, hateful or inflammatory content often receives more reach than respectful discourse, spreading rapidly across networks [14].
- **Coded Language and Memes**: In many cases, homophobia and transphobia are not articulated in direct slurs. Instead, users employ coded language, slang, regional euphemisms, sarcasm, or even popular culture references to express discriminatory views without triggering moderation filters [15]. Memes, in particular, serve as powerful vehicles for hate. A meme mocking someone's appearance, gender expression, or relationship can circulate widely, receive thousands of shares, and perpetuate stereotypes while escaping platform scrutiny due to its "humorous" framing. In the Indian context, especially in languages like Kannada, these coded expressions often include **regional terms that carry derogatory meanings** but are not flagged because they're not part of mainstream hate speech lexicons [16].
- **Polarized Communities and Echo Chambers**: On the other hand, the important factor is the creation of digital echo chambers. Social media platforms are merely the scenario in which the user picks his own bubble of information, encompassing those who share views similar to his own. Here is hateful rhetoric that is accepted and even rewarded. Examples of such rhetoric often demonize LGBTQ+ identities as "unnatural," "Western imports," or threats to tradition and religion, and members of the group find support for any of the views expounded [17]. Traditionally, these communities discourage dissent; they shame allies, thereby creating hostile environments online for queer users.
- **Algorithmic Amplification of Hate**: The design of social media algorithms plays a significant role in determining what content gets visibility. Unfortunately, posts that provoke outrage or strong emotions are often

ranked higher, regardless of whether they are harmful. This means that a comment that attacks a transgender individual or questions the legitimacy of same-sex relationships might receive more attention than a thoughtful post on LGBTQ+ rights [18,19].

In effect, platform design favors engagement over safety. In the absence of effective content moderation, particularly in non-English languages, harmful content stays up longer, spreads further, and shapes public opinion [20–22].

10.1.2 Impact of Online Homophobia and Transphobia

The impact of digital platforms reaches far beyond the system. For members of the LGBTQ+ community, social media is a multifaceted and at times arbitrary space. It is, on one side, avenues to foster relationships, see people within the community, and get support. On the other, it is a medium through which the same ingrained social bias is being amplified, legitimized, and perpetuated. If such baseless biases are allowed to propagate unchecked, then they pose serious threats not only to the people who are afflicted directly but also to the entire social fabric.

10.1.2.1 Individual-Level Harms

The internet has a twofold function for lesbian and gay persons that live in conservative areas, rural lands, or family households, which do not accept gender and sexual diversity. It may appear as a safe space where one can go for octopus and affirmations, where identities are discovered and experiences are shared. That sense of security crumbles whenever an attack of hate is launched. Continual exposure to online homophobia and transphobia has deep emotional consequences for the victims. When users read slurs or derogatory comments with invalidating messages day after day, it starts shaping how they view themselves and their role in society [23].

Common individual-level harms include:

- **Mental Health Distress**: Queer individuals exposed to online abuse often report higher levels of anxiety, depression, loneliness, and suicidal ideation. Studies have shown that even brief exposure to online hate can trigger trauma responses, especially in youth and adolescents [24].
- **Social Withdrawal**: The mechanism begins to pan out with many users withdrawing from the online platform, avoiding discussions, or deleting posts that voice identity. For those in environments that are isolated already, this means reduced access to supportive communities.
- **Self-Censorship and Identity Suppression**: People may avoid using pronouns, hashtags, and even fully expressing themselves online in order to mask their identity and avoid becoming a target. This leads to further diminishing and losing one's genuine opinion.

These feelings are not one-off responses; rather, they are cumulative. Every dismissal, sarcastic meme, and invalidating message serves as a reminder that a person's existence is under continuous scrutiny, mocked, or condemned. For a lot of users, especially those who express themselves in regional languages or subtle and coded language, the trauma often goes unaddressed due to lack of legal or institutional protections.

10.1.2.2 Societal Harms

The impact of online queerphobia goes beyond personal harm. If not moderated, this form of digital vitriol fuels a broader societal atmosphere that preconditions and legitimizes exclusion and discrimination while undermining civic and democratic engagement.

Here are some of the most important examples of social-level damage:

- **Normalization of Hate**: Online queerphobia's most destructive consequence is its increasing normalization. The presence of disdainful and mocking utterances—especially on comments sections beneath posts highlighting LGBTQ+ achievements—without challenge serves to normalize and popularize these opinions. In the long run, this blurs the distinction between free speech and hate speech, in particular with the youth who unfortunately soak these ideas without active engagement [12].
- **Radicalization of Online Communities**: Online communities, especially within private groups or forums, tend to become radicalized and reinforce transphobic and homophobic ideologies. Often starting with "moral" or "cultural" rationalizations, these groups degenerate to a level where they vilify or remove humanity from LGBTQ+ persons. Sometimes, participants from these online communities move from digitally harassing individuals to physically assaulting them, group doxxing, or coordinated online harassment [25].
- **Influence on Policy and Law**: Online narratives shape public opinion—and public opinion, in turn, influences policymaking. In regions where queerphobic content dominates the digital conversation, politicians may avoid supporting LGBTQ+ rights to maintain popularity. Worse, they may use online sentiment to justify discriminatory laws or stall progressive legislation, such as marriage equality, anti-discrimination protections, or gender identity rights [25].
- **Intersectional Consequences**: It is also important to recognize that these harms are not experienced equally by all LGBTQ+ individuals. A Dalit transgender woman in Karnataka, for example, may face multiple layers of discrimination—based on not only gender identity but also caste, language, and geography. Online queerphobia intersects with casteism, sexism, classism, and religious bias, further deepening social inequality [26].

This kind of digital influence has been observed not only in India but across the world where organized online disinformation campaigns target LGBTQ+ individuals and sway public debates. When policymakers and leaders are either influenced by fear of such backlash, the progress of LGBTQ+ rights can be delayed or reversed.

10.1.3 Global and Indian Perspectives

While the fight for LGBTQ+ rights has gained visibility across the world, the digital landscape remains a space of contradiction. On one hand, there has been unprecedented progress in terms of legal recognition, advocacy, and public support in various regions. On the other hand, online queerphobia continues to thrive revealing a significant gap between policy and practice.

10.1.3.1 The Global View

Over the last ten years, many Western democracies have accepted same-sex marriage and adoption rights for queer couples, along with workplace discrimination protections. However, these legislative milestones during the last decade don't seem to ensure cyberspace safety for LGBTQ+ individuals. Countries like the United States, the United Kingdom, and parts of Europe still experience rampant anti-queer content on social media, masked as political discourse or free speech. For instance, certain studies from Gay and Lesbian Alliance Against Defamation (GLAAD) and the Human Rights Campaign suggest that hate speech targeting LGBTQ+ communities has risen sharply after 2016. Online hate during election periods and post-anti-LGBTQ+ legislative debates has skyrocketed too [27]. The rise seems to be pegged as part of the ongoing political divide where queer rights are hot button issues used to advance polarizing agendas.

These governments have openly adopted anti-LGBTQ+ policies, such as declaring "LGBT-free zones" or limiting gender recognition rights, while state-controlled or sympathetic media platforms spread queerphobic content with little accountability. Online spaces in these regions are often hostile to LGBTQ+ expression, with social media algorithms amplifying hate speech under the guise of religious and national values [28]. These global patterns reveal that legal protections alone are not enough. Without active moderation, digital literacy, and inclusive platform design, the internet continues to reflect and magnify the underlying prejudices of society.

10.1.3.2 The Indian Context

In India, the journey toward LGBTQ+ inclusion has been spearheaded by both historical legal milestones and persistent social conservatism. A major milestone was achieved in September 2018, when the Supreme Court read down Section 377 of the Indian Penal Code, de facto decriminalizing same-sex relations. This ruling was a historic one, state-level endorsement of queer rights and individual freedom [29]. However, legal reform has not guaranteed societal acceptance. In many parts of India, especially in semi-urban and rural areas, LGBTQ+ identities are still viewed through a lens of shame, secrecy, or deviance. Religious teachings, traditional gender roles, and dominant political narratives often frame queerness as "unnatural," "Western," or morally corrupt. This complex reality is reflected in Kannada-language social media spaces, where contradictory narratives coexist. On the one hand, some users and influencers advocate for equality, share personal stories, and create supportive online communities. On the other hand, regional slang, coded slurs, spiritual dogma, and nationalistic slogans are used to undermine, ridicule, or outright reject LGBTQ+ identities.

Posts that present queer people as a threat to culture or "Bharatiya values" receive high engagement and are often shared without consequence [16].

Another layer of complexity comes from the limitations of current content moderation systems. Most major platforms like YouTube, X (formerly Twitter), Instagram, and Facebook have policies that prohibit hate speech, but their effectiveness is severely restricted in Indian languages. Indic languages like Kannada are often excluded from early-stage AI model training, meaning that slurs and discriminatory phrases go undetected or unflagged.

Additionally, platform-specific community guidelines rarely include LGBTQ+-specific examples tailored to regional contexts. As a result, even when content is reported, moderation teams may lack the cultural understanding required to evaluate its harm. Furthermore, enforcement of policies in non-English content is often delayed, inconsistent, or completely absent, leading to a digital environment where harmful content remains accessible for longer periods, increasing its impact.

10.1.4 The Need for Detection and Monitoring

As social media remakes the manner in which people communicate, represent themselves, and participate in public discourse, it is also a space where discrimination, prejudice, and hate speech flourish immensely, often with no repercussions. For LGBTQ+ people, especially in areas where being queer is unacceptable or politically risky, the internet both draws and threatens them. In that scenario, finding and tracking anti-queer material on social media is not just a technological challenge; it is also a moral and social imperative.

Discovering homophobic and transphobic content can minimize the damage caused to individuals and groups, particularly those who are more exposed because of their age, place, or social standing. Discovering the type of content is crucial beyond filtering; it is making online environments safer, advocating equal rights online, and providing a foundation for inclusive policies and technical measures.

1. **Prevention of Harm**: Perhaps the most direct advantage of effective detection mechanisms is the safeguarding of vulnerable users from being exposed to offending material over and over again. Studies indicate that repeated exposure to hate speech, slurs, and dehumanizing language may result in psychological trauma, particularly among queer youth, as well as individuals who are in the process of establishing their gender or sexual identity [24]. Platforms that can identify and remove such content proactively before it spreads or trends can minimize the emotional toll on users and reduce the risk of cyberbullying, social withdrawal, anxiety, and self-harm. Timely intervention can break cycles of digital victimization and foster safer online communities.
2. **Ensuring Accountability**: Detection is also closely tied to accountability. Without clear records or mechanisms to identify queerphobic posts, abusive users often go unchecked. Monitoring tools, especially those embedded with machine learning (ML) and natural language processing (NLP) techniques,

can support flagging, reporting, and moderation efforts.[1,2] These tools can assist not only social media companies but also community groups, NGOs, and civil society organizations in documenting hate, demanding platform action, and protecting users in real time. Moreover, detection allows for transparent auditing of platforms. If platforms claim to protect queer users, then real-time monitoring data can either verify those claims or expose moderation failures, forcing them to improve their practices.

3. **Data-Driven Policymaking**: Another crucial role of detection is its contribution to evidence-based policymaking. Often, policy debates around LGBTQ+ rights in digital spaces suffer from a lack of quantitative data. By deploying detection systems that can log the volume, frequency, and context of hate speech, stakeholders can present concrete evidence to support better regulation, legal protection, and community guidelines. For example, insights from automated monitoring tools can be used to influence platform-level moderation strategies, government digital safety laws, funding allocation for mental health services for queer users, and legislative advocacy for marginalized linguistic groups. Such data also helps debunk narratives that minimize or deny the existence of queerphobia, especially in regions where LGBTQ+ lives are systematically invisible.
4. **Promoting Language Justice**: One of the less-discussed but critically important aspects of queerphobic content detection is language justice. The internet in India is multilingual, with users expressing themselves in Kannada, Tamil, Bengali, Hindi, and dozens of other languages. Most existing hate speech detection tools are trained primarily in English or Hindi, leading to under-detection or total neglect of regional language abuse. When homophobia or transphobia is expressed in Kannada, for example, it often involves region-specific slurs, cultural metaphors, and linguistic code-mixing that standard filters fail to catch. Without detection tools tailored to these contexts, millions of users are left unprotected, and the abuse they face remains undocumented. Developing detection models for these languages is a step toward linguistic inclusion in AI, ensuring that all communities, not just those in dominant language groups, receive equal protection online.
5. **Empowering Advocacy and Activism**: Finally, detection systems can empower researchers, activists, and policymakers by generating actionable data. This data helps map patterns of digital hate, understand emerging forms of coded or meme-based queerphobia, and mobilize campaigns to counter disinformation and stigma. For example, if a spike in transphobic memes follows a news report on gender rights, detection tools can help advocacy groups respond faster, design targeted awareness campaigns, and hold media platforms accountable. In essence, technology becomes a tool for resistance and advocacy, not just surveillance.

---

1 What is Azure Content Moderator? - Azure AI services | Microsoft Learn

2 AI Content Moderation Tool | Utopia Analytics

10.1.5 Common Sources of Homophobic and Transphobic Content

Homophobic and transphobic discourse online is rarely accidental or isolated; it often arises from recognizable digital sources and social structures that perpetuate stigma, misinformation, and hostility toward LGBTQ+ individuals. Identifying these sources is crucial for developing effective detection systems, shaping moderation strategies, and crafting counter-narratives that challenge digital hate. While this problem is global in scale, its manifestations are deeply influenced by regional cultures, linguistic practices, and ideological influences. In the Indian context and particularly in Kannada-speaking online spaces, homophobic and transphobic content is embedded in both mainstream discourse and fringe communities. This section highlights key digital sources from which queerphobic content typically originates.

10.1.5.1 Comment Sections under Queer-Themed Content

One of the most visible sources of queerphobic content is the comment sections of online platforms such as YouTube, Facebook, Instagram, and Twitter (now X). Videos, articles, or posts that feature LGBTQ+ characters, news stories, Pride parades, or personal testimonies often attract hateful responses. These comments range from outright abuse and ridicule to calls for censorship or conversion therapy. For example, a Kannada-language news report covering a Pride event may receive replies suggesting that such events "spoil culture," "go against nature," or "deserve to be banned" [16,18]. Because these comments are embedded within fast-moving, high-volume threads, they frequently escape moderation, especially when expressed using code-mixed or sarcastic language.

10.1.5.2 Religious or Political Influencers

Another major source of online queerphobia comes from religious leaders and political figures who have large followings on social media. In some cases, these influencers make direct statements against LGBTQ+ rights, framing queerness as sinful, unnatural, or immoral. In other cases, their rhetoric is more subtle, drawing on spiritual, nationalist, or cultural arguments to delegitimize gender and sexual diversity [16,26]. In Karnataka and other parts of India, such messages are often delivered in vernacular languages, increasing their reach among rural and semi-urban populations. When these figures post videos, reels, or tweets that express disapproval of LGBTQ+ issues, their followers frequently amplify the message, creating waves of secondary hate through shares, duets, stitched content, and reaction memes.

10.1.5.3 Regional Meme Pages and Humor Accounts

Meme culture plays a powerful role in shaping public opinion—especially among younger audiences. Regional meme pages on platforms like Instagram, Facebook, or Telegram are frequently used to create and share content that ridicules queer identities. These memes often target gender non-conforming appearances, mannerisms, voice tones, or relationship dynamics, presenting them as comic material rather than real human experiences. In Kannada meme culture, specific stereotypes are repeatedly circulated—such as portraying transgender women as beggars or mocking effeminate men with slurs. Since this content is disguised as humor, it is less likely to be reported or moderated, even though it reinforces dangerous attitudes. This normalization of hate under the banner of comedy desensitizes audiences and contributes to the idea that LGBTQ+ lives are fair game for mockery.

10.1.5.4 Nationalist and "Traditionalist" Groups

In recent years, some nationalist digital communities have constructed queer identities as threats to Indian culture, family values, and moral integrity. These groups often equate LGBTQ+ activism with foreign influence, labeling it as a "Western agenda" meant to destroy "Bharatiya sanskriti" (Indian tradition). Queerphobia, in these spaces, is repackaged as patriotism or cultural defense. Such rhetoric can be seen in Kannada-language forums, WhatsApp groups, or YouTube channels that discuss topics like "the decay of society," "values in danger," or "protecting children from Western influence." These narratives provide a cultural and moral justification for exclusion, encouraging digital communities to reject or harass queer individuals in the name of national pride.

10.1.5.5 Coordinated Trolling and Harassment Communities

There are also loosely organized online communities that focus on targeted trolling. They often target LGBTQ+ users, activists, and allies. These groups may operate through Reddit threads, Discord servers, or private Telegram channels. Members share content for mass reporting, mass commenting, or group ridicule. These raids are often planned, especially when a queer user shares something that attracts attention. The goal is to intimidate, shame, or silence that person. This kind of digital mobbing is especially harmful because it is ongoing, targeted, and emotionally draining for the victim. Such communities thrive in environments where moderation is weak, especially in regional languages. Code-mixed Kannada-English posts using disguised slurs or layered sarcasm often evade content filters, making these spaces highly unsafe.

10.1.5.6 The Language Challenge

Across all these sources, one common barrier to detection is language and cultural specificity. When queerphobic content appears in Kannada or in Kannada-English mixed text, it bypasses standard moderation tools, which mainly rely on English or Hindi data. These expressions often include local slurs, phonetic spellings, context-specific memes, or culturally rooted metaphors that need careful interpretation. Without systems that understand language and culture, homophobic and transphobic content keeps spreading without resistance. This shows the urgent need for tools that can detect this content based on local language use. These tools should be able to recognize hate, even when it appears indirect, humorous, or symbolic.

10.2 RELATED WORK

Growing internet usage of hate speech has become a serious concern, particularly when such speech is targeted toward marginalized communities, including the LGBTQ+. Homophobic and transphobic speech, in particular, is one specific form of hate speech that is explicitly directed at individuals or groups due to their gender identity or sexual orientation. In contrast to common abusive language, which typically involves the application of profane, obscene, or socially unacceptable words, hate speech is characterized by its focused nature and its capacity to result in discrimination, exclusion, or even violence being perpetrated against specific social groups [30,31].

Due to the availability of free expression in social media, these have become places for such hateful rhetoric thrives. Various empirical studies have been conducted by psychologists and media researchers to highlight the harmful psychological and social consequences of these homophobic and transphobic contents online [32,33]. With the research, it was found that these the impacts are profound for members belonging to the communities like LGBTQ+ who are already a part of the social abuse [51]. Continuous exposure to such speech has been associated with an increase in the stress level, anxiety, and depression among the groups of LGBTQ+ communities, which contributes to a hostile digital environment, undermining the mental health and overall sense of safety [34]. The impact of such hate speech can, however, have effects that move beyond the individual sphere [52]. Acceptance of such language within society itself creates intergroup conflict and undermines efforts at social cohesion and inclusiveness. It has been observed by researchers that repeated exposure to toxic language on the internet can lead to desensitization on the part of broader audiences, reducing their tolerance for discriminatory language and, ironically, increasing tolerance for prejudiced or hateful statements. It does more than reduce public sympathy; it also provides a vehicle through which the incremental radicalization of opinion toward minority groups can take place.

Within the context of internet communication, "toxicity" is a core concept frequently employed to refer to messages or interactions that elicit violent or destructive reactions. Toxic posts are likely to disrupt discussions, increase conflict, and foster a climate of hostility. However, one should also be aware that feelings of toxicity will differ considerably within different social groups and cultural environments because of differences in linguistic norms, usage, and tolerance threshold [35]. Despite such differences, there is a general agreement that the overall toxicity of internet content is increasing, and this trend is seriously threatening.

The prevalence of hate speech aimed at marginalized groups, such as the LGBTQ+ group, has the potential to increase the possibility of social radicalization and can make discriminatory action the norm in online communities. If social media is a common platform for such discussion, people are most likely to be motivated to spread discrimination and violence in online communities. Furthermore, the free circulation of homophobic and transphobic content on online platforms is not just a matter of public health but also a challenge to democratic values and social cohesion.

Internet hate speech, especially transphobia and homophobia, has been of particular interest to researchers from a broad array of disciplines. Researchers have examined the subject from a range of theoretical and conceptual perspectives, such as social psychology, human–computer interaction (HCI), political science, and regulatory and legal models [36]. Interdisciplinary research provides valuable insights about the motivations, effects, and social consequences of target aggression against LGBTQ+ populations in online contexts [54].

The profound psychological damage that online homophobic and transphobic messages can inflict, yet most computational work focuses narrowly on ML- and NLP-based detection [47,50]. Although multilingual transformers such as mBERT and XLM-RoBERTa, along with domain-tuned models like HateBERT, have advanced the automatic flagging of hateful content, they still struggle with the subtle, culture-specific, and implicit expressions of queerphobia that have been found to be especially harmful [57]. This mismatch between social science evidence of harm and the technical limits of current models signals a critical research gap. The problem is even sharper for low-resource Dravidian languages such as Kannada and Telugu [55], where context-aware, culturally attuned detection systems are lacking, leaving at-risk communities exposed. Integrating insights from psychological impact studies with computational techniques could yield NLP tools that are not only accurate but also effective in mitigating the real-world harm of digital queerphobia.

From a computational point of view, identifying and annotating LGBTQ+ hate speech in large online conversations is an enormous undertaking, especially because such material can be subtle and context-dependent. Hate speech tends to be hidden, ironic, coded, or filler language, making it hard to identify using simple keyword strategies. In addition, the malleability of slang, cultural references, and the use of multiple languages in social media posts makes the task even harder. Recent developments in ML and NLP have witnessed spectacular advancements in detecting hate speech automatically. Specifically, the architecture of deep learning models, e.g., convolutional neural networks (CNNs), recurrent neural networks (RNNs), and transformer-based models like Bidirectional Encoder Representation (BERT), has enabled systems to better abstract the complex syntactic and semantic characteristics of hateful language [37,38]. Such models have achieved promising results in detecting hate speech that takes the form of implicit or veiled hostility, which is often encountered in internet homophobia and transphobia.

The study aims to tackle the problem of identifying abusive and offensive language in Tamil–English code-mixed social media posts, a particularly demanding, low-resource scenario within the Dravidian language family. They curate a dedicated dataset and benchmark a spectrum of classifiers, from traditional ML algorithms to modern deep learning and transformer architectures. The transformer-based systems markedly outperform the classical models, largely because they cope better with the code-mixing, transliteration, and unconventional spellings that typify this text [58]. By doing so, the study extends the literature on hateful and offensive speech in Dravidian languages and illustrates the need for computational methods specifically tuned to multilingual, low-resource contexts.

Various ML methods have varying methodologies and definitions in using the term "hate." These definitions are shaped by the data employed, the goals of the research, and the particular community or problem being tackled. The standard test datasets and case studies, annotated corpora, or shared tasks for online toxicity are most often employed for training and testing these models [39]. However, the absence of agreement on definitions and labeling schemes between datasets most often leads to generalizability and replicability hindrances.

Apart from data-driven approaches, theoretically grounded models have come to the fore, combining lexicon-based and embedding-based models. These techniques rely on pre-existing theory from psychology or sociolinguistics to build hate speech detection systems that are not only reactive but also explanatory. For instance, lexicon-based systems rely on diligently curated hate-related word lists, often augmented with contextual rules, while embedding-based models employ word or sentence embeddings such as Word2Vec, GloVe, or BERT's contextual embeddings to represent semantic relationships as well as the nuances of discourse-level meaning. Such techniques are especially important for the identification of targets of hate speech, an essential component of the study of online homophobia and transphobia [40].

The efforts to deal with the challenges of hate speech detection, especially in online scenarios, have mainly pursued the route of text classification techniques based on ML. In computer terms, these solutions range far and wide, from the traditional supervised learning settings to the newer paradigms such as transfer learning and deep learning [41]. Classical ML methods, henceforth, have usually been placed for binary and multiclass classification of hate speech, with Support Vector Machine (SVM), Naïve Bayes, and Logistic Regression being just some examples. Despite their success in many structured text classification problems, these so-called shallow classifiers may fall short at capturing the more subtle semantic aspects of discourse online.

Keyword-based classification was among the earliest methods used for hate speech detection. In these methods, the presence of certain lexicons associated with hateful or offensive language served as signals to flag harmful content. These methods are computationally efficient and easy to implement; however, they do not fare well in scenarios outside the laboratory. This is so because not all hateful speech explicitly contains offensive keywords. On the contrary, most of the hate speech encountered online—almost all of it—against homosexuals and transgenders is expressed implicitly. That is done through coded language, sarcasm, irony, or euphemisms, all interfering with any keyword-based detection technique employed on the surface [42].

Moreover, many of the words traditionally identified as hate indicators can be context-dependent. For example, terms like "swine" or "trash" may not always be used in a hateful sense; they can appear in benign or even humorous contexts. Misinterpreting such usage often leads to a high rate of false positives, which reduces the reliability and usability of these detection systems in practice [43].

Another major limitation in the existing literature is the lack of cross-platform generalization. While a few exploratory studies attempted to train and evaluate a model on data from various online environments, most research still focuses on single-platform datasets. Hate speech is, however, well documented as existing across multiple social media ecosystems such as Reddit, YouTube, Wikipedia, and Twitter. These platforms vary in user demographics, content formats, as well as community norms that greatly contribute to determining the means of expression and perception of hate speech. This implies that models trained on data from one platform often do not fare well when applied to another, which bears out the need for stronger cross-platform training and evaluation mechanisms.

To support this line of research, various annotated datasets have been created. These datasets address different facets of hateful and abusive communication, such as general hate speech identification [16,53], racial bias detection within hate speech [45], counter-hate or anti-hate speech classification [46], hierarchical labeling of hate categories [16], abusive and profane language recognition [48], cyberbullying detection [49], and offensive language identification [17].

Despite the availability of these datasets, challenges remain in standardizing labeling practices, ensuring linguistic and cultural diversity, and handling code-mixed or multilingual data, particularly in under-resourced languages. These limitations are even more pronounced when addressing identity-based hate speech, such as homophobia and transphobia, which often require nuanced annotation frameworks and sensitive ethical considerations.

While significant advancements have been made in NLP to detect binary gender prejudice, hate speech, and abusive or offensive language, the specific subdomain focusing on online harm directed toward LGBTQ+ individuals remains comparatively underexplored. A notable gap exists in understanding how language functions in perpetuating or resisting homophobia and transphobia, especially from a computational and sociolinguistic standpoint.

A study [44] investigated linguistic patterns in LGBTQ+ writing in Chinese. Their results showed that classic types of text-based gender identification techniques are unsuccessful when faced with the complex and fluid expressions of gender and identity that queer discourse entails. This implies that gender prediction models, which are generally trained on the so-called binary assumptions, are hence unable to accommodate non-binary or nuanced gender expressions common within LGBTQ+ communities.

Similarly, Arango et al. [48] have undertaken a cross-linguistic study in creating emotion lexicons in Croatian, Dutch, and Slovene. These lexicons have been used to identify online content that was associated with socially undesirable speech, particularly hate speech on migration or LGBTQ issues. Their approach provides proof of the capabilities of lexicon-based tools in the detection of discriminatory language but also is reflective of the cultural nuances within which sensitive identity issues need to be situated.

Despite such efforts, research in the field remains in its infancy, presenting a number of drawbacks. One of the most problematic issues is the inconsistency that persists with respect to definitions and the categorization of who constitutes offensive language in the sexual orientation and gender identity framework. Offensive language is variously called abusive, toxic, hateful, harmful, or violent in this literature; nevertheless, each term can engender different associations in different geographic-linguistic contexts. This semantic ambiguity renders the concrete modeling of classifiers particularly difficult, since, often, its interpretation relies upon the subjective view of an annotator shaped by her cultural, social, or ideological perspective.

Additionally, the detail needed to differentiate between homophobia and transphobia is frequently absent from current datasets. Automated systems frequently fail to recognize subtle forms of racism, such as coded slurs, stereotypical representations, and microaggressions. The dearth of inclusive training data that can accurately reflect the variety of LGBTQ+ speech and experiences, particularly in non-English or low-resource languages, exacerbates this set of drawbacks.

Furthermore, the attitudes prevailing in society at the time of data collection will permeate both the content of and the interpretation given to the homophobia embedded within such datasets. Hence, issues about temporal bias are raised, and the annotated datasets risk obsolescence given that socio-political changes occur at a very rapid rate. Language considered transgressive in one era or culture may lose its impact in another, necessitating regular updates to training data and annotation guidelines.

10.2.1 Gaps Existing in the Literature

Although there are methodologies to analyze social media data for detecting homophobia and transphobia, gaps still exist in the literature regarding the identification of homophobic and transphobic content on social media:

- **Scarcity of Annotated Corpora**: Current datasets are heavily skewed toward high-resource languages; comprehensive corpora for low-resource regional languages, including the Dravidian family, are still lacking.
- **Complexity of Code-Mixing**: Social media users routinely blend English with their native language, creating code-mixed text that follows neither language's grammar nor syntax. This hybrid structure complicates both linguistic analysis and automated processing.
- **Limited Suitability of Pre-trained Models**: Most pre-trained encoders were trained on high-resource or cross-lingual data but were not explicitly adapted to code-mixed text, diminishing their effectiveness in this setting.
- **Lack of Fine-Grained Analysis**: Existing studies rely on sentence-level classification; none identify the precise hateful span or supply model rationales, which hampers interpretability and the collection of legally admissible evidence.

10.3 METHODOLOGY

This study utilizes an annotated dataset developed in a previous study [56] containing Kannada and Telugu social media comments to detect homophobic and transphobic hate speech. We fine-tuned three pre-trained transformer-based models, such as mBERT, HateBERT, and XLM-RoBERTa, by adding a Bidirectional Long Short-Term Memory (BiLSTM) layer on top of each model's encoder. This BiLSTM layer was used to enhance the models' ability to capture sequential dependencies and contextual cues, which are particularly important for identifying implicit or nuanced expressions of queerphobia. The final classification layer outputs binary labels for hate and non-hate content. The models were trained and evaluated using standard metrics such as accuracy and $F1$-score to assess their effectiveness in low-resource language settings.

10.3.1 Dataset Description

For the identification of homophobia and transphobia contents, we have utilized the corpus developed in a previous study[3] in a low-resource setting. The authors have

[3] CodaLab - Competition

TABLE 10.1
Label Distribution for the Kannada and Telugu Corpuses

Language	Homophobia	Transphobia	None of the Categories	Total
Telugu	4,119	3,823	4,987	12,929
Kannada	3,949	4,058	6,369	14,376

curated the datasets for Telugu and Kannada, along with Gujarati, which were meticulously compiled using a combined approach of manual collection techniques and a specialized YouTube comment scraper. This is the first dataset that has been curated for a low-resource setting that has focused on identifying homophobia and transphobia. The author has followed a rigorous annotation method to maintain high quality and accuracy following the guidelines as discussed. A team of three individuals, consisting of two males and one female, was involved in the annotation process; all the members had a postgraduation degree with proficiency in the language. Labels such as Homophobia, Transphobia, and None of the categories were used to label each comment. In this work, we have considered the Kannada and Telugu datasets. The dataset description is shown in Table 10.1.

For Telugu, the data include 4,119 homophobic, 3,823 transphobic, and 4,987 neutral comments. The Kannada data include 3,949 homophobic, 4,058 transphobic, and 6,369 neutral comments. Both data were split into training, test, and development sets. Telugu data were split into 9,050 training, 1,939 testing, and 1,940 development examples (total 12,929), and Kannada data consisted of 10,063 training, 2,156 testing, and 2,157 development examples (total 14,376). These data were utilized in the CodaLab competition as part of the LT-EDI-2024 shared task at EACL.

In terms of linguistic context, Telugu is a Dravidian language predominantly spoken in Andhra Pradesh and Telangana, with over 80 million native speakers. Kannada, also a Dravidian language, is the official language of Karnataka and is spoken by over 40 million people. Both languages embody India's linguistic diversity and cultural richness. The development of these datasets plays a critical role in fostering more inclusive online spaces by supporting the creation of tools aimed at detecting, monitoring, and mitigating homophobic and transphobic content in social media. These resources can be thought of as linguistic treasure maps, annotated with precision and insight, to uncover hidden pockets of hate speech and better understand the dynamics of online discrimination in Telugu and Kannada discourse.

10.3.2 Preprocessing

The preprocessing of the Kannada and Telugu corpora designed to capture homophobia and transphobia underwent several carefully defined steps to clean and prepare the YouTube comments for training the model. Preliminarily, a language-specific filter was utilized to retain only those comments prominently featuring Kannada or Telugu scripts, satisfying script consistency, and removing unwanted Roman or English entries. The comments were then normalized with normalization of text to

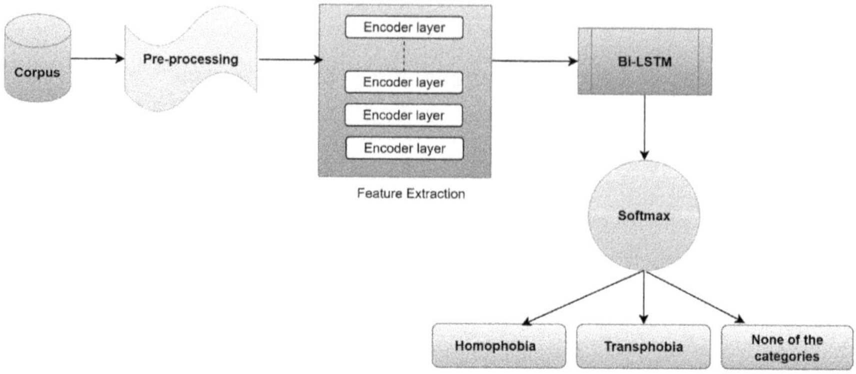

FIGURE 10.1 Architecture pipeline for the identification of homophobia and transphobia.

lowercase, Unicode normalization, removal of character elongation, and normalization of punctuation and numeral system. Non-linguistic artifacts such as HTML tags, URLs, user mentions, and emojis were removed or replaced with textual equivalents when they carried semantic meaning. Tokenization was performed using the built-in tokenizers of transformer models like HateBERT, mBERT, and XLM-RoBERTa, whereas Indic NLP tools were used for additional tokenization for linguistic inspection. Samples with noise, such as those that contained only symbols, were extremely short, or were duplicated, were filtered out to avoid redundancy.

10.3.3 Classification

The architecture of the proposed model is used in Figure 10.1. Three transformer-based models, such as mBERT, HateBERT, and XLM-RoBERTa, were utilized for the proposed work. The experiments on Kannada and Telugu using all the three models were conducted separately. The cleaned and preprocessed text of both Kannada and Telugu were tokenized using the model-specific tokenizers of the respective models. The mBERT model, trained on multilingual Wikipedia data including Kannada and Telugu, generates contextual embeddings capturing structural and syntactic nuances of both languages. These embeddings were further passed to a BiLSTM layer, followed by a softmax layer for classification of the text into any of the three categories, homophobia, transphobia, or none of the categories.

The HateBERT model, trained on English Reddit comments for hate speech detection, utilized its capabilities of abusive language detection in generating the contextual embeddings. These embeddings are passed through BiLSTM layer for capturing bidirectional dependencies and then to the softmax layer for final classification. At last, the XLM-RoBERTa, which has been pre-trained on web data at large scale, fine-tuned on the Kannada and Telugu datasets, is capable of producing rich language-agnostic embeddings. These embeddings were further passed to the BiLSTM and softmax layer for classification of text into Homophobia, Transphobia, and None of the category classes. Each of the three models was trained and tested independently. The hyperparameters used are described in Table 10.2.

TABLE 10.2
List of Hyperparameters

Parameter	Value
Batch size	16
No. of epochs	10
Learning rate	0.001
Optimizer	Adam
Loss function	Categorical cross-entropy

TABLE 10.3
Results Obtained for the Kannada and Telugu Corpuses

		*F*1-Score				
Language	**Model**	**Homophobia**	**Transphobia**	**None**	**Macro *F*1**	**Accuracy**
Kannada	mBERT	0.81	0.82	0.85	0.83	0.84
	HateBERT	0.62	0.60	0.75	0.68	0.67
	XLM-RoBERTa	0.88	0.87	0.89	0.86	0.87
Telugu	mBERT	0.85	0.87	0.89	0.87	0.88
	HateBERT	0.58	0.55	0.72	0.65	0.63
	XLM-RoBERTa	0.90	0.89	0.91	0.89	0.90

10.4 RESULTS AND DISCUSSION

The results obtained from the experiments on the Kannada and Telugu datasets using mBERT, HateBERT, and XLM-RoBERTa demonstrate the comparative effectiveness of multilingual and domain-specific transformer models in detecting *homophobia*, *transphobia*, and *non-hateful* content. *F*1-score and accuracy are used as evaluation parameters. The results obtained are shown in Table 10.3.

For the Kannada data, the best-performing model was XLM-RoBERTa, with a macro *F*1-score of 0.86 and an accuracy of 0.87. This gives an idea of how well this model can generalize through multilingual inputs and develop some contextual nuances in regard to regional languages. The macro *F*1-score and accuracy for mBERT were 0.83 and 0.84, respectively; the model was pre-trained on multiple languages that included Kannada, and it performed better than the task-specific models. HateBERT, on the other hand, despite being trained exclusively on hate speech, gave much lower results (macro *F*1-score: 0.68, accuracy: 0.67), as it is trained purely on English and the resulting transferability issues when applied to Indian languages even after preprocessing.

In the case of Telugu corpus, a similar trend was observed. XLM-RoBERTa outperformed the other two models as in the case of Kannada corpus. With the highest macro *F*1-score of 0.89 and the accuracy of 0.90. mBERT achieved a macro *F*1-score of 0.87 and an accuracy of 0.88. The HateBERT model performed poorly as

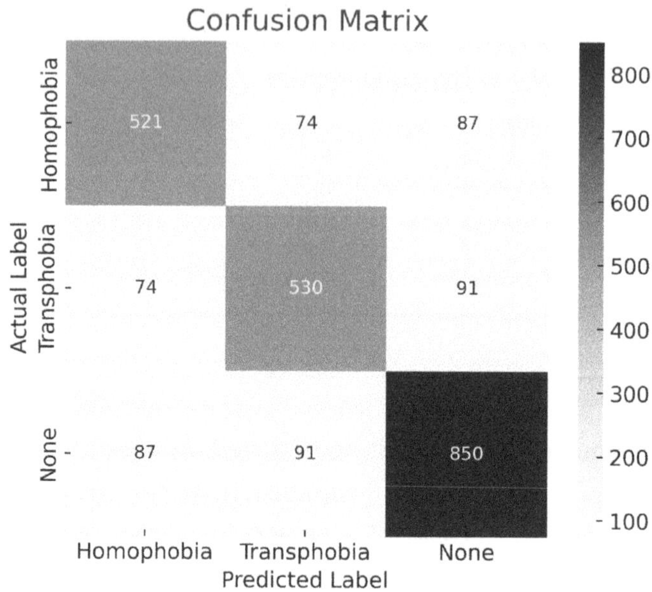

FIGURE 10.2 Confusion matrix for Kannada results.

compared to the other two models, with an $F1$-score of 0.65 and an accuracy of 0.63, indicating its limited capabilities to handle low-resource languages such as Telugu and Kannada despite its domain-specific strengths.

Additionally, these results indicate that multilingual models such as mBERT and XLM-RoBERTa are more effective and reliable for abusive content detection such as homophobic and transphobic contents in low-resource languages such as Kannada and Telugu. This is due to their capabilities to learn cross-lingual representations. Meanwhile, the domain-specific models such as HateBERT require the retraining or adaptation to regional language data to deliver promising results and to match the performance of multilingual counterparts.

The confusion matrices for Kannada results are shown in Figure 10.2; it shows that the model performs well across all three classes, with the highest accuracy for the "None" category. There is noticeable confusion between Homophobia and Transphobia, as well as some misclassification of hateful comments as "None." Figure 10.3 shows the confusion matrix for Telugu results. The confusion matrix for Telugu shows strong classification accuracy across all classes, with particularly high correct predictions for Homophobia and None. Some misclassifications occur between Homophobia and Transphobia, as well as occasional overlap with the "None" category.

The receiver-operating characteristic (ROC) analysis for the Kannada test set underscores the robustness and balance of the XLM-RoBERTa + BiLSTM model (Figure 10.4). All three one-vs.-rest curves, Homophobia (AUC = 0.84), Transphobia (AUC = 0.83), and None (AUC = 0.85), rise sharply toward the upper-left corner before gradually flattening, indicating that the first few threshold settings already recover

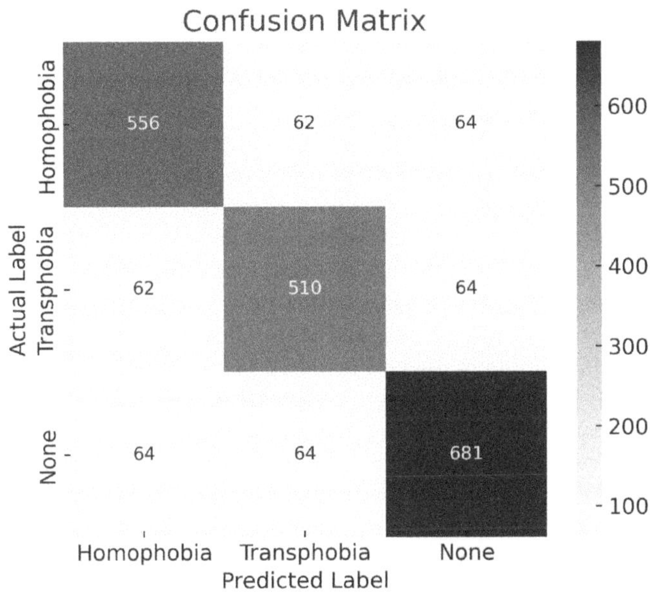

FIGURE 10.3 Confusion matrix for Telugu results.

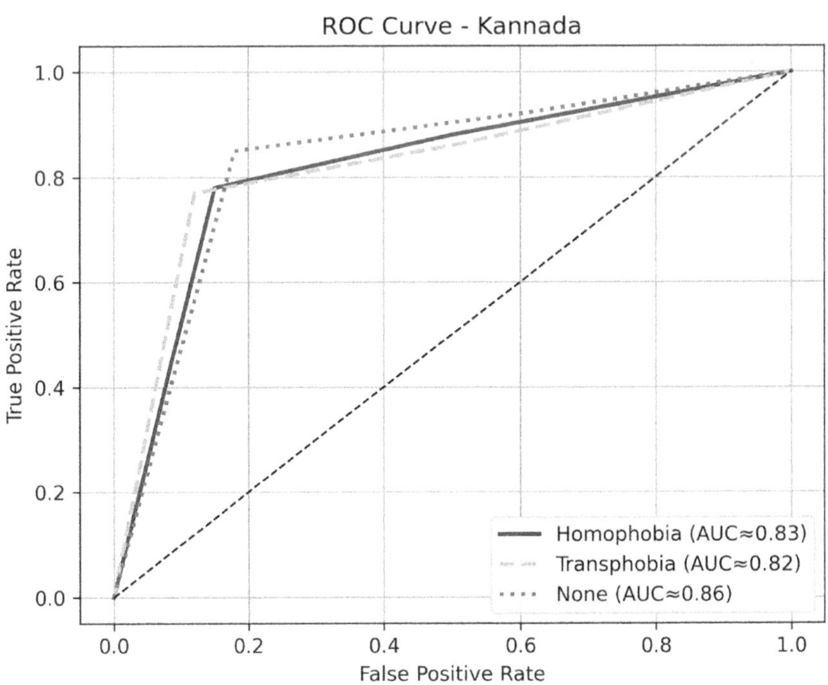

FIGURE 10.4 ROC curve for results on the Kannada corpus.

the bulk of true positives while admitting very few false alarms. The near-overlap of the two hateful classes up to an False Positive Ratio (FPR) of roughly 0.15 reveals that the model distinguishes homophobic and transphobic content with comparable ease, whereas the consistently higher None curve reflects even greater confidence in rejecting benign comments that dominate the corpus. Practically, a conservative threshold yielding an FPR $\leq$ 0.05 still captures about three-quarters of hateful messages, while a more permissive setting (FPR $\approx$ 0.15) boosts recall to about 0.90, which is useful for analyst review queues. The slight plateauing of all curves short of the ideal (TPR = 1) aligns with error analysis insights that sarcasm, rare slurs, and deep contextual cues remain challenging. The ROC profile confirms that our architecture delivers strong discrimination across all three labels and allows flexible threshold selection to balance precision and recall in real-world moderation scenarios.

The ROC curve for the Telugu corpus confirms that the XLM-RoBERTa + BiLSTM model discriminates reliably among the three target labels (Figure 10.5). All class-specific curves climb steeply reaching a true-positive rate above 0.80 and the false-positive rate below 0.10, which signals strong early sensitivity with minimal collateral errors. Area-under-curve values cluster tightly (Homophobia = 0.86, Transphobia = 0.86, None = 0.87), showing that the system treats the two hateful categories almost identically and is even slightly definite when recognizing neutral comments. Such a balanced profile lets practitioners choose thresholds to suit the task: a conservative cut-off (FPR $\approx$ 0.05) captures close to three-quarters of hateful posts, whereas relaxing the threshold (FPR $\approx$ 0.15) pushes recall toward 0.90 for both

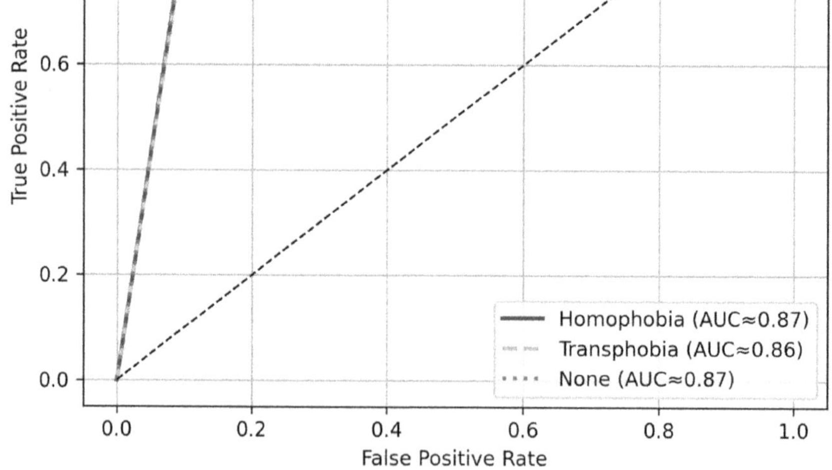

FIGURE 10.5 ROC curve for results on the Telugu corpus.

homophobia and transphobia. The mild flattening of every curve before the ideal (TPR = 1) mirrors the qualitative error analysis, which found sarcasm and rare slurs hardest to catch. The ROC evidence attests that the model offers well-calibrated, robust detection of queerphobic speech in Telugu and can be tuned to balance precision and coverage in real-world moderation pipelines.

10.5 CONCLUSION AND FUTURE SCOPE

The rise of online platforms has significantly amplified the reach of communication but has also turned them into fertile grounds for the proliferation of hate speech, particularly targeting socially vulnerable groups such as the LGBTQ+ community. This chapter examined the spread of queerphobia on social media and the impact of online homophobic and transphobic content. The global and Indian perspectives on these topics were discussed, with an emphasis on the growing need for robust detection mechanisms and continuous monitoring for online platforms. The common sources of transphobic and homophobic content were discussed. Additionally, the unique challenges associated with detecting such content in low-resource languages, specifically Kannada and Telugu, were highlighted. Further, to address these challenges, we conducted experiments aimed at identifying homophobic and transphobic content using pre-trained transformer models. These models included both multilingual representations and task-specific architectures, which were experimented with separately on Kannada and Telugu datasets. Notably, the task-specific model *HateBERT*, despite being fine-tuned for hate speech detection, demonstrated poor performance in both languages. This suggests a limitation in its ability to capture the nuanced linguistic and cultural expressions characteristic of low-resource languages. In contrast, *XLM-RoBERTa*, a multilingual transformer model, achieved better performance across both languages, demonstrating higher $F1$-scores and accuracy. This indicates its relative robustness in handling low-resource linguistic contexts.

Although the transformer-BiLSTM framework yields promising results for Kannada and Telugu homophobia and transphobia detection, its evaluation remains confined to a single, relatively small corpus, offering only partial coverage of platform diversity, code-mixed scripts and Romanized variants. This narrow evidential base, together with the use of general multilingual encoders that lack Dravidian-specific pre-training, restricts the system's capacity to capture subtle, culturally embedded abuse, while the added BiLSTM layer increases computational overhead and thus limits scalability for real-time, large-scale moderation.

Future research should compile expansive, platform-rich corpora that reflect code-mixing, Romanized orthography, and dialectal variation, and pair them with Dravidian-specific transformer models pre-trained on Kannada and Telugu texts. Combining these language-aware encoders with multimodal inputs, conversation context, and lightweight, efficiency-optimized architectures will yield culturally attuned, real-time systems capable of moderating queerphobic content across South-Asian social media platforms.

REFERENCES

1. Kniuraitė, Gabrielė, and Giedrė Paurienė. "The significance of human rights in the context of homophobic and transphobic hate crimes." *Public Security and Public Order* 35 (2024): 171–183.
2. Pirlott, Angela, and Corey L. Cook. "Homophobia." *Encyclopedia of Evolutionary Psychological Science.* Shackelford, Todd K., and Viviana A. Weekes-Shackelford, eds. Encyclopedia of evolutionary psychological science. Cham: Springer International Publishing, 2021. 3795–3802.
3. Tin, Louis-Georges, ed. *The Dictionary of Homophobia: A Global History of Gay & Lesbian Experience.* Vancouver: Arsenal Pulp Press, 2009.
4. Aguirre-Sánchez-Beato, Sara. "Trans Terminology and Definitions in Research on Transphobia: A conceptual review." *Quaderns de Psicologia* 20.3 (2018): 295–305.
5. Colliver, Ben. ""Not the right kind of woman": Transgender women's experiences of transphobic hate crime and trans-misogyny." *Misogyny as Hate Crime.* Routledge, 2021. 213–227.
6. Zhang, Yang Bo, et al. "Adverse childhood experiences, mental health, and resilience in 2SLGBTQIA+ persons: A scoping review." *Adversity and Resilience Science* 4.3 (2023): 211–233.
7. Crawford, Charmaine. "Epistemic Injustice, Sexual Inequality and LGBTQ Realities." *Gender, Sexual Citizenship and Epistemic Injustice in the Caribbean.* Cham: Springer Nature Switzerland, 2025. 39–59.
8. Ward, Nicki. "Social exclusion, social identity and social work: Analysing social exclusion from a material discursive perspective." *Social Work Education* 28.3 (2009): 237–252.
9. Lee, Hyun Jung. "Case Analysis: Non-Criminalization of Same-Sex Relations." *Discrimination Based on Sexual Orientation: Jurisprudence of the European Court of Human Rights and the Constitutional Court of Korea.* Cham: Springer International Publishing, 2022. 187–209.
10. Biradar, Shankar, Sunil Saumya, and Arun Chauhan. "Fighting hate speech from bilingual hinglish speaker's perspective, a transformer-and translation-based approach." *Social Network Analysis and Mining* 12.1 (2022): 87.
11. Kavatagi, Sanjana, and Rashmi Rachh. "A context aware embedding for the detection of hate speech in social media networks." *2021 International Conference on Smart Generation Computing, Communication and Networking (SMART GENCON).* IEEE, 2021. Pune, India
12. Saumya, Sunil, Vanshita Jha, and Shankar Biradar. "Sentiment and Homophobia Detection on YouTube using Ensemble Machine Learning Techniques." *FIRE (Working Notes).* 2022.
13. Barlett, Christopher P., Douglas A. Gentile, and Chelsea Chew. "Predicting cyberbullying from anonymity." *Psychology of Popular Media Culture* 5.2 (2016): 171.
14. Biradar, Shankar, Sunil Saumya, and Arun Chauhan. "Combating the infodemic: COVID-19 induced fake news recognition in social media networks." *Complex & Intelligent Systems* 9.3 (2023): 2879–2891.
15. Hu, Eugene, and Laurel MacKenzie. "Agency within Slurs: An Investigation of Indignant Responses to Slurs on Social Media." (2023).
16. Kavatagi, Sanjana, and Rashmi Rachh. "HASTIKA: Hate speech and target identification in Kannada-English code-mixed text." *Language Resources and Evaluation* 59(2025): 1–46.
17. Balinhas, Daniel. "Bringing critical social psychology to the study of political polarization." *Social and Personality Psychology Compass* 17.1 (2023): e12721.

18. Biradar, Shankar, and Sunil Saumya. "Iiitdwd-shankarb@ dravidian-codemixi-hasoc 2021: mbert based model for identification of offensive content in south indian languages." *arXiv preprint arXiv:2204.10195* (2022).
19. Rachh, Rashmi, Sanjana Kavatagi, and Shridhar Allagi. "Domain Specific Embeddings in RNN Frameworks for Hate Span Detection and Classification." *2023 4th International Conference on Intelligent Technologies (CONIT)*. IEEE, 2024. Huballi, India.
20. Sai, Chava, et al. "Iiitdwd_svc@ dravidianlangtech-2024: Breaking language barriers; hate speech detection in telugu-english code-mixed text." *Proceedings of the Fourth Workshop on Speech, Vision, and Language Technologies for Dravidian Languages.* 2024. Malta.
21. Shankar Biradar, Sunil Saumya, and Arun Chauhan. "mBERT based model for identification of offensive content in south Indian languages." *Working Notes of FIRE 2021-Forum for Information Retrieval Evaluation (online). CEUR.* 2021.
22. Shaik, Zuhair Hasan, et al. "Iiitdwd-zk@ dravidianlangtech-2024: Leveraging the power of language models for hate speech detection in telugu-english code-mixed text." *Proceedings of the Fourth Workshop on Speech, Vision, and Language Technologies for Dravidian Languages.* 2024. Malta.
23. Shaik, Zuhair Hasan, et al. "FeedForward at SemEval-2024 Task 10: Trigger and sentext-height enriched emotion analysis in multi-party conversations." *Proceedings of the 18th International Workshop on Semantic Evaluation (SemEval-*2024*).* 2024. Mexico city, Mexico.
24. Biradar, Shankar, Sunil Saumya, and B. M. Kalpajeet. "Depression clinic: People's mental health prediction using information from online social media networks (OSN)." *International Conference on Computational Intelligence in Communications and Business Analytics.* Cham: Springer Nature Switzerland, 2024. Patna, India.
25. Marwick, Alice, Benjamin Clancy, and Katherine Furl. "Far-right online radicalization: A review of the literature." *The Bulletin of Technology & Public Life* (2022).
26. Ghanea, Nazila. "Intersectionality and the spectrum of racist hate speech: Proposals to the un committee on the elimination of racial discrimination." *Human Rights Quarterly* 35.4 (2013): 935–954.
27. Alfaro, Ange-Marie Hancock. "When Words don't Disappear: An Intersectional Analysis of Hate Speech." *Citizenship on the Edge: Sex/Gender/Race* (2022): 19.
28. Wyers, Katherine, et al. "Identity platforms and anti-LGBTQ+ legislation: Implications for safeguarding personal data." *IFIP Joint Working Conference on the Future of Digital Work: The Challenge of Inequality.* Cham: Springer Nature Switzerland, 2023.
29. Bohra, Shruti. "Decriminalization of Section 377: A Brief Analysis." *Indian JL & Legal Rsch.* 2 (2021): 1.
30. Fortuna, Paula, and Sérgio Nunes. "A survey on automatic detection of hate speech in text." *ACM Computing Surveys (CSUR)* 51.4 (2018): 1–30.
31. Bashar, Md Abul, et al. "Progressive domain adaptation for detecting hate speech on social media with small training set and its application to COVID-19 concerned posts." *Social Network Analysis and Mining* 11.1 (2021): 69.
32. Miok, Kristian, et al. "To ban or not to ban: Bayesian attention networks for reliable hate speech detection." *Cognitive Computation* 14.1 (2022): 353–371.
33. Gámez-Guadix, Manuel, and Daniel Incera. "Homophobia is online: Sexual victimization and risks on the internet and mental health among bisexual, homosexual, pansexual, asexual, and queer adolescents." *Computers in Human Behavior* 119 (2021): 106728.
34. Uyheng, Joshua, and Kathleen M. Carley. "Characterizing network dynamics of online hate communities around the COVID-19 pandemic." *Applied Network Science* 6.1 (2021): 20.

35. Chard, Anna N., et al. "Experiences of homophobia among gay and bisexual men: Results from a cross-sectional study in seven countries." *Culture, Health & Sexuality* 17.10 (2015): 1174–1189.
36. Awan, Imran, and Irene Zempi. "The affinity between online and offline anti-Muslim hate crime: Dynamics and impacts." *Aggression and Violent Behavior* 27 (2016): 1–8.
37. Marret, Mary J., and Wan Yuen Choo. "Factors associated with online victimisation among Malaysian adolescents who use social networking sites: A cross-sectional study." *BMJ Open* 7.6 (2017): e014959.
38. Almerekhi, Hind, et al. "Detecting toxicity triggers in online discussions." *Proceedings of the 30th ACM Conference on Hypertext and Social Media*. 2019. Hof, Germany.
39. DePalma, Renee, and Mark Jennett. "Homophobia, transphobia and culture: Deconstructing heteronormativity in English primary schools." *Intercultural Education* 21.1 (2010): 15–26.
40. Warriner, Katrina, Craig T. Nagoshi, and Julie L. Nagoshi. "Correlates of homophobia, transphobia, and internalized homophobia in gay or lesbian and heterosexual samples." *Journal of Homosexuality* 60.9 (2013): 1297–1314.
41. Tontodimamma, Alice, et al. "Thirty years of research into hate speech: Topics of interest and their evolution." *Scientometrics* 126.1 (2021): 157–179.
42. Poletto, Fabio, et al. "Resources and benchmark corpora for hate speech detection: A systematic review." *Language Resources and Evaluation* 55.2 (2021): 477–523.
43. Pamungkas, Endang Wahyu, Valerio Basile, and Viviana Patti. "Towards multidomain and multilingual abusive language detection: A survey." *Personal and Ubiquitous Computing* 27.1 (2023): 17–43.
44. MacAvaney, Sean, et al. "Hate speech detection: Challenges and solutions." *PloS One* 14.8 (2019): e0221152.
45. Naseem, Usman, Imran Razzak, and Peter W. Eklund. "A survey of pre-processing techniques to improve short-text quality: A case study on hate speech detection on twitter." *Multimedia Tools and Applications* 80.28 (2021): 35239–35266.
46. Gao, Lei, Alexis Kuppersmith, and Ruihong Huang. "Recognizing explicit and implicit hate speech using a weakly supervised two-path bootstrapping approach." *arXiv preprint arXiv:1710.07394* (2017).
47. Kim, Youngwook, Shinwoo Park, and Yo-Sub Han. "Generalizable implicit hate speech detection using contrastive learning." *Proceedings of the 29th International Conference on Computational Linguistics*. 2022. Gyeongju, Republic of Korea.
48. Arango, Aymé, Jorge Pérez, and Barbara Poblete. "Hate speech detection is not as easy as you may think: A closer look at model validation." *Proceedings of the 42nd International ACM Sigir Conference on Research and Development in Information Retrieval*. 2019. Paris, France.
49. Ayo, Femi Emmanuel, et al. "Machine learning techniques for hate speech classification of twitter data: State-of-the-art, future challenges and research directions." *Computer Science Review* 38 (2020): 100311.
50. Burnap, Pete, and Matthew L. Williams. "Us and them: Identifying cyber hate on Twitter across multiple protected characteristics." *EPJ Data Science* 5.1 (2016): 11.
51. Davidson, Thomas, Debasmita Bhattacharya, and Ingmar Weber. "Racial bias in hate speech and abusive language detection datasets." *arXiv preprint arXiv:1905.12516* (2019).
52. Qian, Jing, et al. "A benchmark dataset for learning to intervene in online hate speech." *arXiv preprint arXiv:1909.04251* (2019).
53. Biradar, Shankar, et al. "Pradvis vac: A socio-demographic dataset for determining the level of hatred severity in a low-resource Hinglish language." *ACM Transactions on Asian and Low-Resource Language Information Processing* (2022). Doi: 10.1145/3573199. Florence, Italy.

54. Fortuna, Paula, et al. "A hierarchically-labeled portuguese hate speech dataset." *Proceedings of the Third Workshop on Abusive Language Online*. 2019.
55. Mulki, Hala, et al. "L-hsab: A levantine twitter dataset for hate speech and abusive language." *Proceedings of the Third Workshop on Abusive Language Online*. 2019. Florence, Italy.
56. Kumaresan, Prasanna Kumar, et al. "Dataset for identification of homophobia and transphobia for Telugu, Kannada, and Gujarati." *Proceedings of the 2024 Joint International Conference on Computational Linguistics, Language Resources and Evaluation (LREC-COLING 2024)*. 2024. Torino, Italy.
57. Sánchez-Sánchez, Ana M., David Ruiz-Muñoz, and Francisca J. Sánchez-Sánchez. "Mapping homophobia and transphobia on social media." *Sexuality Research and Social Policy* 21.1 (2024): 210–226.
58. Chakravarthi, Bharathi Raja. "Detection of homophobia and transphobia in YouTube comments." *International Journal of Data Science and Analytics* 18.1 (2024): 49–68.

11 Sarcasm Detection in Code-Mixed Social Media Posts

A Hybrid Perspective

Rajnish Pandey, Abhinav Kumar, and Jyoti Prakash Singh

11.1 INTRODUCTION

The growth of online social media platforms, such as Twitter (now X), Facebook, and Instagram, has transformed human communication, creating vast repositories of unstructured text data [1]. In particular, microblogging platforms have become rich textual data sources where users often employ creative linguistic expressions, humor, irony, and sarcasm to convey implicit meanings [2]. Although such expressions are natural for human cognition, their automatic interpretation by computational models presents significant challenges. Among these, detecting sarcasm is one of the most challenging tasks in sentiment analysis and natural language processing (NLP) [3].

Sarcasm refers to the use of words to convey a meaning that is opposite to their literal sense. For instance, "Oh great, another traffic jam!" may appear positive at a surface level, but its intended meaning is negative [4]. This divergence between literal and intended meaning complicates the sentiment classification task and undermines the reliability of conventional opinion-mining systems. Sarcasm confuses machine learning models and impacts downstream tasks such as sentiment analysis, opinion mining, emotion detection, and fake news identification. Therefore, accurate sarcasm detection is crucial to ensure the reliability of NLP applications in both the commercial and societal domains [5].

An additional layer of complexity emerges when sarcasm is expressed in code-mixed languages. Code-mixing, blending two or more languages within a single utterance, has become highly prevalent in multilingual societies such as India. Among these, Hinglish (a blend of Hindi and English) is among the most frequently used linguistic forms on Indian social media. For example, a Hinglish tweet such as "Bhai, tum toh genius nikle! Ek number ka kaam kiya hai" can often be sarcastic depending on its context [6]. Detecting sarcasm in such cases is more difficult because code-mixing introduces linguistic irregularities, non-standard spellings, transliterations, and grammatical variations. Furthermore, sarcasm in code-mixed text often depends on semantic understanding and cultural context, which conventional models fail to capture.

 DOI: 10.1201/9781003611110-11

While effective in monolingual settings, traditional machine learning approaches encounter significant limitations in multilingual and code-mixed contexts. Features such as bag-of-words (BoW) or term frequency-inverse document frequency (TF-IDF) fail to capture semantic nuances and context dependencies. Deep learning models, including Long Short-Term Memory (LSTM) networks and Convolutional Neural Networks (CNNs), improve the situation by capturing sequential and local contextual patterns. However, they too struggle with complex linguistic phenomena such as irony and sarcasm when applied to highly noisy code-mixed text. Recent advances in transformer-based architectures (e.g., Bidirectional Encoder Representations from Transformers (BERT), mBERT, and XLM-RoBERTa) have demonstrated substantial improvements in contextual representation, making them promising candidates for this task. Nevertheless, the challenge persists: sarcasm often requires integrating local *n*-gram features, long-term dependencies, and contextual embeddings, which no single architecture achieves optimally.

In this chapter, we focus on hybrid methodologies that integrate the strengths of traditional machine learning, deep learning, and transformer-based architectures to detect sarcasm in code-mixed Hinglish social media data. The proposed framework begins with rigorous preprocessing, including language identification, transliteration normalization, and tokenization using multilingual models. We then explore different feature representations such as GloVe embeddings and contextual embeddings from mBERT, followed by experimental evaluations using a diverse set of models ranging from Support Vector Machines (SVM) and Random Forest (RF) to advanced deep learning and transformer models. Furthermore, we emphasize hybrid architectures that combine conventional and modern techniques to leverage the complementary strengths of different approaches.

The contributions of this chapter are as follows:

1. We highlight the unique challenges of sarcasm detection in Hinglish code-mixed data, a problem underexplored in mainstream NLP research.
2. We provide a comparative evaluation of conventional, deep learning, transformer-based, and hybrid models on sarcasm detection.
3. We demonstrate how hybrid approaches can outperform single-model paradigms by effectively capturing linguistic and contextual features.

Through this exploration, the chapter aims to advance the state of research in code-mixed NLP, offering insights and methodologies that can be generalized to other multilingual and low-resource settings.

The rest of the paper is structured in the following way: Section 11.2 presents a review of the related works, Section 11.3 describes the proposed methodology in detail, Section 11.4 describes the experiment steps, Section 11.5 discusses the findings of the proposed model, and finally, Section 11.6 concludes the chapter in terms of future directions.

11.2 RELATED WORK

The detection of sarcasm is an active NLP research topic that has been developing for more than ten years, starting with simplistic lexicon-based methods of detecting sarcasm, up to advanced deep learning and transformer-based frameworks. This chapter is a systematic review of the literature that has been published to date, focusing on the development of methods and its applicability to code-mixed data.

11.2.1 Early Approaches: Machine Learning with Handcrafted Features

Initial attempts at sarcasm detection relied on rule-based and statistical learning approaches, where textual cues such as interjections, emoticons, and sentiment shifts were employed as discriminative features. Commonly used techniques included n-gram models, TF-IDF representations, and part-of-speech (POS) tagging, combined with classifiers such as Naive Bayes (NB), SVM, Logistic Regression (LR), and Decision Trees (DT). For example, Davidov et al. [7] exploited semi-supervised pattern recognition for sarcasm detection. In contrast, Gonz´alez-Ib´an˜ez et al. [8] used features such as sentiment polarity shifts to capture sarcastic intent. Although effective for short texts, these methods struggled with contextual ambiguity and required extensive feature engineering.

Due to the irregular grammar and spelling variations, handcrafted features were even less effective in multilingual and code-mixed contexts. Despite these limitations, such conventional models remain important baselines for evaluating modern approaches.

11.2.2 Deep Learning Approaches

The advent of deep learning brought significant advancements in sarcasm detection. Recurrent neural networks (RNNs), particularly LSTM networks, were widely adopted to capture sequential dependencies in text. Studies such as Ghosh and Veale [9] demonstrated the ability of LSTMs to model sarcasm by learning implicit semantic patterns. Extensions like Bidirectional LSTM (BiLSTM) and attention-enhanced LSTMs further improved contextual understanding. Simultaneously, CNNs were employed to capture local n-gram features, crucial for sarcasm, where word combinations often signal irony. CNN-based approaches [4,10,11] have been successfully applied to short texts such as tweets and comments, where local patterns dominate the semantics. However, both LSTM and CNN models required high-quality word embeddings, leading to the adoption of pre-trained embeddings such as GloVe and Word2Vec.

Despite their advantages, deep learning models often faced challenges in dealing with code-mixed text due to out-of-vocabulary (OOV) words [12], transliteration issues [13], and cultural expressions [14]. This limitation paved the way for contextual embedding models.

11.2.3 Transformer-Based Models

The introduction of transformer architectures [15] revolutionized sarcasm detection by enabling contextualized word representations. Models such as BERT, mBERT (multilingual BERT), and XLM-RoBERTa leveraged large-scale pre-training to capture nuanced semantics across multiple languages. Researchers have reported significant improvements in sarcasm detection accuracy using these models [16,17], particularly for multilingual and low-resource scenarios. For code-mixed languages, transformers offer the advantage of multilingual tokenization and subword-level modeling, which mitigates issues of transliteration and spelling variation. Khanuja et al. [18] have shown that mBERT and XLM-R are effective in code-mixed classification tasks. However, fine-tuning strategies and hybrid combinations often yield better results than standalone transformer models.

11.2.4 Hybrid Approaches

Hybrid models represent a promising direction by combining the strengths of different architectures. For example, CNN-LSTM [19] hybrids can simultaneously capture local features and long-term dependencies, while transformer-enhanced models [20,21] integrate deep contextual understanding with domain-specific embeddings. Some studies have even explored ensemble frameworks [22,23] combining conventional and neural models for improved robustness.

The consensus in recent literature suggests that no single model is sufficient for sarcasm detection, especially in code-mixed settings. Hybrid approaches that leverage handcrafted features, deep architectures, and contextual embeddings appear most promising in balancing performance with generalizability.

11.3 PROPOSED METHODOLOGY

This section describes our study methodology by incorporating the data collection and preprocessing as the first step, followed by feature representation, and finally, the experimental design that incorporates conventional machine learning, deep learning, transformer-based, and hybrid models. The design of every stage was in response to the specific dilemma of code-mixed Hinglish text and delicate task of detecting sarcasm.

11.3.1 Data Collection and Preprocessing

This study used a publicly available Hinglish code-mixed dataset [24] collected from X (formerly Twitter). The choice of Twitter as the primary source of data is deliberate: it provides short, informal, and often context-rich utterances where sarcasm is more likely to appear. Unlike long-form text, microblogging posts are inherently noisy and creative, making sarcasm detection a particularly challenging yet meaningful task.

The raw dataset contained posts written in Hindi and English, often with irregular grammar, phonetic spellings, and transliterated terms. To ensure reliable input for computational models, we employed a multi-stage preprocessing pipeline:

- **Stopword Removal and Punctuation Handling**: Common stopwords (e.g., "is," "hai," "the") were filtered out, while punctuation was handled carefully. In sarcasm, punctuation marks such as exclamation points or repeated question marks can carry significant meaning; hence, we normalized excessive punctuation for consistency instead of complete removal.

- **Tokenization**: The cleaned text was tokenized using multilingual tokenizers such as XLM-RoBERTa. These tokenizers operate at the subword level, particularly useful in code-mixed data where non-standard spellings are common.

11.3.2 Feature Representation

A critical aspect of sarcasm detection lies in how text is represented before being fed into models. We explored two complementary categories of embeddings:

- **GloVe Embeddings**: We used character- and word-level embeddings. Character-level embeddings help capture subword information, which is highly relevant for noisy Hinglish text with spelling variations. Word-level embeddings, on the other hand, encode semantic information, aiding in understanding meaning at the lexical level.
- **Contextual Embeddings**: We leveraged multilingual BERT (mBERT) along with Cross-lingual Language Model, a robustly optimized BERT variant (XLM-R), which provides dynamic embeddings that vary according to context. Unlike static embeddings, contextual embeddings allow the same word to be represented differently depending on its surrounding words. This is especially useful in detecting sarcasm, where meaning often shifts with context.

By experimenting with static and contextual embeddings, we aimed to compare their effectiveness and explore the potential benefits of combining them in hybrid models.

11.3.3 Conventional Machine Learning Models

As a baseline, we employed conventional machine learning classifiers such as SVM, RF, NB, K-Nearest Neighbor (KNN), LR, DT, and Gradient Boosting (GB). The text was first vectorized using the TF-IDF approach, producing a BoW representation. This simple representation captures the relative importance of terms across documents. The overall flow of the work for conventional machine learning models can be seen in Figure 11.1.

These models provided a foundation for comparison against more advanced deep learning and transformer-based approaches. While limited in their ability to capture context or sequential dependencies, they remain essential benchmarks due to their efficiency and interoperability.

11.3.4 Deep Learning–Based Models

Given the intricate nature of code-mixed text, we investigated multiple deep learning architectures to capture its underlying patterns more effectively.

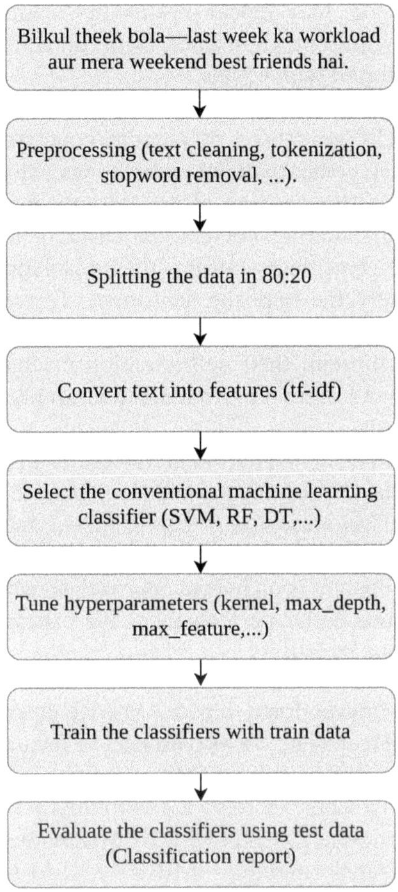

FIGURE 11.1 Workflow for the conventional machine learning classifiers for the sarcasm identification.

- **LSTM and Its Variants**: LSTM networks are designed to capture sequential dependencies in text. We extended the basic architecture to BiLSTM, which reads input in both forward and backward directions, and LSTM with attention (LSTM-A), which allows the model to focus on significant tokens. We used character-level and word-level embeddings for sarcasm detection in Hinglish as input to LSTM, BiLSTM, and LSTM-A architectures. Character-level embeddings were particularly beneficial for handling spelling variations common in social media text.
- **Convolutional Neural Networks**: CNNs were employed to capture local *n*-gram features. Since sarcasm often emerges from specific word combinations, CNNs are well-suited for identifying such patterns. Both character-level and word-level embeddings were tested with CNNs. CNNs were used to detect local *n*-gram patterns that often signal sarcasm. For example,

phrases like "great job" may appear positive in isolation but can convey sarcasm when paired with contextual clues. Both character-level and word-level embeddings were tested with CNNs.

- **Transformer-Based Models**: Pre-trained transformers such as mBERT and XLM-RoBERTa were used to capture contextual semantics. These models provide deep contextualized embeddings, which are critical in sarcasm detection since the meaning of an utterance may only be clear when considering the surrounding context. Sarcasm is inherently contextual. A statement that appears neutral or positive in isolation may, under certain circumstances, imply the opposite sentiment. Transformer-based models such as mBERT and XLM-RoBERTa are particularly well-suited to capture such context through their self-attention mechanism. These models were fine-tuned on our dataset to evaluate their ability to handle sarcasm in code-mixed Hinglish.
- **Hybrid Models**: We designed hybrid architectures that include the mBERT and XLM-R models. Combining various deep learning–based models such as CNNs with LSTMs allows us to capture local and sequential features, while transformer-enhanced hybrids add a contextual dimension. The primary focus of this chapter is on hybrid approaches, which combine multiple paradigms to achieve better performance. We experimented with various hybrid combinations, including:

  - Conventional–Conventional (e.g., SVM + RF ensembles)
  - Conventional–Deep (e.g., SVM with LSTM features)
  - Deep–Deep (e.g., CNN + BiLSTM)
  - Conventional–Transformer (e.g., LR with mBERT embeddings)
  - Deep–Transformer (e.g., CNN with XLM-R embeddings)
  - Transformer–Transformer (e.g., mBERT + XLM-R ensemble)
  - Full Hybrid (integrating all categories of models)

Through these combinations, we aimed to explore whether integrating complementary strengths—such as the interpretability of conventional models, the sequential learning ability of LSTMs, the local feature detection of CNNs, and the contextual depth of transformers—can result in superior performance for sarcasm detection in noisy code-mixed text. The overall flow of the proposed hybrid model consisting of XLM-RoBERTa and mBERT can be seen in Figure 11.2.

11.4 EXPERIMENTAL SETUP

All experiments were conducted using Python 3.10 with deep learning frameworks such as TensorFlow and PyTorch on a workstation equipped with an NVIDIA RTX 3080 GPU (16 GB memory), an Intel i9 processor, and 64 GB RAM. The dataset was preprocessed through standard NLP pipelines, including tokenization, stopword removal, and normalization, followed by embedding generation using character and word-level representations. For sequence-based models (LSTM, BiLSTM, and their attention variants), the maximum sequence length was fixed to 100 tokens to ensure

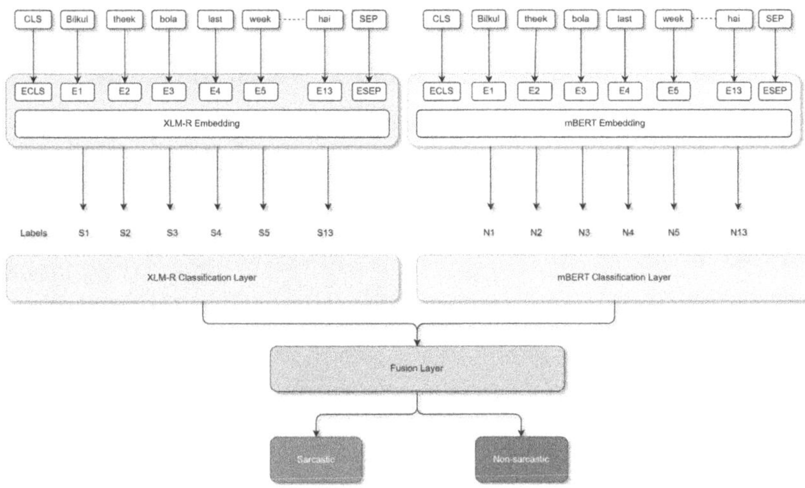

FIGURE 11.2 Workflow of proposed mBERT-XLM-R hybrid model for sarcasm identification.

uniformity across experiments. In convolutional models, 1D filters with varying kernel sizes were employed to capture local contextual dependencies. Transformer-based baselines, such as mBERT and XLM-R, were fine-tuned with a learning rate of 2×10^{-5} and a batch size of 32.

Each model was optimized using grid search as to the hyperparameters to compete against each other. The patience used to prevent overfitting was early stopping with the validation loss of five epochs. Precision, Recall, and $F1$-score were used to assess model performance on a class-wise and weighted average basis. The ablation study was performed by systematically removing or altering key components (e.g., embeddings, attention layers) to quantify their contribution to overall performance. This consistent setup ensures a fair comparison across different architectures while highlighting the effectiveness of hybrid and transformer-based approaches in sarcasm detection on code-mixed Hinglish datasets. The overall hyperparameters of the proposed hybrid model can be seen in Table 11.1.

11.5 RESULTS AND DISCUSSION

Various conventional machine and deep learning–based results can be seen from Tables 11.2 and 11.3. Transformer-based models significantly outperformed BiLSTM and CNN architectures, indicating their superior ability to model contextual semantics in code-mixed text. Error analysis revealed that sarcasm expressed through cultural references and idioms remains challenging. The hybrid model achieved a weighted precision of 0.93, recall of 0.94, and $F1$-score of 0.94, outperforming conventional and standalone deep learning baselines. These findings confirm the robustness, reliability, and superiority of the mBERT + XLM-R hybrid model for sarcasm detection on the Hinglish dataset (see Table 11.3).

TABLE 11.1
Hyperparameters of the Proposed mBERT + XLM-R Hybrid Model

Component	Hyperparameter	Value	Justification
Tokenizer	Max seq. length	100	Balances efficiency and context coverage
mBERT encoder	Model	BERT-base-multilingual-cased	Captures multilingual embeddings for Hinglish
	Trainable layers	Last 4	Allows task adaptation without overfitting
XLM-R encoder	Model	XLM-RoBERTa-base	Provides strong multilingual contextual embeddings
	Trainable layers	Last 4	Same reasoning as mBERT
Fusion layer	Method	Concatenation of [CLS]	Effective combination of representations
Dense layer	Units	128	Compresses fused features
	Activation	ReLU	Introduces non-linearity
Dropout	Rate	0.3	Prevents overfitting
Output layer	Units	1 (binary)/#classes	Matches classification setup
	Activation	Sigmoid/Softmax	Standard for classification
Optimizer	Type	AdamW	Widely used for transformer fine-tuning
	Learning rate	2×10^{-5}	Empirically effective for transformers
Loss function	Type	BCE/CCE	Matches binary or multiclass setup
Batch size	Value	32	Fits GPU memory, stable training
Epochs	Value	5	Typical range for convergence

TABLE 11.2
Performance Comparison of Conventional Machine Learning Models on Hinglish Dataset

Models	Class	Precision	Recall	*F*1-Score
	S	0.91	0.41	0.56
RF	NS	0.93	0.99	0.96
	WA	0.93	0.93	0.91
	S	0.63	0.16	0.26
LR	NS	0.90	0.99	0.94
	WA	0.87	0.89	0.86
	S	0.65	0.14	0.24
KNN	NS	0.90	0.99	0.94
	WA	0.87	0.89	0.86

(*Continued*)

TABLE 11.2 (*Continued*)
Performance Comparison of Conventional Machine Learning Models on Hinglish Dataset

Models	Class	Precision	Recall	*F*1-Score
	S	0.51	0.14	0.22
NB	NS	0.85	0.98	0.91
	WA	0.79	0.83	0.74
	S	0.85	0.08	0.14
GB	NS	0.88	0.99	0.93
	WA	0.86	0.89	0.86
	S	0.71	0.06	0.11
DT	NS	0.86	0.99	0.92
	WA	0.79	0.88	0.73
	S	0.94	0.94	0.94
SVM	NS	0.92	0.99	0.95
	WA	0.90	0.91	0.89

NS, non-sarcasm; S, sarcasm; WA, weighted average.

TABLE 11.3
Performance Comparison of Deep Learning Models on Hinglish Dataset

Models	Class	Precision	Recall	*F*1-Score
	S	0.84	0.83	0.83
DNN	NS	0.87	0.83	0.85
	WA	0.85	0.83	0.84
	S	0.80	0.86	0.85
LSTM (Char)	NS	0.90	0.91	0.93
	WA	0.85	0.85	0.87
	S	0.72	0.85	0.78
LSTM (Word)	NS	0.90	0.91	0.93
	WA	0.85	0.85	0.85
	S	0.96	0.94	0.96
CNN (Char)	NS	0.76	0.86	0.87
	WA	0.92	0.90	0.92
	S	0.95	0.96	0.96
CNN (Word)	NS	0.74	0.85	0.88
	WA	0.91	0.92	0.92
	S	0.70	0.70	0.70
Hybrid (mBERT + XLM-R)	NS	0.96	0.96	0.96
	WA	0.93	0.94	0.94

NS, non-sarcasm; S, sarcasm; WA, weighted average.

TABLE 11.4
Ablation Study of the mBERT+XLM-R Hybrid Model

Variant	Description	Accuracy	*F*1-Score	Observation
Full model (proposed)	mBERT + XLM-R fusion	0.94	0.94	Best performance
Only mBert	Removed XLM-R branch	0.92	0.92	Performance drops, XLM-R adds context
Only XLM-R	Removed mBERT branch	0.93	0.93	Better than mBERT alone, weaker than fusion
Fusion w/o dense layer	Direct concat → output	0.91	0.90	Dense layer refines representation
No dropout	Dropout removed	0.87 (train), 0.89 (test)	—	Overfitting observed
Lower LR (1×10^{-5})	Halved learning rate	0.87	0.86	Stable but slower convergence
Higher LR (5×10^{-5})	Increased learning rate	0.82	0.81	Training unstable

11.5.1 Ablation Study

An ablation study was conducted to systematically analyze the contribution of each component within the hybrid model. The results confirmed that the full mBERT + XLM-R fusion consistently outperformed individual branches, achieving the highest accuracy and *F*1-score. Removing the XLM-R branch resulted in a significant performance drop. In contrast, the XLM-R-only model performed slightly better than the mBERT-only model, highlighting the stronger contextual representation of XLM-R. Eliminating the dense layer and relying solely on raw concatenation reduced performance, demonstrating the importance of feature refinement. Similarly, removing dropout led to clear overfitting, with higher training accuracy but poor generalization on test data. Variations in the learning rate showed that overly low values slowed convergence, while higher values destabilized training. These findings emphasize that encoder branches, dense layers, and dropout are crucial for the robustness of the proposed hybrid model (see Table 11.4).

11.5.2 Comparison with Other Works

To evaluate the effectiveness of our proposed hybrid architecture, we compared its performance with existing benchmark approaches on the Hinglish sarcasm detection dataset. The results demonstrate that conventional machine learning classifiers, while effective in capturing shallow lexical cues, lag significantly behind deep learning and transformer-based methods in handling the nuanced, context-dependent nature of sarcasm. CNNs and LSTM variants improved the performance by modeling local *n*-gram patterns and sequential dependencies, respectively. Transformer-based architectures such as mBERT and XLM-R further enhanced contextual representation

TABLE 11.5
Comparison of Existing Hinglish Sarcasm Detection Models with the Proposed Hybrid mBERT-XLM-R Model

Authors	Dataset	Features/Models	Performance
Swami et al. [24]	Hinglish Tweets (code-mixed EN–HI)	TF-IDF features + Random Forest	$F1 = 0.78$ (10-fold CV)
Aggarwal et al. [25]	Hinglish sarcasm dataset (custom)	Bilingual embeddings (FastText, Word2Vec) + CNN, LSTM, BiLSTM, Attention BiLSTM	Acc. = 78
Proposed Hybrid mBERT+XLM-R	Hinglish sarcasm dataset	**Contextual embeddings**	$\boldsymbol{F1 = 0.94}$

learning, outperforming traditional deep learning models. However, our hybrid mBERT + XLM-R framework achieved the best overall performance across accuracy and $F1$-score, indicating that the fusion of complementary transformer representations captures both semantic richness and cross-lingual contextual cues more effectively. This establishes our model as a state-of-the-art approach for sarcasm detection in code-mixed Hinglish text (see Table 11.5).

11.6 CONCLUSION AND FUTURE WORK

In this work, we proposed a hybrid transformer-based framework that fuses mBERT and XLM-R to address the challenging task of sarcasm detection in Hinglish text. By exploiting the complementary strengths of these multilingual pre-trained models, our approach successfully captures semantic richness and cross-lingual contextual information inherent in code-mixed discourse. Experimental results on the Hinglish dataset demonstrate that the proposed model consistently outperforms conventional classifiers, deep learning baselines, and individual transformer models, achieving notable improvements in accuracy and $F1$-score. The ablation study further highlights the significance of model fusion, dense representation learning, and regularization strategies in enhancing robustness and generalization.

Despite these encouraging results, certain limitations remain. The hybrid model incurs high computational costs, making real-time deployment on resource-constrained platforms challenging. Additionally, while representative, the dataset may not fully cover regional variations, informal spellings, or the multimodal nature of sarcasm (e.g., emojis, memes). Future work will therefore focus on reducing model complexity through knowledge distillation and pruning and extending the framework to multimodal sarcasm detection. Furthermore, we aim to evaluate the approach on larger and more diverse code-mixed corpora and adapt it for other low-resource languages, thereby contributing to broader advancements in multilingual NLP.

ACKNOWLEDGMENT

We acknowledge the support of Dr. Rammanohar Lohia Awadh University for providing computational resources.

REFERENCES

1. Tahereh Saheb, Mouwafac Sidaoui, and Bill Schmarzo. Convergence of artificial intelligence with social media: A bibliometric qualitative analysis. *Telematics and Informatics Reports*, 14:100146, 2024.
2. Zheng Lin Chia, Michal Ptaszynski, Marzena Karpinska, Juuso Eronen, and Fumito Masui. Initial exploration into sarcasm and irony through machine translation. *Natural Language Processing Journal*, 9:100106, 2024.
3. Jamin Rahman Jim, Md Apon Riaz Talukder, Partha Malakar, Md Mohsin Kabir, Kamruddin Nur, and M.F. Mridha. Recent advancements and challenges of nlp-based sentiment analysis: A state-of-the-art review. *Natural Language Processing Journal*, 6:100059, 2024.
4. Rajnish Pandey, Abhinav Kumar, Jyoti Prakash Singh, and Sudhakar Tripathi. Hybrid attention-based long short-term memory network for sarcasm identification. *Applied Soft Computing*, 106:107348, 2021.
5. Walabin Subait, Mashael M. Asiri, Muhammad Swaileh A. Alzaidi, Me-shari H. Alanazi, Menwa Alshammeri, Ayman Yafoz, Raed Alsini, and Alaa O. Khadidos. Artificial intelligence-based natural language process-ing for sarcasm detection and classification on Arabic corpus. *Alexandria Engineering Journal*, 125:320–331, 2025.
6. Rajnish Pandey and Jyoti Prakash Singh. BERT-LSTM model for sarcasm detection in code-mixed social media post. *Journal of Intelligent Information Systems*, 60(1):235–254, October 2022.
7. Dmitry Davidov, Oren Tsur, and Ari Rappoport. Semi-supervised recognition of sarcasm in twitter and amazon. In *Proceedings of the Fourteenth Conference on Computational Natural Language Learning*, pages 107–116, Uppsala, Sweden, 2010.
8. Roberto Gonz´alez-Ib´anez, Smaranda Muresan, and Nina Wacholder. Identifying sarcasm in twitter: a closer look. In *Proceedings of the 49th Annual Meeting of the Association for Computational Linguistics: Human Language Technologies*, pages 581–586, Portland, Oregon, USA, 2011.
9. Aniruddha Ghosh and Tony Veale. Fracking sarcasm using neural network. In *Proceedings of the 7th Workshop on Computational Approaches to Subjectivity, Sentiment and Social Media Analysis*, pages 161–169, San Diego, California, 2016.
10. Oxana Vitman, Yevhen Kostiuk, Grigori Sidorov, and Alexander Gel-bukh. Sarcasm detection framework using context, emotion and senti-ment features. *Expert Systems with Applications*, 234:121068, 2023.
11. Avinash Kumar, Vishnu Teja Narapareddy, Veerubhotla Aditya Srikanth, Aruna Malapati, and Lalita Bhanu Murthy Neti. Sarcasm detection using multi-head attention based bidirectional lstm. *IEEE Access*, 8:6388–6397, 2020.
12. Johannes V Lochter, Renato M Silva, and Tiago A Almeida. Deep learning models for representing out-of-vocabulary words. In *Brazilian Conference on Intelligent Systems*, pages 418–434. Rio Grande, Brazil, Springer, 2020.
13. Gauri Takawane, Abhishek Phaltankar, Varad Patwardhan, Aryan Patil, Raviraj Joshi, and Mukta S Takalikar. Language augmentation approach for code-mixed text classification. *Natural Language Processing Journal*, 5:100042, 2023.

14. Paras Tiwari and Sawan Rai. Mind your tweet: Abusive tweet detection. In *International Conference on Speech and Computer*, pages 704–715. St. Petersburg, Russia, Springer, 2021.
15. Ashish Vaswani, Noam Shazeer, Niki Parmar, Jakob Uszkoreit, Llion Jones, Aidan N Gomez, Lukasz Kaiser, and Illia Polosukhin. Attention is all you need. In *31st Conference on Neural Information Processing Systems (NIPS 2017)*, Long Beach, CA, 30, 2017.
16. Ganesh Jawahar, Beno^ıt Sagot, and Djam´e Seddah. What does Bert learn about the structure of language? In *ACL 2019–57th Annual Meeting of the Association for Computational Linguistics*, Florence, Italy, 2019.
17. Joan C Timoneda and Sebasti´an Vallejo Vera. Bert, roberta, or deberta? Comparing performance across transformers models in political science text. *The Journal of Politics*, 87(1):347–364, 2025.
18. Simran Khanuja, Sandipan Dandapat, Anirudh Srinivasan, Sunayana Sitaram, and Monojit Choudhury. Gluecos: An evaluation benchmark for code-switched nlp. *arXiv preprint arXiv:2004.12376*, 2020.
19. Paul K Mandal and Rakeshkumar Mahto. Deep CNN-LSTM with word embeddings for news headline sarcasm detection. In *16th International Conference on Information Technology-New Generations (ITNG 2019)*, pages 495–498. Las Vegas, Nevada, USA, Springer, 2019.
20. Rolandos Alexandros Potamias, Georgios Siolas, and Andreas-Georgios Stafylopatis. A transformer-based approach to irony and sarcasm detection. *Neural Computing and Applications*, 32(23):17309–17320, 2020.
21. Soroush Javdan, Behrouz Minaei-Bidgoli, et al. Applying transformers and aspect-based sentiment analysis approaches on sarcasm detection. In *Proceedings of the Second Workshop on Figurative Language Processing*, pages 67–71, 2020.
22. Jens Lemmens, Ben Burtenshaw, Ehsan Lotfi, Ilia Markov, and Walter Daelemans. Sarcasm detection using an ensemble approach. In *Proceedings of the Second Workshop on Figurative Language Processing*, pages 264–269, 2020.
23. Priya Goel, Rachna Jain, Anand Nayyar, Shruti Singhal, and Muskan Srivastava. Sarcasm detection using deep learning and ensemble learning. *Multimedia Tools and Applications*, 81(30):43229–43252, 2022.
24. Sahil Swami, Ankush Khandelwal, Vinay Singh, Syed Sarfaraz Akhtar, and Manish Shrivastava. A corpus of english-hindi code-mixed tweets for sarcasm detection. *arXiv preprint arXiv:1805.11869*, 2018.
25. Akshita Aggarwal, Anshul Wadhawan, Anshima Chaudhary, and Kavita Maurya. "Did you really mean what you said?": Sarcasm detection in Hindi-English code-mixed data using bilingual word embeddings. In *Proceedings of the Sixth Workshop on Noisy User-generated Text (W-NUT 2020)*, pages 7–15, Online, November 2020. Association for Computational Linguistics.

Index

T

U

V

W

X

Y

For Product Safety Concerns and Information please contact our EU representative GPSR@taylorandfrancis.com
Taylor & Francis Verlag GmbH, Kaufingerstraße 24, 80331 München, Germany

www.ingramcontent.com/pod-product-compliance
Ingram Content Group UK Ltd.
Pitfield, Milton Keynes, MK11 3LW, UK
UKHW020158200926
475702UK00004B/514

* 9 7 8 1 0 4 1 0 0 6 9 0 9 *